Redefining the Market–State Relationship

This book offers an interdisciplinary overview of the role of law in modern capitalism in the context of financial crisis. In this work, the reader will find a discussion of key issues relevant to the crisis that have occupied the pages of the financial press since 2007, including an assessment of the meltdown of the sub-prime mortgage market, the credit crunch, the European debt crisis and the turmoil in Greece, plus a series of theoretical contributions that are aimed at challenging perceptions of the market–state relationship and the place of law within it.

The book includes a methodological defence of the state–market dichotomy, a critique of the tenets of neoclassical economics and an evaluation of what the financial crisis heralds for the future of the political economy of western democracies. Ioannis Glinavos argues that it is a mistake to associate markets with freedom and states with oppression, and suggests that more choice for consumers can – and does – mean less choice for citizens. The book suggests that a new social contract is needed to ensure the survival of both capitalism and democracy.

In contributing a unique, legal perspective to the underlying dynamics of the financial crisis, this book will be valuable to scholars and students of regulation, financial markets and economic development.

Ioannis Glinavos is Lecturer in Law at the University of Reading, UK.

Routledge Research in Finance and Banking Law

Available:

European Prudential Banking Regulation and Supervision
The Legal Dimension
Larisa Dragomir

International Secured Transactions Law
Facilitation of Credit and International Conventions and Instruments
Orkun Akseli

The Legal and Regulatory Aspects of Islamic Banking
A Comparative Look at the United Kingdom and Malaysia
Abdul Karim Aldohni

Banking Secrecy and Offshore Financial Centres
Money Laundering and Offshore Banking
Mary Alice Young

Fiduciary Law and Responsible Investing
In Nature's Trust
Benjamin J. Richardson

Forthcoming:

Competition Law and Financial Services
David Harrison

Redefining the Market-State Relationship
Responses to the Financial Crisis and the Future of Regulation
Ioannis Glinavos

Redefining the Market–State Relationship

Responses to the financial crisis and the future of regulation

Ioannis Glinavos

Routledge
Taylor & Francis Group
LONDON AND NEW YORK

First published 2014
by Routledge
2 Park Square, Milton Park, Abingdon, Oxon, OX14 4RN

Simultaneously published in the USA and Canada
by Routledge
711 Third Avenue, New York, NY 10017

Routledge is an imprint of the Taylor & Francis Group, an informa business

British Library Cataloguing in Publication Data
A catalogue record for this book is available from the British Library

Library of Congress Cataloging-in-Publication Data
A catalog record has been requested for this book

ISBN: 978-0-415-69128-4 (hbk)
ISBN: 978-0-203-71879-7 (ebk)

Typeset in Garamond
by Cenveo Publisher Services

MIX
Paper from responsible sources
FSC® C013604

Printed and bound by CPI Group (UK) Ltd, Croydon, CR0 4YY

For Sophie

Contents

Preface

This book offers an overview of the role of law in modern capitalism in the context of financial crisis. In these pages, the reader will find a methodological defence of the state–market dichotomy, a critique of the sacred tenets of neoclassical economics and an evaluation of what the financial crisis (and responses to it) herald for the future of the political economy of western democracies. This work, in summary, combines a presentation of the economic calamities that the world has suffered since 2007 with a reflection on the role of law and delivers a powerful political message. This message is that democracy is suffering under financialised capitalism and that a new social contract is needed to ensure the survival of both capitalism and democracy. In this work, the reader will find a discussion of most of the key issues relevant to the crisis that have occupied the pages of the financial press since 2007, plus a series of theoretical contributions that are aimed to challenge the way we view the market–state relationship and the place of law within it. The book will argue that we are mistaken in associating markets with freedom and states with oppression, and suggests that more choice for consumers can – and does – mean less choice for citizens.

Since my first book *Neoliberalism and the Law* was published in 2010, the world has become a very different, and not necessarily better, place. Concerns about the purposes of law reform, the role of law in modern capitalism and the links between justice, equality and security that were common in discourses about countries emerging from communism have now become prevalent discussions in western democracies. What has intervened, of course, between the time of the research that produced my first work and this book is the financial crisis in its many forms, ranging from the sub-prime mortgage collapse in the USA to the credit crunch and the European sovereign debt crisis. This book argues that there is a continuum between works on the role of law in post-communist transition and examinations of the effects of the financial crisis. The link is provided by the stranglehold economic orthodoxy has over our understanding of the balance between markets and states and the scope for policy discretion over economic decision-making allowed by neoclassical assumptions. This book, as a result, offers an indictment of the de-politicisation of economic decision-making that is so central to economic orthodoxy, arguing that the distancing of democratic politics from norm creation in regulatory fields leads to the dissolution of liberal democracy.

Why should the reader choose this work over many others about aspects of the financial crisis that have since 2010 littered the shelves of bookshops? This work is novel because it discusses the background to the financial crisis by focusing on the role of law. Current literature on the crisis focuses on economics or politics but little on law. Key to understanding the nature of contemporary capitalism and in proposing reform, however, is a re-evaluation of the function and purposes of law. The book adopts an interdisciplinary approach to the issues under consideration, bringing together economic theory and political reflection within a normative legal framework. The book does not seek to offer yet another review of the crisis, but an explanation of underlying dynamics. The book concludes by proposing a mechanism for achieving a new organisation of the market–state relationship based on reinvigorating democracy in western societies and offers an avenue towards the creation of a new social contract wherein markets serve as a mechanism for the attainment of social goals chosen via the democratic process. In short, the book centres on the role of law in interpreting current regulatory phenomena and recommends a vision for the future.

The central underlying theme of the book is that legal changes implementing reforms with a pro-market direction reduce policy options and as such dilute the public's ability to influence economic decision-making. Law therefore becomes an instrument of de-democratisation – resulting in extremis in a dictatorship of finance. This book is at the same time a call to arms, carrying a significant political message and a contribution to academic knowledge about the nature of law and the lessons of the financial crisis. The political message is that if we wish democracy to survive, we need to have a discussion about the nature and purpose of law in modern capitalism. We need to engage in a debate that will end in a new social contract whereby a commitment to liberal democracy is reaffirmed. This debate will only be one of substance if different balance points in the market–state relationship are envisaged. We need to break out of the confines of neoclassical thinking, dispel the myths of a *homo economicus* and regain control over our fates as citizens in a democratic polity. The book also explains why the slide to 'technocracy' carries the danger of a tumble towards fascism or anarchy. The crisis, in summary, is a game changer that we can either use to reaffirm our commitment to a future of shared prosperity, or we can squander it, with unpredictable consequences.

The contribution to knowledge from an academic point of view comes from the dissection of the role of law in capitalism and from unpacking the various notions that comprise the constitutive myths of financialised capitalism. The book challenges fundamental notions about the nature of markets, the role of law and the place of democracy that have been dominant for so long we have forgotten how they came into existence. The book also offers a novel exploration of the ideology behind policy formation pre- and post crisis.

While it is beyond the aims of the book to offer an exhaustive list of policy responses to the crisis in a multi-jurisdictional environment, this work presents some illustrative examples of reform, exploring the reasons behind policy changes, and enquires into the origin (and likely destination) of current shifts in our perception of the role of law and the place of the state in regulatory frameworks.

The book has been written in what is hoped to be accessible language that will appeal to both an audience well versed in the relevant literature and to the interested lay person. There is no benefit to be gained from overtly technical language if the result is that it does not communicate its meaning effectively. Every effort has been made therefore to explain technical concepts when they are used, and this applies both to legal and economic/financial terms. The consequence of this method of writing is that the style of the book may appear simple to scholars, but it is not simplistic. Also, the book aims to use contemporary sources, while making a theoretical contribution that will outlast the newsworthiness of the content used. The purpose is not just to inform about what we have experienced from 2007 to 2013, but to put current developments in a wider context, to draw messages about the nature of law and regulation that will be relevant long after this crisis is (hopefully) past. The sources for this work are a combination of published literature, current affairs commentary and personal reflection and experience. I owe the greatest gratitude to the authors of my sources, even to those I disagree with, and I assume responsibility for any mistakes and misunderstandings. As with every cross-disciplinary work, especially one that straddles law, economics and politics like this one, readers well versed in only one of the fields involved may find the analysis occasionally lacking, superficial or partial. The aim of the book is not to offer a comprehensive examination of the literature on regulation in each field, but to combine knowledge in order to suggest something novel. To find truth we need to break through disciplinary barriers, despite the dangers of oversimplification that may lurk.

The realisation offered in this work that market-friendly reforms can have corrosive unintended consequences on the health of our democracy, even in core capitalist states, links together the many examples and themes of the book that are explored in three main parts. Part 1 introduces the main concepts that the book deals with and defines its main objective, which is to locate what the role of law should be in western capitalist democracies and to enquire into appropriate balance points between market freedoms and state policy discretion. Chapter 1 contains the main methodological defence for the book and explains why, despite the intermingling of states and markets since the 1980s, the distinction between state and market is still a methodologically sound one. The chapter delves into the theory on market intervention and then offers a reflection based on ethics. Taking one of the key illustrations used in the book, the concept of executive remuneration, Chapter 1 explores the legal, economic and ethical justifications behind inequalities in modern capitalism. The chapter concludes by a reflection on the relationship between law and justice in financialised capitalism. Chapter 2 goes to the core of the discussion linking law with economic governance, challenging neoclassical assumptions as to the nature and purpose of finance, money, credit. This reflection then allows the chapter to proceed to an investigation of ideas and their role in policy-making, unmasking the central role ideas and ideology have in issues that are presented by the current orthodoxy as a result of apolitical, scientific enquiry.

Building on the theoretical bases set thus far, Part 2 of the book reaches into the core of the motivation behind this work, an investigation of the financial crisis and what it means for law in western political economy. Chapter 3 continues the work of unpacking neoclassical assumptions by offering a history of the state–market relationship, doubting the received wisdom that regulation is a modern concept that descended upon previously free markets after the shock of the Great Depression. Viewing history through a critical lens, the chapter argues that what we think we know about the role of law in economic management and the historical origins of laissez-faire needs to be taken with much caution. This re-examination of the historical record leads then to a presentation of the financial crisis in Chapter 4. Chapter 4 presents the main features of what we call the Great Recession and is split into two main sections. The first section presents the financial part of the crisis, from the sub-prime mortgage market collapse in the USA to the credit crunch. The second section is less historical and more contemporary as it addresses the European sovereign debt crisis. Chapter 4 explains in some detail events surrounding the Greek problem, which is taken as the focal point of the sovereign debt crisis, and uses Greece as an illustration of the dangers of legislating free market policies, especially when the law is used to distance market-friendly frameworks from the reach of normal legislative and political processes. The chapter concludes with a reflection on a very controversial issue, the ability of member states of the Eurozone to leave the monetary union, either voluntarily or involuntarily.

The presentation of the two facets of the crisis, the financial and the sovereign debt problems, is followed in Part 3 by an investigation of the meaning of policy responses to the crisis in the USA and Europe, a reflection on how the political economy of capitalist states may change as a result of the shock delivered by the crisis and a discussion on emerging trends in policy responses. Chapter 5 presents regulatory reform initiatives first in Europe and then in the USA, taking special note of responses to the perceived problem of excessive remuneration for top executives, especially in the financial sector. The message taken from measures so far in response to the crisis, the chapter argues, does not suggest a change in the philosophy that motivates reform. It seems that, to date, we cannot discern a challenge to an ideological background to economic governance that sees market mechanisms as the default basis for organising our economic lives. Chapter 6 uses this realisation to test how dispute resolution processes affect the evolution of norms and the respective space left to states to regulate market activities. The chapter also asks whether the focus on law, that this book has, is in fact unnecessary and whether self-regulation and voluntarism present a lasting alternative to state regulation of market activity. The chapter suggests that unless we re-empower democratic institutions to define the nature of the market–state balance, unless we reach a new social contract to support capitalism in the future, we risk the dissolution of liberal democracy. The book concludes by challenging the current turn towards 'technocracy' by calling on citizens to embrace the opportunities presented by our great crisis in order to reclaim policy space, to demand that choices are opened to us as citizens rather than just as consumers in a market.

Acknowledgments

The author would like to thank the journal *European Business Law Review* published by Kluwer and the *European Journal of Law Reform* published by Eleven, as well as Routledge for allowing the reproduction of the author's material previously published with them.

List of abbreviations

ABS	asset-backed security
APR	annual percentage rate
BBA	British Bankers Association
BIT	bilateral investment treaty
CAC	collective action clause
CEBS	Committee of European Banking Supervisors
CEIOPS	Committee of European Insurance and Occupational Pensions Supervisors
CESR	Committee of European Securities Regulators
CDO	collateralised debt obligation
CDS	credit default swap
CEO	chief executive officer
CRD	Capital Requirements Directive
CSR	corporate social responsibility
EBA	European Banking Authority
ECB	European Central Bank
ECJ	European Court of Justice
EFAMA	European Fund and Asset Management Association
EFSF	European Finance Stability Facility
EIOPA	European Insurance and Occupational Pensions Authority
EMU	Economic and Monetary Union
ESA	European Supervisory Authorities
ESMA	European Securities and Markets Authority
EVCA	European Private Equity and Venture Capital Association
FDIC	Federal Deposit Insurance Corporation
FSA	Financial Services Authority
FSB	Financial Stability Board (formerly FSF)
FSF	Financial Stability Forum
GATT	General Agreement on Tariffs and Trade
GDP	gross domestic product
ICSID	International Center for the Settlement of Investment Disputes
IEA	Institute of Economic Affairs

IMF	International Monetary Fund
ISDA	International Swaps and Derivatives Association
MFN	Most Favoured Nation
MP	Member of Parliament
NAFTA	North American Free Trade Agreement
NEET	Not in Employment, Education or Training
NGO	non-governmental organisation
NRSROs	Nationally Recognized Statistical Rating Organizations
OECD	Organisation for Economic Cooperation and Development
OFT	Office of Fair Trading
OTC	over-the-counter
PSI	Private Sector Involvement
SEC	Securities and Exchange Commission
TARP	Troubled Asset Relief Program

Part I

Theory

Contrary to much popular perception, scepticism about the place of markets in society is not the exclusive domain of anti-globalisation, anti-capitalist agitators. This book is premised upon the central idea that in order to ensure the survival of capitalism and the perseverance of free markets, we need to reconsider the balance between the state and the market. This is not a call for revolution or a suggestion that non-capitalist ideas are necessarily viable. It is rather a pragmatic observation that a progressively less democratic capitalism is unsustainable. The suggestion that de-politicised economic decision-making does not ensure long-term stability is critically reinforced by the financial crisis. Market advocates, even more than market sceptics, therefore, stand to gain from the realisation that a growing disconnect between public support and free markets, embedded in legal structures, does more to undermine markets than state sponsored attempts at re-regulation. The nexus of this discussion is the role of politics (via law) in economic governance. The reason why the debate about better economic management and more legitimate economic decision-making is essentially a political question is because, as this book claims, it is only political processes that can determine the overall aims of policy with a degree of legitimacy and permanence that ensures the long-term survival of the capitalist project. Economic policy design currently, however, is largely being considered as an issue of technical competence, a scientific endeavour. The market (allegedly) has rules that are akin to scientific rules. These rules demand certain things of the state–market relationship and set frameworks that mandate what is beneficial and what is damaging to the market and, by extension, to the society as a whole. This perception, however, equates market needs with social needs. When social needs diverge from what is best for the market, the currently dominant analytical framework described above requires that social requirements take a back seat to the needs of the market. Determining a hierarchy of needs and goals for government policy, however, cannot be made the prerogative of so-called scientific economic analyses. The explanation for this is that lacking legitimacy and public support, any system of government is unstable and potentially incapable of keeping the peace. It is politics, which this book regards as representative democratic politics, which should determine the aims of a system of governance, not markets or economic theories. As a democratic society, we aspire to live in a state governed by law determined in reflection of the popular will. A society governed by laws created on the basis of their compatibility with 'technical competence' are inching away from democracy, towards what we could, in the context of contemporary capitalism, call a 'dictatorship of finance'.

In discussing where should the balance between markets and states be found, and what is the role of law within such a balance, we need to address the question of what is capitalism aimed to achieve? Indeed, what is the market aimed to achieve? We need to find what the goals of policy should be, before we start debating the means employed to reach those goals. These questions are, of course, inherently political questions. Once we answer the question of what capitalism is for and what is the role of markets then we can use economic efficiency arguments to determine the means to achieve these objectives. To reiterate a point made earlier, this book does not recommend that a command economy along Stalinist lines of control (a historical alternative to capitalism) could ever replace a free market or lead to better social outcomes. The book, however, does argue that economic considerations, in the guise of science or not, should not determine every aim of policy. It is our prerogative as citizens to determine what the market is for, what the state should do and the shape of the structure of our economies. The acceptance of free markets as an effective way to achieve optimal outcomes should not mean that the public is robbed of choices. Even conceding that one would rather live in a capitalist, as opposed to a command, economy does not make capitalism the end of history. Viewed in this way, the discussion offered in this book becomes a discourse on choice. Not the choice that right-leaning governments (like the Conservative-Liberal coalition in the UK) want us to have (consumer choice), but a choice about more fundamental questions as to how we live our lives. A choice as to the aims of the system around us and as to the outer legal boundaries of that system.

Are these questions naive? Is not what is being described here (a democratic state) what we already have? Unfortunately the answer to both these questions is no. These questions are not naive if we go beyond the theory as to how our state should operate and actually confront how it does operate. I live in Britain which is a democratic state, but perhaps democratic in name is not the same as democratic in nature. What is the use of the label 'democracy' if choices about the things that matter are not subject to the democratic process? What this book seeks to achieve is to spark a discussion as to what sort of capitalism we want. The financial crisis is a unique opportunity in this regard in opening up a discussion shorn of the conceptual shackles of a neoliberally defined recent past. When I was writing *Neoliberalism and the Law* (2010a) I dealt with the way economic theory shaped the role of law, resulting in a distortion of democratic dynamics in states emerging from Communism (primarily in Russia). I did not anticipate at the time that the same questions as to the balance between state and market, and the role of law in elevating choices in economic governance beyond the reach of the political process, would become so prominent in discussions about regulatory reform worldwide, only a few years later. The financial crisis allows us to revisit the capitalist settlement that crept upon us after the collapse of 'applied' socialism. If capitalist societies have a good look at themselves, as democratic polities, perhaps they will be able to determine whether this settlement is appropriate for the twenty-first century.

1 Methodological framing

Resistance to regulation negates democratic choice because it entails a rejection of democratic politics.

1.1 Introduction

The first chapter of this book sets the methodological bases of the discussion. The chapter offers an explanation for the choice of the market–state relationship as a valid methodological tool and reflects on the nature of market and state. In doing so, the following discussion draws from political, legal and philosophical debates in investigating which sources of coercion in society can be considered as legitimate. Chapter 1 also offers a discussion as to the nature of law and its relationship with regulation, exploring theories of market intervention in economic processes. This presentation sets the background for a consideration of ethics in a capitalist economy. Why is it, the chapter asks, that the wealthy in society reject claims to their wealth as violations of rights? The answer is not to be found in avarice, but in understandings of the nature and function of property rights that are intrinsic to capitalism. If this is the case, then, does capitalism require the existence and persistence of inequality, and how do western concepts of legality deal with the problem of inequality? In addressing these issues, Chapter 1 acts as an introduction to western political economy and as an entry point to a thesis about the place of law in modern capitalism. We begin our discussion by considering the nature of the divide between state and market.

1.2 The state–market relationship

1.2.1 The state–market dichotomy

This book is based on a dichotomy between the market and the state. The choice of this dichotomy as a methodological tool requires some justification. While commonplace, the terms state and market are not automatically accepted as a valid categorisation for advanced capitalist economies. It has been argued, for instance, that this distinction is far too abstract to lead to the kinds of policy work that the financial crisis necessitates we engage in before finding a lasting resolution to problems of systemic stability. Could there be a sensible way to talk about banking regulation, for example, in terms of a bifurcation between state and market?

Randall Germain (2010) argues that while market- or state-based control structures were useful definitional tools in the past, they are not adequate descriptions of later twentieth-century forms of economic governance. Talking about dis-embedded economic orders (structures of economic governance distinct from their social backgrounds) in the era of advanced financialised capitalism (Lapavitsas, 2009) suggests, according to authors like Germain, a need to consider hybrid forms of governance. These hybrid forms are neither entirely private and national in sphere, nor solely public and international. They combine elements of public-private and national-international in a potentially unstable mix. The asymmetrical expansion of power, in some places country-specific while in others global, in some market-based while in others state-based, is consistent, according to Germain, with Karl Polanyi's (1957) observation of a double movement. This double movement, Polanyi argued, is one where the effects of self-regulating markets force political movements to counter the socially destructive consequences of profit-seeking activities. This effort to find balance (or, as economists say, to reach equilibrium) and to counter market freedoms with regulation generated for Polanyi the conditions for a Great Transformation to a new social, political and economic stability. This stability crystallised from the 1950s to the 1970s in a highly regulated cooperative model of oligopolistic capitalism. Robert Reich (2009) describes this compromise as a 'not quite golden age' of capitalism. The reason for the 'not quite' is the persistence of differences in the life chances of population groups according to gender and race that, according to Reich, makes it misleading to call this a society-wide golden age. Nonetheless, the 'compromise' that characterised the result of Polanyi's movement is hailed by most commentators as the pinnacle of capitalist success in the twentieth century.

Even focusing on the state as the source of 'regulation' is considered outdated. Morgan and Yeung (2007: 4) challenge what they view as the three key assumptions behind focusing on the state as the source of regulation. First they argue that non-state institutions, including commercial enterprises and non-governmental organisations (NGOs), operate as sources of social influence and as fora of public deliberations. As a result, the state is challenged in its role as the primary forum for articulating the collective goals of the community. Second, the idea that the state has final authority expressed in a vertical sense, from ruler to subject, is increasingly challenged by the emergence of multiple centres of governance, national and international, public and private. Third, legal rules may not be as effective in controlling behaviour (it can be challenged that commands and command structures are the main drivers of human motivations), plus there is in advanced economies potential for alternative techniques of policy implementation, such as self-regulation and voluntary codes of conduct that are becoming a lot more common, as we will see in Chapter 6.

It is acknowledged that modern forms of regulation have acquired hybrid forms, combining public and private elements, aspects of hard law and self-regulation; however, this does not negate the methodological value of a categorisation of the sources of controls of economic activity as market-based or state-based. While one cannot deny the emergence of 'decentred regulation', it can be argued that the phenomena described above change the relationship between the state and other actors, without dislodging the state from its central role. Also, such developments do not eliminate the relevance of law, nor the importance of a legal perspective on regulation. This book will show in the coming chapters how the state remains the prime conduit of political choices to economic governance by using the responses to the financial crisis and the political turmoil that underlies them as evidence. As balances in the market–state relationship are struck (where expanded market freedoms meet with stronger political resistance that pushes the state to act to protect non-profit interests, in accordance with Polanyi's double movement) it is the force of democratic choice that lends credence to the resulting political economy. In other words, it is the core force of politics as opposed to the profit-making motive of markets that explains the shape of economic governance arrangements. There are political as opposed to economic imperatives therefore that maintain the need to talk about states as distinct from markets even in the current political economy, which is admittedly characterised by hybrids. This argument will be resisted by those who view politics and market interests as one and the same; after all, do politicians not reflect the wishes of markets as opposed to the vaguely expressed interests of constituents? We can ask, therefore, why shouldn't politics be subsumed into the will of the market?

One of the key problems we have in understanding the relationship between the state and the market is the obscuring effects of 'economism'. We can define economism as the orthodox interpretation of economics that employs an almost Marxist inspired pyramid of social relations, placing economic relations at the basis of all social interaction. The problem with this economic determinism is that it leads us to mistake the approximation of human relations in the form of market exchanges with the totality of human interactions. In a sort of odd Platonic 'allegory of the cave' therefore, we mistake shadows with reality and then proceed to structure our entire system of rules upon a false basis of economic exchange. Because markets 'leave their mark' (Sandel, 2012) we come increasingly (to borrow Oscar Wilde's quote) to know the price of everything and the value of nothing. This makes societies less likely to 'counter-move' à la Polanyi. The law, however, can help us out of this trap and offer hope to those who wish to counter-move (Perry-Kessaris, 2011), because the law can re-establish the link between the popular will and economic governance.

A further reason why not all political motivation is 'captured' or tends to market needs is that not all political initiative has market imperatives. There remain centres of power outside the market, which makes the state the crossroads of political activity. We see this in those states worst hit by the crisis, states like Greece, where politics has assumed the role of a buffer between the impositions of economic orthodoxy on the one hand and popular frustration on the other. Perhaps another way to explain a sustained focus on the state–market division as a valid methodology is to argue that losing sight of the dichotomy between state and market is dangerous because, as noted by Stigler (1971), it concedes to private interests coercive powers that should be the sole privilege of the state. If the reader is wondering why coercion should remain the prerogative of the state (and isn't in any case economic coercion as important as the power to exercise physical force?), this book argues that coercion should remain a state prerogative because only the state, to the extent that it is the product of a democratic political process, can use its privilege of coercion legitimately. The link to legitimacy or the perception of a link to legitimacy via democratic expressions of the popular will dampens the destabilising effects of the exercise of coercion, especially in times of crisis. If the aim of the political debate is to sustain capitalism, to sustain free markets, something more than the realpolitik of force (economic or physical) is necessary. The nihilism of abandoning the ideal of democratic control over economic decision-making can lead to the loss of both democracy and markets, something that again we see emerging in crisis states like Greece in the last few years.

While the state at least aspires to legitimation therefore, the market on the contrary uses its privilege of wealth to coerce without needing to appeal to higher ideals (even though a link has been suggested between wealth and moral entitlement as we will see later on in this chapter, followed by an evaluation of the argument that markets are inherently democratic and that product choices are a method of people voting with their wallets later on in the book). The move from state-based regulation to hybrid forms and self or voluntary regulatory structures is explored fully in Chapter 6; however, it is important to state now that if economic governance comes, at least on a philosophical and theoretical level, under the control of hybrid structures, then political legitimacy is defused and the subjugation of social needs to the profit imperative is in danger of becoming total. Vesting ability to exercise coercion to private forces de-legitimises the state, and de-legitimising the state leads to a corruption of social cohesion. We should not therefore be quick to agree to conceptualise regulation outside the notion of the state because that can lead us to relinquish permanently our status as citizens in favour of our status as consumers.

It is our status as consumers in fact that comes to define much of our social and political interaction. Perhaps as a consequence, in twenty-first-century Europe many citizens would consider their lives to be at the mercy of market forces, a reality that Olli Rehn (2011), European Commissioner for Economic and Monetary Affairs, all too well recognised in a speech in January 2011.

Indeed, a Eurobarometer survey (European Commission, 2011) in November 2011 found the most negative perceptions of European citizens to the internal market to be related to too unequal competition, loss of identity to the detriment of smaller countries, inequality between countries and labour issues. The problem is that Mr Rehn used this danger as an argument for further fiscal consolidation, despite most Europeans' distaste for European integration by necessity rather than by choice. We will return to the issue of economic policy by 'technical expertise' instead of democratic choice later on in the book, but before we can do that, the following section seeks to explore further how control is exercised over economic governance by delving deeper into the issue of elevating the state to the position of sole legitimate holder of coercive powers.

1.2.2 Sources of legitimate coercion

The preceding discussion has portrayed the state as being in the position of primary carrier of legitimate powers over decision-making in society. Why is it that the state should be entrusted with such a function, and are sources of legitimate governance residing in other spheres of social interaction, like the market? The concept of legitimacy is used here to denote the extent to which a broad community (in the sense of the principal organisations affected by policy and the general public) acceptance of a regulatory regime comes into being. Legitimacy in turn is linked to the notion of accountability, which is conceptualised as a set of mechanisms and processes that impose an obligation to reveal, explain and justify regulatory actions and is therefore instrumental in securing regulatory legitimacy (Morgan and Yeung, 2007: 11).

In placing the state centre-stage in the debate as to governance and legitimacy the book adopts John Locke's view of the state as a social contract (expressed in the Second Treatise on Civil Government, 1690), the product, in other words, of a conscious decision to defer coercive powers to an entity distinct from other citizens – a politically constituted institution. This view of the state leads to a perception of democracy as government by laws which are arrived at after deliberation by properly chosen representatives of the people and which are promulgated so that all citizens may become acquainted with them. We find a parallel here with discussions as to the nature and meaning of the rule of law, discussed in some detail in *Neoliberalism and the Law* (Glinavos, 2010a). A lot of this discussion on the nature of command structures and the place of law has to do with rights over property, as laws are often evaluated via their impact on the possession of wealth. Indeed Locke's emphasis on private property rights shows that economic rights are the ones most strongly determining the flavour and quality of any governance regime, including a democratic one. According to Locke, therefore, the whole purpose of government is to make laws for the regulation and preservation of property, and for the defence of the community (Popkin and Stroll, 1986: 80).

A key argument of this book is that as the preservation and use of private property rights rests at the core of our conception of the role of the state (which is why private property rights form the cornerstone of the legal framework that enables capitalism), a discussion needs to be had as to the way society uses these rights to effect social outcomes. The discussion in this chapter started by critiquing the current political economy for distancing economic decision-making from political processes. In order to reverse this phenomenon of de-politicisation, the social outcomes of property relations should become once more the overt subject of political discussion. It is argued that this is not the case in contemporary debates, as evidenced, for example, by the inability to discuss openly the uses taxation can serve, especially in Anglo-American jurisdictions. We will address issues of wealth distribution, including the role of taxation, in various parts of this book, in particular in our examination of compensation structures in the financial industry. In arguing for a debate about property rights and wealth, it is important to highlight, however, where my argument deviates from Locke's political philosophy. This book does not treat property rights as natural rights that precede the creation of the institutional structures that constitute the state. In this respect, the analysis here may be closer to Hobbes and Rousseau who viewed property as a creation of society instead of an independent 'natural' state of being. Nevertheless, while implications of viewing property rights as politically constituted bundles of rights are explained fully later on in this discussion, for current purposes Locke's analysis is useful as it offers a philosophical cornerstone for the importance of the state as the centre of a political and economic universe that mediates between social interests.

How does state power translate via regulation of market activity? An argument in favour of regulation can be made by taking the view that mandatory rules backed by legal enforcement, despite their disadvantages, remain the best means to control market behaviour in a way that guarantees the common good. A key reason why this is so rests with the realisation (explained in detail in the following chapters) that laws are the end results of deliberate processes on the part of citizens and their representatives that cannot be understood as the mere aggregate of private preferences in a marketplace. Sunstein (1993) argues that the choices people make as political participants are different from those they make as consumers. Democracy therefore calls for an intrusion on markets. Not only should we not equate consumer with citizen, but we should also be concerned that the evolution of capitalism to a form of 'supercapitalism' (Reich, 2009) (what this book refers to as financialised capitalism, borrowing the phrase from Lapavitsas) elevates the profit-making motive of markets beyond the reach of democratic politics. As citizens, people may seek the aid of the law to bring about a social state in some sense higher than what emerges from market ordering (Sunstein, 1999: 22), but this may no longer be possible in our current political economy. When markets become completely disembedded from their social and political backgrounds, the state (as the protector of the public good) may need to intervene to forcibly re-embed markets into the rest of the social structure. The financial crisis is in this view a Polanyian moment, where the double movement (state intervention) is inevitable in peacefully restoring balance between competing social interests. The emphasis on maintaining the peace is important and pragmatic. As our latter discussion on Greece and the impacts of the crisis there will show, maintaining the peace is no longer the premise of political philosophers but a very real governance problem.

The realisation that the state sometimes has to force market processes back in synch with social expectations has two main consequences. One is that the dichotomy of state and market is revalidated as a methodological tool in interpreting relations in twenty-first-century capitalism. A second consequence is the realisation that deregulation (the main vehicle for disembedding market processes from social controls) needs to be reversed. In summary, therefore, the book seeks to demonstrate that not only a larger role for the state is necessary as a way out of the current crisis, but also that only a larger role for law can guarantee a reconnection of popular control with economic decision-making. This book therefore identifies two main tasks for law. The primary task is to link government to the public via a process of democratic legitimation. In the words of Tony Prosser (1986), law should no longer be seen as isolated from politics, forming an outside constraint on political life. It should be seen rather as a sub-branch of politics, defined by its purpose of legitimation. The law therefore is a means for achieving social ends, as those are determined by the people. This of course is not meant to suggest that we should be in favour of the politicisation of law or promote a legal system akin to that of soviet Russia in antithesis to Hayek's (1960) conception of the rule of law (Hayek viewed law as general rules known in advance which have equal application to everyone) that forms the basis of western legal systems. Under communism, law was explicitly regarded as political and enforced by reference to principles of political justice rather than by reference to abstract concepts of formal justice, such as Hayek's rules of just conduct (Glinavos, 2010a). Prosser's comment means, rather, that we should acknowledge that the basis of legitimate law creation rests in democratic political process. The secondary task for law is to provide a series of stopgaps to prevent market-based economic processes from generating disasters such as the current financial crisis. The explanation for this rests with Minsky's insight into the endogenous dynamics of capitalism to propel itself towards crisis, which we will discuss in the following chapters.

Our discussion so far has assumed that the reader has a conventional understanding of the terms regulation and law. Even these terms, however, are not without controversy in their definition. The following section seeks to explore the intricacies of the very concept of market intervention through law.

1.2.3 Means and outcomes: law and regulation

Barton (1989) argues that there are three ways to conceptualise regulation. One is derived from the neoclassical tradition and focuses on micro-economic concerns (the behaviour of economic units – households and businesses – in making decisions regarding the allocation of resources). The second can be linked to more recent scholarship on institutions and can be called systemic. The third is cultural and has to do with the values each society ascribes to factors of production. Whichever view is chosen, however, it is not necessary that an economic problem is coupled with an economic methodology (Barton, 1989: 43). Hancher and Moran (1989) defined regulation as a feature of any system of social organisation, premising the existence of a social order on the presence of rules. One can argue that the central feature of economic regulation in advanced capitalism is its domination by large, sophisticated and administratively complex organisations performing a range of social tasks. The behaviour of these organisations takes place against a background of extensive state intervention in the form of rules. The exercise of public authority through rules therefore rests on legal authority and this in turn is legitimised by appeals to the popular will. While not all regulation is cast in the form of legal rules (self-regulation and market standard setting can be seen as being outside, or alongside, state-created rules for instance), the principle of constitutionalism (that legal authority flows from the people to the state via the democratic process) means that the range and form of regulation is deeply influenced by the particular conception of the scope and purpose of law which prevails in any particular community at any particular time (Hancher and Moran, 1989: 273). It is this link between social conceptions of the purposes of law and the aims of regulation that this book argues has been eroded by decades of de-politicisation of economic decision-making.

Regulation, however, is inevitably a process by which public control is exercised over the workings of a private power in the marketplace with the aim of taming this power. To take a historical example (Kolko, 1963), regulatory agencies were created during the New Deal in the US as the outposts of capitalism designed to control the market lest capitalism by its own greed, fear, avarice and myopia destroy itself. Within this concept of regulation one finds a divide between the public and the private sphere, with the public seen in opposition to the private and the state seen as the product of a liberal constitution with a public core bounded by law and distinct from the market (Lowi, 1979). This relationship of opposition nonetheless does not imply hostility towards the market, but represents the reflection of a social desire to contain market impulses that give capitalism its propensity towards crisis. In this way, we can see a clear link between the desire to regulate in order to enable market operations to achieve the goal of producing socially beneficial outcomes. To combine once more the different streams of literature on this topic, we see a parallel between legal scholars and Keynesian economists (like Minsky) in attempting to use a framework of rules to stabilise market operations.

Following this view of regulation as a 'product' of state action aiming to constrain capitalist impulses, we can define as regulation any control system that contains at least three components: first, some capacity for standard setting, to allow a distinction to be made between more or less preferred states of the system; second, some capacity for information gathering or monitoring to produce knowledge about current or changing states of the system; and third, some capacity for behaviour modification to change the state of the system (Hood et al., 2001: 23). Determining the scope of action for such a control system, however, is far from a straightforward task. Richard Posner (1974), for instance, recognised the explanation of the pattern of government intervention in the market (another definition for economic regulation) as a major challenge to social theory. Posner, viewing regulation from the point of view of a law and economics scholar, defines the term regulation as referring to taxes and subsidies of all sorts as well as to explicit legislative and administrative controls over rates, entry and other facets of economic activity. We can elaborate on the view of regulation as a constraint on market activity by viewing regulatory intervention as a set of deliberate attempts by the state to influence markets towards socially valuable behaviour by establishing, monitoring and enforcing legal rules (Morgan and Yeung, 2007: 3).

Following from this conception of regulation as a product of law, we can conclude that when we talk of law we refer to the means employed to achieve a regulatory outcome. Law in this sense is an instrument (means) used by the state to achieve the community's collective goals (regulatory product). Law in the context of a democratic state is seen then as a set of authoritative rules backed by coercive force, exercised by a legitimately constituted nation state. In this sense therefore law is a process, while regulation is a product of that process. Law in fact is a part of a wider process that facilitates the operations of a capitalist economy, forming part of the infrastructure that links the state to the market, to the community and to individuals.

The law is present both when rules prohibit or mandate behaviour and when rules delineate the boundaries of acceptable behaviours. For example, while the law comes to mind when an action is declared illegal (e.g. dumping toxic waste), the law is also central to economic activity when an action is allowed yet regulated (e.g. in the case of trading licences to pollute via carbon trading schemes). George Stigler (1971) considered that the state (the machinery and power of the state) can be both a potential resource and a threat to every industry in the society. With its power to manipulate law in order to prohibit or compel, to take or give money, the state can and does selectively help or hurt a vast number of industries. In employing law, in other words, the state produces regulatory outcomes that alter market relations. Yet in using law in such manner the state engages in a process that has a political and moral subtext. By providing the framework within which economic and social interaction takes place, law cannot help but interact with morality and politics (Morgan and Yeung, 2007: 6). Law creation therefore is an inherently political process. As a consequence, in capitalism, law rests at the centre of the political economy of a state. It expresses the result of political actions and it legitimises the operation of state institutions that in turn impact on political processes. Said otherwise, the key power of the state – the power to coerce – is channelled through a legal path that simultaneously explains the source of power and legitimates it. As part of this dual dynamic (law as the result of politics and the boundary to politics), the law both constructs and constrains democratic institutions that articulate collective choices. As a result, law acquires (in a democratic state) a normative dimension and can be understood as institutionalising and giving expression to certain values that democracy itself presupposes. These values then are reflected in choices made by processes of adjudication when resolving disputes on conflicting visions of rights. It is important to remember, however, that while this power of coercion is, in democratic states, channelled via courts and other dispute resolution mechanisms, regulation should not be limited (as we argue in Chapter 6) to being a product of law creation via the judiciary.

The discussion so far has set us on a course that will lead to an interpretation of the role law has in effecting regulatory outcomes. Before we proceed further, however, we need to pause and examine the nature of the state, to look deeper into justifications for the exercise of state coercion. This discussion involves an analysis of the way regulators and courts see themselves. A reflection is therefore offered below on the literature explaining theories for market intervention. We will also explore further the balance between sources of regulatory creation (state, courts, voluntarism) in the final chapter of the book (Chapter 6) when we will look at the possibilities for regulatory reform post crisis.

1.2.4 Theories of market intervention

In discussing rationales for state intervention, we need to reflect on the nature of the state itself. There are four main views of the state one can find in the literature. A juristic view of the state, most closely associated with the writings of Hans Kelsen (1967), views the state as the product of a system of rules where compliance is ensured via un-derived structures of authority. A Hegelian view of the state on the other hand sees the institutions of the state as a directing intelligence bringing order to the rest of society (Damaska, 1982-3). Hobbes and Locke are at the opposite end of Kelsen and Hegel, seeing coercive authority as the product of a social compact, a situation where state power emanates from the people via an almost contractual process of delegation of power (Mashaw, 1982-3). The Marxist view takes the contractual point to its extreme, treating a social compact as an unobtainable ideal and viewing state authority as a violation of social compromise, an instrument for the domination of one social class by another. What we see around us today is a state-capitalist model that adopts the language of a compact between the people and authority, while operating like a directing intelligence, proffering to express technocratic knowledge on issues of economic governance. This technocratic 'intelligence' can in turn be portrayed in Marxist class-conflict terms as serving the interests of the (few) wealthy against the interests of the (many) poor. While in a contractual model there is a strong link between regulation and democracy, in the current state-capitalist model (if we wish to call it that) government becomes the handmaiden of economic determinism, with regulation becoming distanced from democracy. This growing distance, that we often deplore in this book, brings to the fore the need for a discussion of values. What are the cultural aspects, the values, of regulation in a technocratic model of governance? Barton argues (1989: 62) that if economic determinism is rejected, then a dialogue can begin on questions of equality both distributional and spiritual. How did we arrive, however, at a state model that views regulation as the expression of technocracy?

The history of regulation reveals a tension between the evolution of rules via the courts and through the legislative process. The history of US intervention in market processes offers a useful illustration of how regulation evolved from being virtually non-existent to being a newly acquired function of the courts and later a function of the state itself. As we will see in more detail in Chapter 3, before 1900 significant commercial disputes in the United States were generally resolved through private litigation. Courts ruled on corporate liability in industrial accidents, on anti-competitive practices (involving the railways for example), on the safety of foods and medicines and even on the constitutionality of income tax. In the three decades between 1887, when the US Congress passed the Interstate Commerce Act, and 1917, when participation in the First World War put an end to the progressive movement (one of the first efforts to bring socially harmful market practices under state sanction) (Hofstadter, 1960), this situation changed radically. Over thirty years, reformers eroded the nineteenth-century belief that private litigation was the sole appropriate response to social wrongs. During this era, regulatory agencies at both the state and the federal level took over the social control of competition, anti-trust policy, rail-transport pricing, food and drug safety, and many other areas. At the same time, the US experienced other important changes, such as reform of the civil service, use of voter referendums to decide local issues, direct election of senators, recall of judges and the growth of government administrative agencies (Glaeser and Shleifer, 2003: 404).

What brought about this increasing willingness to regulate, however, and why was it deemed necessary to intervene in markets at all? Posner (1972), explaining the relationship of law to economics in the twentieth century identified two main theories of economic regulation that had come into prominence by the mid-1970s. One was the public interest theory, which holds that regulation is supplied in response to demands by the public for the correction of inefficient or inequitable market practices. The second theory was the capture theory, which in turn holds that regulation is supplied in response to the demands of interest groups struggling among themselves to maximise the benefits of their members. The standard public interest theory holds that regulation deals with market failures and externalities (defined as uncompensated costs of market activities that fall on the rest of society, for instance environmental degradation) (Stiglitz, 1989). While there is agreement, however, that market failures do exist (this would in fact be difficult to deny in the face of the current crisis), there is very little consensus as to whether such failures require regulatory intervention, and if they do, what form it should take and to what extent it should reach.

Let us take financial markets as an example of a prime target for regulation. One can identify two main explanations for the need to intervene, especially in this area. The first is control and avoidance of systemic risks, suggesting that regulation may be necessary to prevent imbalances that may endanger the stability of the entire economic system. An example of this sort of prudential regulation is setting capital-base requirements for banks, so that they do not find themselves insolvent in a liquidity crisis or during other economic shocks, a suggestion that is much in vogue as a response to current difficulties. The second is the use of a regulatory system to correct information asymmetries. As examples one can think of rules mandating that companies to disclose certain information to their shareholders or the rules banning insider dealing. Such intervention ensures that the market operates on a level playing field and justifies regulatory involvement as a necessary step to ensure that those in control of information do not take advantage of their position of power to abuse other market actors. (A current example of this sort of attitude to intervention are proposals to bring more areas of the market under control, for example by creating central clearing houses for over-the-counter derivatives.)

Even if the aim is to eliminate market imperfections by regulating, however, one still has to discern how to use the legal mechanisms available to do so. Should the courts be tasked with regulatory aims, is this a matter for the legislature, or should industry rely on voluntary mechanisms to minimise harmful social consequences? The public interest theory, according to its critics, does not explain why either contract or tort law could not successfully address these problems in the first place (Coase, 1960) and, as a consequence, does not offer an answer to the question as to who should be responsible for securing socially beneficial behaviours. Posner (1972) and Shavell (1984) discuss the choice between litigation and regulation from an efficiency perspective (we discuss the role of voluntarism later on in the book in Chapter 6 when we see how different mixtures of control regimes can be part of a reformed regulatory environment). Posner identified two key assumptions as being at the centre of the public interest theory (1974: 336). One assumption was that markets are extremely fragile and apt to operate very inefficiently (or inequitably) if left alone; the other was that government regulation is virtually costless. With these assumptions, it was easy to argue against the gradual and constraining effects of litigation and in favour of direct legislative interventions in the economy (examples include trade union protection, public utility and transport regulation, agricultural subsidies, occupational licences, the minimum wage). These interventions could simply be seen as government responses to public demands for the rectification of palpable and remediable inefficiencies and inequities in the operation of the free market. Behind each scheme of regulation therefore one could discern a market imperfection, the existence of which supplied a complete justification regulation which is assumed to operate effectively and without cost (Posner, 1974: 336).

Since practically everyone accepts the idea of market failures, why is it then that direct state intervention in the marketplace (in the form of law-making) is being resisted? One explanation is the relative failure of law-based regulation to affect desired outcomes (correcting the identified market imperfections). The idea that regulatory agencies are created for bona fide public purposes, but are then mismanaged with the result that those purposes are not always achieved, has been thoroughly dissected in the literature. It is alleged that a serious misgiving about any version of the public interest theory lies in doubts about the mechanism through which any perception of the public interest is translated into legislative action, a topic to which we will return to consider in Chapter 2, where we examine the role law plays in markets. Critics of public interest theories, like Posner, argue that while a classical understanding of markets explains how the efforts of individuals to promote their self-interest through transacting bring about an efficient allocation of resources, there is no comparable articulation of how a public perception as to what legislative policies or arrangements would maximise public welfare is translated into legislative action. Negating the capacity of democracy to accurately reflect public wishes, therefore, critics of public choice theories argue that there is insufficient evidence that legislative action works in ameliorating market inefficiencies and also that there is insufficient theory to link popular choice, political expression and policy outcomes (Posner, 1974: 340).

The force of criticism of the public interest theory as hinted above resulted in the development of so-called 'capture' or 'special interest' theories of regulation, mentioned above as an analytical category brought to public attention primarily by Posner. Stigler (1971) and Posner (1974) made a significant contribution to the development of the theory of regulation by questioning the motives and the capabilities of regulators (Glaeser and Shleifer, 2003: 405). Posner, however, was hostile to the early versions of a capture theory that dismissed regulation as an instrument of domination, suggesting that economic regulation is not about the public interest at all, but is a process by which interest groups seek to promote their (private) interests. Taking this view, it is possible to believe in the existence of market inefficiencies and to ascribe a legitimate role to the state to intervene, while being sceptical of the state's capacity to intervene successfully. Even among authors least enamoured with the market, there is still a great degree of scepticism about the state's capacity to translate a public perception of the public good into law. An example is offered by Reich (2009) who argues that the spillover of corporate money into politics has created a rotten cycle of influence peddling by lobbyists and corporate interests that corrupted politics in a way that has turned the legislative process into a mechanism for delivering the wishes of the highest bidder. In Reich's view this situation is systemic as firms in highly competitive environments have no choice but to try and capture the regulatory agencies that affect their ability to make money. Posner himself was sympathetic to the idea that over time regulatory agencies come to be dominated by the industries regulated. Posner, however, preferred overall an economic explanation of regulation, one based on rational choice on the basis of individual self-interest. He suggested that viewing regulation as a product allocated in accordance with basic principles of supply and demand directs attention to factors bearing on the value of regulation to particular individuals or groups, since, other things being equal, we can expect a product to be supplied to those who value it the most (1974: 344).

The message emanating from this short description of the evolution of regulatory theory from the public interest to the capture theories helps us answer the question we set at the beginning of this subsection. How did we arrive at a state model that views regulation as the expression of technocracy? The effect of the critique of the link between the political process and efficient regulatory outcomes as explained by Posner (whether inefficiency is due to the inability of regulators to translate mandates to effective rules, or due to capture and the resulting loss of sight of regulatory goals) is to cast doubt on the entire link between democratic politics and regulatory systems. If the articulation of political aims becomes lost in the fog of actually managing regulatory systems, then wouldn't it be better to dispense with politics altogether? If the study of post-communism (to borrow from the analysis in *Neoliberalism and the Law*) has taught us anything, it is not to underestimate the power of the technocrat's belief that the truth is not out there, but in the academic textbooks. Who can, after all, argue against equations? But if technocracy is an escape from the toils of the political process, what about ethics? How could values be represented in regulatory systems that are designed on the basis of 'economic' as opposed to political truths?

1.3 Ethics of regulation

In order to begin discovering the values of a regulatory system, we need to enquire into the ethical justifications that support the practice of surrendering the reigns of policy-making to market-friendly technocracies. Whichever theoretical justification for regulatory action on the part of the state one chooses to advocate, market actors consistently raise a series of objections to the use of legal mechanisms to direct market behaviour. These objections can be roughly categorised in two groups, one external and one internal to legal process. The first group has at its core economic justifications, making it seem as if proposals to extend regulation infringe upon a 'natural state of being' of market operations that has them free of interference. We will explore in Chapter 3 the source of the myth that markets 'at the beginning' were unregulated and then became corrupted by state interventions. The second group utilises legal notions, like private property rights, to make a link between entitlements and moral values. This discussion draws on my work published in an edited collection entitled *Socio-Legal Approaches to International*

Economic Law (Perry-Kessaris, 2012). The following part of this chapter offers an overview of objections to regulation, first presenting the economic and then the legal grounds. Most examples used here to illustrate industry responses to proposals for reform have been drawn from an examination of controls over compensation structures in the financial sector, which is fully explored in Chapter 5 of the book. While objections to regulation often adopt the same style, the particular responses to recommendations on reforming compensation structures presented at the EU level in the guise of a set of guidelines by the Committee of European Banking Supervisors (CEBS) in 2010 are especially illustrative of the thinking of industry actors. Chapter 5 will describe these guidelines as a mild attempt to temper the bonus culture in the financial sector by attempting to align compensation with long-term firm performance, without in fact aiming to outstep the status quo as existed pre-crisis. For the time being, we will not dwell on the intricacies of controls over compensation, but on the moral subtext of reactions to calls for regulation. It is via examining the underlying rationales for resistance to regulation that we begin to understand how de-politicisation has come to define our thinking about the state–market relationship in fundamental ways. The following discussion does not offer a comprehensive presentation of all arguments against regulation, but focuses on the most commonly voiced arguments by free-market advocates.

1.3.1 Economic arguments against regulation

The first part of our exploration of the philosophical bases of resistance to state intervention will look at the economic justifications for markets free from interference. While the rhetoric varies, objections to regulation (especially from the financial industry) revolve around a series of headline arguments that could be grouped under three categories: future, past and present. The argument that looks to the future has to do with the value of innovation. The argument drawing lessons from the past relates to the dangers of excessive regulation. Finally, the argument that deals with the present focuses on comparative advantage, antipathy to taxation, regulatory competence and complexity. The following discussion presents each one of those key arguments in attempting to unearth the thinking and moral subtext of resistance to state intrusion into market activity; the reason for this analysis is of course the argument made earlier in this book: that resisting state intrusion entails a rejection of politics that leads to a negation of democratic choice. Our reference point for this discussion is the focal point of the crisis, the finance industry.

The purpose of finance is said to be the facilitation of economic activity across space and time. A great number of objections by the finance industry to regulation therefore centre on the idea that inhibiting financial innovation jeopardises future growth. The innovation argument against regulation is in other words suggesting that regulation impedes the industry's capacity to evolve. For example, the European private equity and venture capital industry representative body noted that under the circumstances of the current financial crisis, capital gains incentives are necessary to encourage long-term risk-taking in fledgling companies that stimulate the economy. This means that the private equity and venture capital industry should not be hampered in its ability to create companies, industries and technologies. Controlling market operations, like compensation structures, is seen as an example of inappropriately restricting activity, at a time when the private equity and hedge fund industry is (according to itself) without equal in guaranteeing alignment of remuneration to performance (EVCA, 2010). One would hope that the 'innovation' they have in mind is not that of securitisation of asset-backed securities in the form of collateralised debt obligations (which were then repackaged into further products) that allowed the endless recycling of debt, spiralling leverage and augmented risk, leading to the collapse of value that caused the credit crunch, as we will see in detail in Chapter 4. Wolfgang Munchau in *The Meltdown Years* (2009) offers an excellent and accessible explanation of the consequences of 'innovation' arguing that most financial engineering was just a consequence of attempts to evade the Basel capital adequacy rules rather than an organic process of evolution towards financial products that offer better value to customers and investors.

The industry's vehement dislike of regulatory intervention is not only based on assumptions about the value of innovation to future economic performance, but is also born supposedly from historical fact. Past experience, the industry tells us, is brimming with examples of state failure and catastrophic regulatory assaults. Drawing from this claimed experience (mirroring the theoretical critique as to the inefficiencies of regulation we saw earlier in this chapter), a so-called excessive regulation argument suggests that efforts to regulate are flawed because they inevitably take a too broad-brush approach and catch unintended targets. The fault with intervention therefore is not that it is not needed, but that it is directed at the wrong parties. This point is exemplified by the European Fund and Asset Management Association (EFAMA) which, while agreeing with the need to promote effective risk management by including, for instance, principles on remuneration in regulatory instruments, felt that remuneration structures in the asset management industry should not have as their main objective the promotion of effective risk-taking as asset managers by definition do not take risk against their balance sheet but instead manage client portfolios in accordance with detailed rules agreed with their clients (EFAMA, 2010).

In the same vein, commercial banks claim that they are prudent and point the finger at hedge funds as being responsible for share price fluctuations that lead to market instability. Investment banks and hedge funds argue that they are only facilitating the operations of their clients, so they ought not to be regulated. Giant consolidated financial institutions, such as insurance firms like AIG, claim that their integrated structures promote efficiencies. Everyone claims that the state can only intervene where negative externalities are clearly identified and where instances of market failure are acute, while at the same time warning that the capacity of state actors to comprehend the market and act independently is compromised. To return to the point made earlier, we see clearly here how the corrosive critique of scholars like Posner serves to pull the rug from under states' feet, undermining the theoretical and practical reasons for intervention in market processes. In consequence, even when the state has to intervene, the argument is put forward that its action is likely to make matters worse rather than better. To summarise then, what does the past teach us about regulation according to the members of the financial industry? The lesson is that no matter how the market deals with things, it is still better than involving the state. This conclusion is reached despite the conclusions of institutional economists like Douglass North and Oliver Williamson which show how misguided this view is and offer a framework for explaining (in a contemporary setting) how state action and a foundation of law are complementary to a successful market (Groenewegen et al., 2010). Never mind, the industry says. A market free from state interference is a matter of science, and when that fails to convince, it becomes a matter of values. Before we move onto the invocation of 'values', however, there remains a final set of economic arguments to address.

Arguably, the forward-looking and past impressions of the purpose and value of regulation do not offer a full picture of economic arguments against regulation. Many of the financial industry's objections to regulation relate to the here and now, to how state intervention can change the present, for the worse. A key component of this theme is a 'comparative disadvantage' argument which is being repeated ad nauseam, and proposes that no action should be taken before a global consensus on regulatory reform is reached. Since a global consensus on any level other than grand rhetoric is nigh-on impossible in the field of market regulation, this is a wonderful recipe for inaction. The motivator behind this objection is that the country, or the region, or the continent as a whole is disadvantaged. For example, the UK's Financial Services Authority's (FSA) consultation on the interpretation of the CEBS compensation guidelines in national law offers a summary of the industry's objections that is of special relevance to the comparative disadvantage argument presented here. According to the consultation document, on the issue of retention awards (bonuses) several respondents to the FSA said that limiting or not permitting retention awards for current employees would place existing employers at a disadvantage when seeking to retain key talent, in particular in situations where they wish to counter an offer of employment elsewhere. Some respondents specifically said that the loss of such staff could place the UK at a competitive disadvantage. One trade association commented that the proposed rules on limiting bonuses would produce a 'poacher's paradise' as it would incentivise firms to focus on external hiring rather than developing and rewarding their own talent. Similarly, on the issue of deferral of bonuses, most respondents agreed in principle with the FSA deferral proposals, but some were concerned that the deferral rules were too prescriptive regarding structure and levels of award, once again highlighting that this would put UK firms at a potential competitive disadvantage as other jurisdictions have taken a lighter approach (FSA, 2010: 18–19).

An offshoot of the above argument is the regulate/tax us and we'll leave dilemma, a favourite of banking executives. The British Bankers Association (BBA) said that while the industry recognises that effective measures of remuneration are important, it is concerned that if they are not progressed in a practical and proportionate manner, there is a risk that key personnel will either seek to relocate outside the EU, or be reluctant to move to the EU. Over time, this would allegedly have an increasingly significant impact on the amount of financial services jobs, activities and revenues located in the EU (BBA, 8 November 2010). The threat to up sticks and move to more business-friendly jurisdictions brings to mind the fanatical ramblings of characters in the novels of the free market crusader Ayn Rand. In *Atlas Shrugged* Rand imagines a world eerily like our own, but one where brave men of industry rebel against government intrusion into the free market and 'go on strike' by leaving. In the words of the character John Galt (Rand, 1957: 680):

> We've heard it shouted that the industrialist is a parasite, that his workers support him, create his wealth, make his luxury possible – and what would happen to him if they walked out? Very well. I propose to show the world who depends on whom, who supports whom, who is the source of wealth, who makes whose livelihood possible and what happens to whom when [the industrialist] walks out.

What would happen indeed if all the bankers left simultaneously for an offshore 'haven' like Guernsey? Would it bring about an apocalypse as that imagined by Rand, or just ease congestion in Kensington? The thinly veiled threats of modern-day (actual) financiers have not impressed all equally, especially European policy-makers. Speaking with MPs on the British Treasury Select Committee, the European Commissioner Michel Barnier said that the guidelines would not see 'a flight of talent towards Asia or elsewhere'; he added that he would not be overly impressed by attempts to blackmail governments to prevent regulatory actions using a hyped-up risk of executive flight from the EU (Treanor, 2010). Comments such as Barnier's, however, have not deterred firms from threatening to pack their bags since.

The above comments lead to a related point put forward at the time of the nationalisation of Northern Rock and the effective nationalisation of RBS in the UK in 2008: the argument that even if one accepts the case for state intervention in finance (in particular), the state does not know how to run banks. At that time, the market was supposedly worried that the Brown government had developed an appetite for nationalisation. The government defended itself by saying that it never intended to do such a thing, as it would not be able to find the expertise to run the nationalised banks. This argument, as to the lack of expertise or competence of government to interfere in the running of the financial sector, runs into a wider objection to financial regulation that we came across when considering regulatory theory earlier, which could be described as the complexity argument. Kurt Andersen in *Time Magazine* (2009) summarised the problem by saying:

> The financial crisis came about because we got complacent, depending on all knowing financial experts – mortgage lenders, Wall Street sharpers, the Federal Reserve – to run our system expertly. But then the experts did the same thing, imagining that they had laid off all their risks on other experts. Until finally, the last expert down the line turned out to be just another greater fool, and the system crashed.

The worrying conclusion from this observation is that if things are too complex for the experts to understand, what are the chances that politicians and regulators can devise adequate mechanisms to deal with financial market regulation? We come back therefore to the question posed earlier: if politics cannot manage, isn't it best to leave things to the markets? Is it better indeed to leave these things to the experts, despite the fact that self- or light-touch regulation seems to have failed (for more on the failure, death and resurrection of light-touch regulation see Chapter 6)? For an entertaining account of the way complexity reached levels at which not even the financial industry fully understood the 'products' it was creating, see Michael Lewis *The Big Short* (2011). Admitting complexity, however, does not solve our key problem of what to do about it. The thesis that the market is imperfect but the state is worse operates to create false dilemmas such as: does one regulate before fully understanding or does one let the market 'innovate' and then mop up the consequences? The FSA's swing from principles-based regulation to law-backed enforcement and then back to principles-based regulation is a good example of a fear that the cure for market imperfections may be worse than the disease. As Lipshaw (2010: 315) observes, however, in order to regulate prospectively, we need to explain retrospectively. The reaction of regulators to any crisis will be to reduce the financial crisis to cognisable (and if possible legally translatable) instances of social scientific cause and effect, in preparation for imposing the 'technological' cure of a regulatory scheme. Such cures abound in the literature, and they need not be wrong. One can look, for example, at Hyman Minsky's work *Stabilizing an Unstable Economy* (2008) to see why financialised capitalism is unstable and how it can be brought under control so that it does not continuously endanger prosperity via violent booms and busts. Should we really be content allowing the market to continue to operate on patterns that create persistent crises due to fears (backed by flimsy empirical evidence) that the state does not have adequate expertise to devise effective regulatory frameworks?

While these arguments have been countered in economic terms by many, including the authors mentioned above (Joseph Stiglitz, in his latest work *Freefall* (2010), offers a wonderful dissection of the flaws of contemporary economic orthodoxy), there is a common philosophical thread that runs through them that goes perhaps to the core of objections to regulation in a way that individual arguments do not. This common thread is the industry's assumption (to return to our compensation structures example) that differences in compensation and the subsequent wealth inequalities are justified (beyond economics) from a legal and ethical point of view. This is where law, economics and ethics come together in a way that transcends divisions between disciplines. It is exactly the morphing of the argument from textbook economics to values and ethical considerations that betrays the need to consider the nature of law creation and its links with economic governance. Looking at the issue of regulation from the perspective of a lawyer, but drawing on the empirical and analytical expertise of an economist within a normative legal framework, allows us to truly appreciate the consequences of different forms of market organisation on the rest of the social structure. The following section addresses the very concept of the purported justice of entitlements over wealth in a way that brings forward the values embedded in the law as an underlying justification for much of the surface economic arguments against regulation.

1.3.2 Legal explanations for inequality

A major premise of the argument that economic relations ought to be contractually determined without interference from government is that private property rights are unassailable and that redistribution of wealth is a violation of personal freedom. The classical economic argument central to Adam Smith's theory of the 'invisible hand' (proposed in the *Wealth of Nations* in 1776) and elaborated on by Ronald Coase (1960) is that people are entitled to their wealth as they are responsible for its creation. Apart from some original distribution of wealth that is taken for granted, the solidifying of entitlements in the form of private property rights means that wealth is not only securely owned, but also justly deserved, giving ownership a moral aspect as well as a legal one. The point of the following discussion is not to question the overall capitalist settlement that accepts inequalities of wealth. It is rather to challenge the legal and philosophical underpinnings of *extreme* inequalities of wealth and the *extreme* rewards that characterise the financial sector. It is this excess that defines the crisis. In a way this discussion links back to the ancient Greeks and the Aristotelian notion of a good society, defined mostly as a society in which moderation is a key moral virtue – a virtue that is in stark absence today. The following part of the discussion begins by addressing the argument that the state ought not interfere with private property rights, as this entails a violation of freedom.

1.3.2.1 Property rights and freedom

The notion of incontestable private rights of property protected by law against both private and governmental interference is of pivotal significance to capitalism and is linked to fundamental notions of individuality, democracy and freedom. Property rights are also fundamental to western liberal theory as they provide an explanation for the existence of a framework of law. Friedrich von Hayek delineated the implications of property as a legal concept for state economic policy and for individual freedom. For Hayek (1944) government regulation and laws that respect freedom need to be general and formal. He argues that the rule of law demands that the government is bound by fixed rules announced beforehand. By contrast, he claims, economic planning is fundamentally contrary to the rule of law because of the ad hoc decision-making power which is necessarily granted to planners. If the state wishes to abide by the rule of law it should confine itself to establishing rules applying to general types of situations and should allow individuals freedom to determine their actions in everything which depends on the circumstances of time and place (Hayek, 1944: 80).

Following Hayek's thinking, especially as developed in *The Constitution of Liberty* (1960), one can reach the conclusion that requiring firms to behave on the basis of state regulations should be seen as a violation of the rule of law. Putting to one side the question of the allocation of entitlements in society, Hayek claimed that the predictability of 'the rules of the game' and their strict application protect individual entitlements from all kinds of interference, including from the state. Hayek thus attempted to sidestep questions arising out of the substantive injustice of gross inequalities of wealth. In a similar fashion, borrowing from the Austrian tradition, orthodox economists nowadays suggest that the distribution of wealth generated by unhindered market processes is inherently just, whatever its final form, because factors of production, including labour, receive their true worth reflecting what they actually contribute to production (Glinavos, 2010a: 20).

Hayek's contributions to the literature represent an evolution of the theory that gained prominence since the publication of Adam Smith's *The Wealth of Nations* (1776) which introduced the idea of people as autonomous economic agents. Classical economics as a whole represent a conceptual structure premised on the assumption that rational human beings, on the basis of available information, make the best choices on how to produce more efficiently and take advantage of the opportunities presented by the markets in which they operate. Both social and political activity is subjected to this overarching rationality. This notion led to the creation of the concept of a *homo economicus*. For an example of how these assumptions translate to policy prescriptions one can follow the evolution of the theory of rational markets into the efficient market hypothesis (Fama, 1970). All decision-making is meant to be conducted on the basis of economic objectives and Smithian theory is cemented in this economic determinism. Smith saw society progressing from one form to another, driven by an evolving division of labour. Indeed, an embryonic Darwinism contained in Smith's work is central to contemporary market theory, with its tendency to see economic systems as engaged in a competitive struggle for supremacy, with the consequence that the free market is seen as a system inherently and even evolutionarily superior to all others (Glinavos, 2010a: 146).

Modern capitalists, such as the respondents to the consultations on regulatory interventions discussed above, with their belief in the inherent superiority of market mechanisms, assume therefore (however subconsciously) that history is simply the process whereby impediments to the operation of markets are gradually removed, a process which releases man's natural tendencies (Glinavos 2010a: 146–7). To paraphrase Francis Fukuyama (1992), history comes to an end when all market impediments are lifted. We revisit this belief in Chapter 3 when we take a critical view of the history of state interventions in the economy. It is almost inconceivable, therefore, for capitalists to envisage regulation in anything other than negative terms. Some commentators on the behaviour of elites (such as David Harvey in *A Brief History of Neoliberalism* (2007) for example) tend to ascribe distaste towards regulation to personal self-interest, and blame the institutional inability to curtail market excesses to a conspiracy of political and market interests in the corridors of power. While there inevitably is some truth in these claims, this work proposes another explanation as most probable. It is to a great degree the ideological make-up of market actors and their skewed understanding of the purpose of law that leads them to abhor regulation. Where is it though that orthodox opinion is wrong?

Critics of both Smith and Hayek reject the economic determinism inherent in the ideas described above (and their treatment of 'the economic' as a spatially separate sphere to the social and political). Karl Polanyi (1957) rejected Smith's assumptions about human nature arguing that the dynamics of history are produced not so much by certain natural human tendencies but by the pressures exerted by prevailing property relations. Faced with critique, market advocates retort that the beneficial, wealth maximising, economic logic of the market cannot fully operate until all 'unnatural' impediments to its operation are removed. From this perspective, the failure of financial capitalism that we are currently experiencing has less to do with the avarice of bankers and their specific behavioural characteristics and more to do with politically inspired impediments to market operations imposed by the state (Glinavos, 2010a: 147). This thinking surfaces in arguments blaming the financial crisis on failures of regulation rather than on failures of the market. Bankers are claiming, among other things, that the reason for the crash was that the government either made them behave in ways that were risky (for example by encouraging them to offer loans to lower-rated borrowers in order to increase home-ownership) and/or failed to stop them from making unwise investments when credit was becoming overextended. A summary of arguments along these lines is offered in Davies' *The Financial Crisis* (2010). A fuller explanation is offered in this volume in Chapter 4.

Already in this chapter we have come repeatedly across the very powerful idea that state regulation leads to less effective markets. This belief is a constant block to progress in discussions on reform of regulatory frameworks.

Added to the above is the fact that neoclassical models of 'rational economic men' fail to acknowledge real-life motivations for economic decisions. Economists unfortunately are often characterised by their refusal to address differences between theoretical models and empirical evidence (Krugman, 2008: 182), resulting in overwhelming support for ill-backed theories such as supply-side economics (the idea that economic growth comes from enabling production only via deregulation and tax cuts, rather than by stimulating demand). One area where this lack of interest in the pragmatic is most obvious is the refusal (implicit in the financial industry's reaction to the regulation of remuneration for example) to acknowledge how incentives for managers in the finance industry prior to the crash led them to behave in ways detrimental to the interests of their firms, the economy and society. Orthodox economic theory built around libertarian economic beliefs (which still remains the main yardstick of government policy as we will see in our discussion of the remedies proposed for the European sovereign debt crisis in Chapter 5) largely lacks adequate interpretive tools to assess this perceived 'irrationality' that had as its ultimate result the financial crisis (Roubini and Mihm, 2011: 54).

A key tool in escaping the theoretical sclerosis of neoclassical constructs is the realisation that property rights are not independently existing natural phenomena, but legal constructs *preceded* by political interventions which allocate rights. Property rights should be seen in fact as nothing more than social relations of constraint (Cohen, 1994: 16). By extension, money itself is nothing more than a legal fiction or construct, a notion to which we will return in Chapter 2. Markets are, to use Chang's (2002) phrase, premised upon 'rights-obligation structures' that are politically constituted. Karl Polanyi rebelled against the myth perpetuated in capitalism that labour, land and money are 'commodities'. He noted that:

> Labour is only another name for a human activity which goes with life itself, which in its turn is not produced for sale but for entirely different reasons, nor can that activity be detached from the rest of life, be stored or mobilized; land is only another name for nature, which is not produced by man; actual money, finally, is merely a token of purchasing power which, as a rule, is not produced at all, but comes into being through the mechanism of banking or state finance. None of them is produced for sale. (1957: 72)

The problem with this view, from the point of orthodox theory, is that it undercuts the idea that 'the market' is somehow apolitical or can be politically neutral, and the notion that the rationality of the market is somehow 'purely economic', separate from politics.

Despite the elaborate arguments against regulation woven around the idea of private property, bankers are not in fact entitled to their bonuses, neither are they entitled to determine their own pay structures as a matter of some natural law. Contract is not free and wealth is not private due to some universal, ahistorical imperative. It is the capitalist legal system that defines property rights and distributes wealth on the basis of those rights that allows all this to happen. It is our agreement, as citizens, to give legal effect to privately determined contracts that allows private agreements to operate. In sum, it is a political decision to respect property rights and contractual agreements that rests at the basis of the legal system, not some God-given or naturally determined law. This may sound radical or novel in this era of unthinking acceptance of pro-market soundbites, but it is neither. Wealth, contracts, property rights, as the products of political agreements, do not have some mythical unassailable status. Society can decide otherwise and the law can be amended to allow for a different treatment of contractual agreements and changed balances in the distributions of rights. This does not mean that one should disrespect property and seek to confiscate wealth. On the contrary, an appreciation of the 'synthetic', legally constituted nature of our political economy allows us to debate whether this particular form of organisation (financialised capitalism) is chosen in the interests of society and enables us to choose different ways of organising our economy through a process of democratic consultation.

Also, a temporal legal entitlement does not equate to a moral right, and despite what people like the orators of the Institute of Economic Affairs try to tell us, redistributing wealth is not equivalent to theft. In fact this is not some shocking revelation: all capitalist legal systems contain rules that can help ameliorate the consequences of private bargains when they are socially harmful. The rules of Equity in English law are but one example. Perhaps it is time to acknowledge that what makes property rights and contractual expectations unassailable is the political power that the upper class commands as opposed to any moral imperative. This is not of course a new idea – it has been the cornerstone of Marxist critique and has animated challenges to the myths of capitalism since the nineteenth century. However, it is worth restating for those who have forgotten that bankers can (for example) choose to pay themselves whatever they want as bonuses, but only with the acquiescence of the democratic majority. Such a majority will probably seek to determine issues of distribution and market freedom by reference to a sense of justice. What should we understand, however, as being just?

1.3.2.2 What is justice?

Attempts to rationalise entitlement to wealth are commonly supplemented by the economic 'logic' of a trickle-down effect of wealth from the very privileged to the less so. According to Hayek (1960: 44–9) inequalities of wealth are justified because high rewards to highly producing individuals further incentivise those individuals to create, resulting in an increase in aggregate social wealth. This wealth then finds its way to all levels of society, also improving the lives of the less well off. This is the oft repeated (and empirically resoundingly misplaced) argument of Thatcherite conservatism that has been resurrected by executives at the centre of the financial storm seeking to defend their high rewards. If wealth therefore is legally right and inequalities of wealth are economically beneficial to all, isn't wealth also morally justified? We have no option at this point but to attempt, at least in a summary fashion, to grapple with a definition of justice.

Justice is often defined through its absence via the use of negative terms, such as calls for compensation, redress, revenge for a wrong that has occurred. According to Wolgast (1987: xii) the grammar of justice is intimately connected with the invocation of justice when we object to wrong. This view of justice is strongly conservative, in the sense that conformity to norms and existing social orders seems to be part of the very definition of what is just. It is a deviation from the existing order and the 'harm' that such departure causes that activates the correcting influence of 'doing' justice. Justice, however, is not only limited to a negative definition. A positive definition can be sought when one looks at the legitimising power of calls to achieve justice. Wrapped in the language of legitimacy, the notion of justice can be used to validate political power, especially at the stage of its creation or consolidation via revolution or upheaval. In this latter view, justice is an issue of law and public policy more than something solely associated with economic and private matters (Campbell, 2001: 4).

The public connotations of justice and its interpretation as a facilitator of freedom led legal scholars like Robert Nozick (1974) to conclude that justice places individual rights as the irreducible basis for social organisation. Justice therefore should be seen as a normative structure within which individuals can pursue their own goals without – of course – infringing the rights of others. Nozick's libertarian justice consequently is more concerned with liberty than with equality. A slightly more distributionally 'aware' notion of justice is the one proposed by John Rawls (1971), at least to the extent that it refers to the sum of happiness and well-being of all persons and to the alleviation of the sufferings of the poor and disadvantaged. Such justice can be achieved, it is alleged, via the management of society in order to produce a fair overall distribution of goods and evils within a system of equal basic rights. This type of utilitarianism has been used in the construction of arguments in favour of individual liberty in contexts where there are protected opportunities for unfettered exchange between individuals as the principal mechanism for attaining welfare maximisation (welfare here meaning the greatest happiness of the greatest number). Richard Posner's defence of private rights is a product of this tradition, one that Campbell (2001: 8) describes as an alternative to Nozick's scheme of rights as the justification for libertarian views on limiting the role of the state.

Rawls's (1971: 10) concept of justice (as a set of related principles for identifying the relevant considerations which determine a balance between competing claims) has specific distributional outcomes that largely depend on what rights and obligations each person has. A simplified reading of his thesis may suggest that justice requires that each is given his due. Miller (1976: 20), for instance, claims that if a just state of affairs is one where each person has exactly those benefits and burdens which are due to him, then the crucial question is how do we determine what a person is due? Answering this question leads to the predictable political/ideological divisions between left and right and links back to the arguments against regulation presented earlier in this section. If then defining justice cannot be disconnected from an understanding of entitlements, could we determine whether justice can exist in conditions of inequality?

1.3.2.3 Unequal justice?

Lord Griffiths of Fforestfach (Griffiths et al., 2001: 40) argued that the concept of the corporation as a moral community is a crucial facet of business life. It is rarely high on the agenda because, he acknowledged, its impact is difficult to measure; however, the explicit establishment of a moral standard within a company can bring significant benefits to everyone associated with the company. Nonetheless, Lord Griffiths also defended lavish bonuses in Goldman Sachs in 2009, in his capacity as its vice chairman, using arguments discussed earlier, suggesting that the general public should tolerate the inequality as a way to achieve greater prosperity for all, and that we should not be ashamed of offering compensation in an internationally competitive market which ensures the bank businesses here and employs British people (Quinn and Hall, 2009). How can, however, company entitlements be described as 'moral'?

It is difficult indeed to ascribe moral content to legal fictions, such as the idea of separate corporate personality. It is perhaps easier to construct an ethical argument supporting the maintenance of inequalities of wealth in society, not paying particular attention to whether this wealth is in the hands of real persons or legal ones. An influential illustration of the argument in favour of inequality was put forward by John Rawls in *Justice as Fairness* (Avinieri and de Shalit, 1992: 186) in the form of his 'difference principle' which suggests that inequalities of wealth are acceptable so long as they improve overall social welfare or do not make the poorer less well-off. While there are many philosophers and political scientists who have attempted to construct justifications for inequality, Rawls is particularly suited to our analysis here as he has exerted considerable influence on legal scholars and offers the most identifiable point of opposition to the egalitarian message of G. A. Cohen discussed below.

As an extension of Rawls's argument, one may contend that it is petty to complain about high earners when their rewards do not reduce the size of the overall pool of funds available for everyone else. This is, however, a point where the current crisis has made a difference. The money offered to the banks as assistance during the credit crunch has come from the taxpayer. Therefore maintaining high payments for executives in the financial sector has come at the expense of everyone else, and arguably did make the poorer sections of the population worse off. When the British government, for example, is implementing a programme of harsh austerity to deal with what it calls 'high levels of public debt' caused by its choice to pour billions into the banking system (into the RBS banking group for instance), we do have an almost unprecedented example of one section of the population losing massively in order to enrich another (already wealthy) section of the population. On a strict Rawlsian analysis based on the 'difference principle' therefore high payments to the bankers that increase wealth inequality cannot be defended from a moral point of view, at least in the circumstances prevailing in the immediate aftermath of the credit crunch and bank rescues.

Furthermore, the very notion of using inequality of wealth as an incentive to production (because, as was pointed our earlier, it is said to motivate people to work harder) entails a denial of community that is at the same time stark yet commonplace. We are so used to capitalist incentive structures that it does not immediately strike us as odd that people are badly off at the same time that others are very highly well off. While inequality, and the acceptance of inequality, is not a unique feature of capitalism, it is only in capitalist societies that it is elevated to a virtue. For all the shameless divisions in communist societies, at least the rhetoric aspired to equality. In our case, we take it as a given that some among the people, like bankers for instance, are outside the community or society of which they should be part. The cruel nature of the incentives argument, however, as the following discussion demonstrates, should make it unacceptable for any society that aspires to a balance of interests. Even if one accepts the Rawlsian analysis, when the result of inequality violates the difference principle and results in some sections of the population being directly worse off as a result of higher rewards for others (as is the case in the current crisis), then the moral defensibility fades and exposes the moral bankruptcy of arguments seeking to rationalise inequality. One wonders why we should keep listening to arguments against regulation based on the idea that regulation depresses growth, such as the propaganda that extraordinary rewards are necessary to incentivise bankers to do their jobs.

We can expose the suspicious ethical dimensions of rejections of regulatory initiatives, such as the bankers' arguments in favour of the self-regulating nature of their compensation packages, by adapting Cohen's kidnapper parable (Cohen, 1991: 276). The argument made here is that bankers (when they are arguing against caps on compensation) are not describing a natural phenomenon (what motivates rational persons), they do not present a situation independent of them, they in fact create the dilemma (leave us be, or we will leave). In other words, the ethical balance of the debate is skewed by bankers' expressed desire to accumulate limitless wealth. It is therefore the misuse of the idea of economic rationality that offers a parallel with the parable of the kidnapper. This parable is presented as follows. If someone kidnaps a child and contacts the parents to ask for ransom, then the following considerations play out: children should be with their parents; unless the kidnapper is paid, the child is not going to be returned to her parents; therefore parents ought to pay. Put in this way, deciding what to do in this situation is a matter of rational calculus or, as the economists would put it, rational utility maximisation. The child is more valuable than any amount in ransom, therefore the rational choice is for the parents to pay – and this is not a particularly morally charged calculation. Consider, however, the same situation put in the first person. If the kidnapper calls the parents and says: 'children ought to be with their parents; I will not return the child unless you pay; so you should pay me', then there is a strong moral reaction. While the argument is the same as before and rational calculus still dictates that payment will be made, there is strong discredit that attaches to anyone who makes such a statement in an interpersonal setting. Isn't this, however, what is happening currently, with bankers arguing that regulating their compensation will make them work less well or even make them leave their jobs?

Let us reconsider the proposition substituting banker for kidnapper. The argument goes like this: unregulated compensation offers incentives to higher production; controlling compensation will reduce production; therefore compensation arrangements should remain unregulated. Rational calculus would point to an acceptance of this position, assuming we accept the link between compensation and incentives. Let us rework the argument bringing it to the first person: 'unregulated compensation offers me incentives to higher production; controlling compensation means I will produce less; therefore the compensation structure must remain unregulated.' What we see is that what makes for an economic argument in the abstract makes for blackmail in the first person. Are bankers really telling us that if we do not condone their excessive money-making, they will work less well; that they will intentionally do a worse job? Is the 'kidnapper' blackmailing or explaining the likely consequences of different options? Are we really accepting an argument that suggests: 'I will only do my job properly if you agree to let me have whatever rewards I choose'? Would we accept this argument if it were made by a nurse, or a teacher, or a police constable? If not, why do we choose to accept it from finance executives?

A society that is just in the way Rawls explains, in which the difference principle ensures that everyone is as well off as they could be, is illusory. Cohen rightly notes that the poor in such a society are as well off as the selfishness of the rich allows them to be (1991: 320). Is a vision of society where the super-rich refuse to improve the lot of the less fortunate if they don't receive kickbacks for doing so one that we aspire to? To use another one of Cohen's parables, consider someone who goes fishing for sport. He derives satisfaction from fishing but does not need to eat the fish to survive. If the fisherman meets another person who needs to eat, but does not have a fishing rod, would it be acceptable for the fisherman to say: 'my satisfaction from fishing exceeds your need to eat'? To bring this in alignment with our financial industry discussion, is it acceptable for bank executives to say: 'our satisfaction in having multi-million-pound bonuses exceeds poor people's need to benefit from basic services'? If society accepts to grant those bonuses to incentivise production in an abstract sense, this could be defensible, but for bankers to ask the question is morally repugnant. Maybe we should ask ourselves: are we always to prefer a bargaining conception of social relationships over a community one?

There is some evidence, however, that the perception we have of what top executives want may not be an accurate one. For instance, Andrew Witty, CEO of pharmaceutical giant GlaxoSmithKline, warned in March 2011 that the drive for profits is undermining public trust in big companies and is reported in *The Observer* newspaper (Clark, 2011) as saying:

> It is 'completely wrong' for businesses to view themselves as 'mid-Atlantic floating entities' with no connection to society ... One of the reasons why we've seen an erosion of trust broadly in big companies is they've allowed themselves to be seen as being detached from society and they will float in and out of societies according to what the tax regime is ... While the chief executive of the company could move, maybe the top 20 directors could move, what about the 16,000 people who work for us? It's completely wrong, I think, to play fast and loose with your connections with society in that way.

Research by Desmet et al. (2011) of the Rotterdam School of Management suggests that at least Dutch executives do not claim they want more money for themselves, they rather see the potential of offering large compensation packages as a recruitment tool. This is close to presenting the argument for non-regulation in the abstract 'markets expect something' as opposed to using the first person proposition: 'I expect something'. While this may make Desmet et al.'s interviewees nicer people to talk to, does it really reflect reality, or change the moral dimension of this argument in the face of constant 'tax us and we'll leave' arguments against regulation? To borrow the expression of Wilhelm Röpke (1960: 125):

> The market, competition and the play of supply and demand do not create ethical reserves; they presuppose and consume them. These reserves must come from outside the market ... Self-discipline, a sense of justice, honesty, fairness, chivalry, moderation, respect for human dignity, firm ethical norms. All of these are things which people must possess before they go to market and compete with each other.

The current crisis has proved that all these are qualities in short supply in the financial sector.

1.4 Conclusion

This chapter has employed a rather complex analysis seeking to address a series of methodologically centred reservations the reader may have about the underlying bases of the arguments in the book. Despite the elaborate arguments in support of the idea that we are entitled to talk about the state–market relationship as a living, breathing, actual dichotomy that determines policy responses, the chapter talks about some simple truths. We live in an era where democracy has become a label, a nice rhetorical construct within which we can debate our tastes, likes and dislikes about some things but not others. The arena for political discussion, even in Europe, is becoming one to debate how to best prevent horse meat making its way into our burgers (a topical issue in Britain in 2013) and whether we should allow gay weddings (topical in France). I do not mean to say that horse meat and gay weddings are not issues to discuss in politics. What I am trying to say is that politics should be a forum for discussion for everything that matters to people. Yet some of what matters is becoming taboo. We are not meant to talk about economic policy lest we alarm the markets. We cannot discuss taxation lest we scare away internationally mobile executives. We cannot threaten unchecked accumulation of wealth, as this is a violation of what our law holds most dear: property rights.

There comes a point though when we need to wake up and face reality. When even billionaire investor Warren Buffett realises that there is something wrong with paying less tax than his secretary (Tienabeso, 2012) we should pause and reconsider the nature of our political economy. The great crisis we are living through gives us the chance to have another look at the market–state dichotomy, to rethink the sources of coercion in our society (and their legitimacy) and to deliberate on the goals of regulation and the means to achieve those goals. Crucially, we can take this opportunity to develop, or rediscover, an ethical stance towards the realities of applied financialised capitalism. We have earned the right after the sacrifices asked from us all (via austerity and cutbacks) to question arguments against regulation and explanations for inequality. Buffett's secretary and the NEETS (Not in Employment, Education or Training) of London can ask when finally will the wealth trickle down, or why is our law (by definition) a tool for the preservation of privilege? I will state once again what was noted at the beginning of this work. This book is not a call to revolution, but it is a call to something revolutionary: a true debate about the place of law in economic organisation. The analysis in the following chapters offers a beginning to this debate.

2 The role of law in markets

Giving governments the ability to determine balances of interests on the basis of political values is based on a recognition that economic relations are not governed by autonomous mechanisms resembling those driving physical processes.

2.1 Introduction

One of the media-beloved scandals of political life in Britain in 2012 involved a Conservative minister who was allegedly infuriated by a policeman's refusal to allow him to ride his bike into the House of Commons. The minister reacted by allegedly calling the officers at the gate 'plebs' (Wintour and Sayal, 2012). This chapter explains why we are all considered 'plebs' by those initiated in the workings of contemporary financialised capitalism, why the system of advanced finance makes even the most educated of us feel like meaningless cogs in a large obscure machine. It also helps explain one of the key features of the technocracy that Chapter 1 claimed threatens the nature of modern democracy: we live in an economic system run by experts and supposedly understood only by experts. The chapter will examine why this is so and reflect on whether technocracy is an inevitable consequence of the complexity of modern capitalism. The following discussion will attempt to unpack the notions of credit, finance, money and liquidity in a way that will demonstrate why economic efficiency often becomes a mechanism for increasing unfairness in society. In seeking to define the aims of finance we will explore the role of law in modern capitalism, without dismissing popular misgivings about the 'virtual' nature of finance as the product of a lack of sophistication or the deficient understanding of 'plebs'. The chapter will explain the central place of credit in the economy and the consequent importance of liquidity; it will show how liquidity as the basis of finance is responsible for making capitalism appear immaterial, unreal and therefore something at the mercy of sentiment and the whims of markets. We will argue that a market system with liquidity as its basis serves to de-materialise the foundations of the economy. After setting this background, the chapter continues by exploring the role of ideas in economic policy-making, dispelling the myth of 'orthodox' policy as apolitical and non-ideological. We will argue that the current politics of sound macro-economics is not a struggle to establish efficient institutions, but a struggle to legitimise self-appointed authority on the basis of technical expertise. This discussion will conclude with a reflection on whether the financial crisis is nothing more than a crisis of modernity, a postmodern struggle between abstractions: the conflict between the reality of poverty and austerity against the virtual meta-notions of high finance.

2.2 A story about sardines

One of the key themes of this chapter is the discontinuity between the projected nature and the realities of the operation of the financial system. In seeking an illustration of how a system can be corrupted and result in absurdity, we can refer to a wonderful essay written by Lord Justice Kerr (1987) in which he sought to dispel myths as to the inherent superiority of international commercial arbitration as a dispute resolution mechanism for international trade, as opposed to litigation in national courts. Kerr LJ recalled in his essay a legendary dispute, known as the Macao Sardine case, which came out of a claim for breach of contract against a Macao sardine manufacturer which we will now present in outline. The Macao manufacturer was producing tins of sardines for many years, but was going through hard times due to increases in production and raw material costs. When they received a large order from a Taiwanese company for 400 tons of sardine tins, they were presented with a lucrative opportunity, but lacking the ability to finance the purchase of the fish, they found themselves in an impossible conundrum. Unfortunately, the Macao Company resolved the problem by resorting to what most people would call fraud. They produced the tins, but did not fill them with sardines in oil. They filled them instead with mud collected from a nearby river bank. When the tins had been sealed, labelled and checked in the usual manner, the consignment was shipped on a vessel travelling in the Pacific nominated by the Taiwanese customers. The bill of lading was issued to the order of the buyers and duly negotiated against their documentary credit established in Hong Kong. The Macao Company's cashflow problems were resolved and the company returned quickly to profitability. The consignment of sardines was sold by its Taiwanese owners and then resold multiple times on a steadily rising market. It became, in fact, a recognised standby 'spot' parcel throughout South East Asia. It was usually sold while in transit and rarely unloaded. About four and a half years later, however, things went wrong. An earthquake in the Philippines produced a sudden food shortage. Together with staple commodities, the sardine cargo was hurriedly bought 'spot' from its then Japanese owners by a government trading agency in the Philippines and was ultimately taken into stock by a chain of supermarkets based in Manila. As one can imagine, when the hungry earthquake victims got their hands on the tins, they were not amused to discover they had been packed with mud. This led to a cascade of legal actions following the long list of contracts. At the end of the litigation chain was the original Taiwanese buyer and the Macao manufacturer.

As their contract contained an arbitration clause, the matter was settled by arbitration. The well esteemed and expert arbitrator conducted a thorough analysis of the contractual chain drawing on the evidence and his own unparalleled knowledge of international trade. He also drew extensively on well-regarded academic literature. The arbitrator drew upon his learning in pointing out that the concept of 'merchantability' – itself directly evocative of the *lex mercatoria* – was indubitably derived, forensically and etymologically, from the concept of the 'marketability' of the goods in question, in other words from their capacity of being sold and resold in the course of trade. As to this, the arbitrator said, the evidence spoke for itself. This consignment of tins had passed through the (metaphorical) hands of hundreds of owners during the four and a half years of its life, not once having a single tin being opened with a view to consumption. In fact, in the arbitrator's own experience there wasn't a single occasion he was aware of where a traded parcel of sardines had been landed and opened anywhere in the Pacific. The arbitrator dismissed contrary opinions as emanating from those with scant knowledge of how international trade works in practice. Tins of sardines are a tradable commodity with the functions of a currency – they are in essence a store of value, not food. The arbitrator therefore dismissed the Taiwanese claim for breach of contract and ordered costs against them, saying that the goods had performed their intended function in its entirety.

Thus the moral of the story is that international trade had evolved from a mechanism that allowed the meeting of seller and buyer with the purpose of conveying goods, to a completely closed and self-referential system which aims to generate profits without any other ultimate goal. By this point the reader will have guessed the point of elaborating upon this rather silly example (Kerr LJ does not say this clearly, but the scenario is in all probability fictional). Would a result such as that reached by the arbitrator be ridiculous? Of course it is. Unappealing as tins of sardines may be to many, they are food, not a form of currency (despite the elastic definitions of the latter as we will see below). Kerr LJ in fact made up this story to shake his audience out of the complacency of relying on experts and industry insiders. If we dare challenge one insider's (this arbitrator's for example) view of the 'way things really work', however, aren't we able to extend out scepticism to other fields? Do we dare ask what is the purpose of finance, for instance? Is it to allow the meeting of the creditor and the debtor in order to enable the production and sale of goods and services, or is finance a closed and self-referential system which seeks to perpetually delay the settlement of debts with no ultimate end rather than the generation of profits for those participating in finance itself? Why is it ridiculous to propose that sardines can be a form of currency, yet it is ignorant to suggest that securitisation is a sham? To use a less aquatic example, why can you not buy fire insurance on your neighbour's house, but you can buy insurance (in the form of a credit default swap) on an asset you do not own?

The answer to these questions can be found in the law. The discussion that follows reveals the reason why the whole structure of finance seems to the 'non-initiated' artificial and exposes the role of law in propping up the artifice of financial capitalism. This chapter also seeks to address the question of what finance is for and once this is determined, it asks what is the role of law in ensuring that finance stays focused on the attainment of its goals?

2.3 What are money, credit, finance?

This book proposes a leading role for law in shaping our political economy. This focus on law is explained through the need for a legitimate backing to economic policy-making. The book argues that it is only via law resulting from the actions of elected representatives that the public gains ownership of governance. Through such ownership, efforts to increase the reach of regulation and law over economic processes are a way to relegitimise and recapture economic governance from an amorphous and unrepresentative market. Despite the myth that the market represents everyone, the sad truth is that the market represents those with wealth. In particular, financial markets primarily represent those with extreme wealth. The assertion that we all have a stake in capitalism because we all, in one way or other, are dependent on capitalist success (as shareholders directly or via pension funds, as stakeholders – employees, customers, suppliers of firms – or as consumers of the products and services of companies) is a popular piece of pro-market propaganda. As Michael Sandel argues, however, in his influential book *What Money Can't Buy: The Moral Limits of Markets* (2012) a reliance on market mechanisms as the primary means of social organisation fails to distinguish between the willingness to pay and the ability to pay. Yes, the distribution of public goods can be determined by market mechanisms (such as the 'efficient markets hypothesis' presupposes), but only when those who desire the goods are able to purchase them. Lacking the ability to buy, the ability to select becomes meaningless. It is a fallacy therefore to hear the siren calls of pro-marketeers that would have us believe that we all have a stake in financial markets due to our pension funds. The inclusiveness and representation of markets is one of the grossest misrepresentations that we need to dispel before we can comprehend the functions of law in bringing about legitimate economic governance.

In the same way that we can dismiss the claim of market representation, we are not obligated to accept Richard Posner's (1972) aggregate consumer willingness to pay as the official measuring rod of human satisfaction. If we were to take such a limited view of human relations (drawn from the philosophical bases of utilitarianism) and accept 'satisfaction' as a good, then we could legitimately accept economic efficiency as a goal of economic policy. If, in turn, we accepted efficiency as a goal, we could accept willingness to pay as a proxy for what achieves satisfaction. Why, however, do economists and scholars like Posner accept these assumptions, and moreover why do they embrace them while being blind to an environment of stark inequalities of wealth? The answer is that if we confront inequality and we acknowledge that existing distributions of wealth are unfair, then we realise that economic efficiency becomes a mechanism for increasing unfairness (Baker, 1975). If the goal on the other hand is truly to increase satisfaction, or maximise utility, then we would be forced to redress inequalities of wealth as opposed to simply increasing efficiency. As we mentioned in the previous chapter, a stark paradox of capitalism is that more choice for consumers means less choice for citizens. More choice for citizens is possible via the expression of democratic choices in the law, not via picking products in supermarket aisles. A pro-choice agenda therefore cannot only be expressed as expanding consumer choice, but can be presented as expanding policy discretion.

This focus on law is explained in various ways throughout this discussion, but it is worth repeating here that the law is a crucial determinant, not only of economic outcomes, but also of the incidence of crises in markets. The link between law and crisis as provided by deregulation will be presented in detail through our historical analysis in Chapter 3. It will illuminate matters, however, to focus here on a reflection on the nature and purpose of finance, and particularly on one central conduit from deregulation to crisis that is central to our understanding of modern finance: the concept of liquidity.

2.3.1 What is the purpose of finance?

This section draws on the excellent work of Amato and Fantacci (2011) who argue that the reliance of modern capitalism on liquidity (defined as the severance of the link between borrower and lender that aims at the settlement of debts – the 'end' or purpose of finance, as they say) is responsible for market movements disconnected from the real economy and increasingly serious crises. The present book builds on their realisations to argue that reliance on 'market sentiment' is a destabilising force in our political economy because it simultaneously makes market operations erratic and because it wrests policy-making away from legitimate democratic institutions, placing it on shadowy market players. The notion of liquidity is what allows 'market sentiment' to play such a prominent role in controlling market fluctuations. The following discussion demonstrates how a reliance on liquidity has allowed financial markets to detach themselves from real economic processes and has let our political process reduce to a game of 'catch-up' with market wishes, trying to anticipate what market actors might want, undermining in the process democratic legitimacy and severing the link between public control and economic decision-making.

The current crisis is not just an economic crisis but in particular it is a financial crisis. In order to fully appreciate therefore what this crisis means for our understanding of law, the economy and democratic politics, we need to spend some time elaborating upon the concept of finance itself. Finance could be defined as the framework that allows the meeting of a creditor with a debtor and is almost universally considered essential in allowing business to take place in a market economy. This necessity for finance arises for the simple reason that every productive activity needs funds to commence, and funds need to originate somewhere, more often than not away from the control of the business requiring them. It is unusual for business activity to commence only after the accumulation of funds by the producers themselves. It is far more common that the funds originate someplace else and are then channelled to what investors consider fruitful endeavours. To take a commonplace example, a farmer with a few chickens could save the money he makes from selling eggs and slowly accumulate enough funds to purchase a cow. This would take a long time and economists would consider it inefficient. The farmer in question could alternatively borrow the funds to purchase the cow, then slaughter it, take it to market, make enough to repay the original loan and use the excess to purchase a new cow without a further need to borrow. While this example is reminiscent of arithmetic lessons offered to primary school children, the reader should resist being contemptuous of its simplicity as such 'dumbing down' is commonly proffered in support of the infinitely more complex edifices of finance.

The following discussion deals with these concepts in more detail and will enquire into the nature of the creditor–debtor relationship, the concept of accumulation, liquidity and crucially the meaning of 'money'. In giving definition to all these concepts, law is central. It is the law that allows the commodification of money (a key process as we will discover) which then allows liquidity (in the current expression of financialised capitalism) to define the ability of creditors to lend to debtors. In offering these frameworks to market activity, law also determines the policy space left to politicians to mould economic governance. Law in other words serves to limit policy discretion in ways that reduce the choices left to citizens to determine their destinies.

2.3.2 What is the role of law in shaping finance?

It is often observed that the 'common man' perceives finance and the structures of modern capitalism as highly artificial: people talk of 'fake' wealth produced by nothing, which then in time disappears into nothing. This sense of a virtual economy of high finance disconnected from the 'real' economy of the high street or main street is usually dismissed by economists and those involved in finance as being due to the ignorance of the uninitiated 'man on the street'. We should not, however, be so quick to dismiss popular misgivings about the artificiality of finance, because a lot of what is seen today as the pinnacle of capitalist innovation is in fact a superstructure premised upon a series of legally constructed and therefore challengeable bases. Furthermore, it is the way the system is constructed, rather than some automatic, natural propensity rooted in the failings of humanity, that leads to instability and crisis. Amato and Fantacci (2011), for instance, argue that instability at the core of financialised capitalism is due to money being used as a commodity and on the ever expanding definition of credit. As we mentioned above, the central place of credit in a modern economy and the consequent importance of liquidity is what makes the base of financial capitalism to appear immaterial, unreal and therefore something at the mercy of sentiment and whim. In other words, the reliance on market sentiment and its link to the notion of liquidity explains feelings of artificiality and accounts for much of the instability one associates with modern capitalism. It is this very virtual domain that this discussion seeks to expose, drawing on literature on the nature of money that has come to prominence in the later stages of the current financial crisis.

If finance is understood as the meeting of creditor and debtor that is essential for business to happen in a market economy, then the creditor–debtor relationship should be understood as a relationship whose aim is the payment of the debt – the settlement of the obligation. It is the delay in payment, in some instances the perpetual delay, that characterises the modern incarnation of finance, that creates a situation in which money is seen as a commodity in itself, where money equals debt (via mechanisms such as securitisation). If debts are not to be repaid, but sold and resold like products (hence the equation of money with a commodity) then the continuation of market transactions depends on the ability to buy and sell debt. This ability to buy and sell is not only a legal ability, but practically implies the willingness of sellers to sell and buyers to buy. This in one word is called liquidity and for some (Warburton, 2000) has come to describe the volume and speed of financial transactions or market turnover rather than the content of those transactions.

Treating money as a commodity and using liquidity as a measure of the value of an economic system rests on a particular attitude towards the concept of risk. In a marketplace that deals in debt, the ability to handle that debt (to eventually pay if necessary) is represented in the concept of valuing risk. Market liquidity then can also be defined as comprising the spatial, intertemporal, cognitive and social processes of valuing risk (Carruthers and Stinchcombe, 1999: 353–4). As Nesvetailova (2010: 114) argues, liquidity is the absolute essence of all market exchanges and is paramount to the functioning of any financial system. Liquidity is synonymous therefore with the wider meaning of capitalism itself, the desire to own and transfer one's claims to wealth (Berle and Pederson, 1934). In an era of financialised capitalism every eventuality is supposed to be capable of being priced, securitised and transferred to others in the marketplace (Shiller, 2008).

Modern finance then (what we could call a mechanism for the perpetual delay of settlement) is dependent on liquidity, which in turn is dependent on sentiment and the psychology of this amorphous mass of market actors (the people who need to feel confident enough to sell and buy debt in the marketplace). It is worth repeating here that in a system where debts are not meant to be repaid, the ability to sell them on becomes vital. The funding of a large number of market participants involved in the securitisation process depends crucially on market liquidity being permanently sustained

(Banque de France, 2008: 11). The design of modern capitalism assumes a constantly maintained liquidity of markets, but this, Nesvetailova (2010: 122) says, is a dangerous illusion. Assuming that everything can be bought and sold in the financial markets is simply wrong, in the same way that assuming market turnover to be perpetually sustainable and hence synonymous with liquidity is also wrong. A market system having liquidity as its operating basis de-materialises the foundations of the economy. It turns economic activity from a matter of fact into a state of mind, a collective and cognitive achievement where buyers and sellers all need to maintain a deep conviction that commodities contained in the large flow of financial instruments changing hands are really worth something. The consequence is that, stripped of its relation to the underlying assets (what really goes into the financial 'products'), market liquidity is increasingly taken to be synonymous with the shared appetite for trading, an appetite commonly equivalent to a desire for speculation (McCulley, 2008). It is this very link between liquidity and sentiment that makes modern capitalism so volatile and the operations of the financial markets so detached from the real economy. Nesvetailova (2010: 130) concludes that the liquidity of the financial system is an artificial construction, created by the rarely questioned theorems of self-regulating, efficient and optimising market strategies and the collective behaviour of investors. To return to the sardine example with which we started our discussion, it seems that in the same way that Kerr's arbitrator confused sardines with money, financialisation leads us to confuse liquidity with wealth. Can we be wrong about the sardines being a form of money yet correct about liquidity being a proxy for wealth?

Where is the law in this system, one may wonder? The law is involved in two main ways in the creation and operation of the system. First, the law is what allows the process of commodification of money via deregulating – or via the failure to regulate – capital movements and exchange rates and by de-linking money from a physical anchor like gold. Second, the law allows operations that create or restrict liquidity, both by allowing private actors like banks to extend credit and create money (the whole essence of fractional reserve banking, explained below) and by allowing public actors like central banks to expand the money supply via (for instance) quantitative easing, commonly known as printing money. We can discover the role of law in finance therefore by examining the relationship between law and the definition of money.

2.3.3 What is the role of law in 'money'?

As Philip Coggan noted (2011: 23), given that mankind has been using money for thousands of years, it is perhaps surprising that money is still such a nebulous concept. A general definition of money is that money is anything (even tins of sardines one may argue) that people accept as payment for goods and services based on the belief that they can use the proceeds to buy goods and services from someone else, or as Meyrick Chapman (2009) said succinctly, money is the belief that someone will pay you back. For economists, money is capable of performing three functions simultaneously, as a means of exchange, as a measure of value and as a store of value. Historically, the use of money as a medium of exchange has been the most important, a use which in John Law's view (see below) was the prime function of money. The second use, money as a unit of account, is one of convenience: expressing the price of all goods and services in relation to one common denominator is a lot easier than figuring out the barter value of each good against every other. Using a single currency in Jerusalem in biblical times would have eliminated the need for 'money-changers' that in the opinion of Jesus polluted the Temple according to the Gospels. The third use, the store of value, is useful (one would not want to be obligated to spend immediately whatever is earned), but is also the most problematic. In fact, it is this latter characteristic of money as a store of value, that is responsible for the many peculiar characteristics of modern financial markets.

As Keynes pointed out, money saved, rather than spent, reduces demand for goods and thus depresses employment. The economy can be trapped therefore in a circle where too much is saved, too little is spent and too few jobs are available (Coggan, 2011: 11). John Law, the eighteenth-century Scottish mathematician and early economist, claimed that money is not the value *for* which goods are exchanged, but the value *by* which they are exchanged. The use of money, he continued, is to buy goods, money in itself is of no other use (Law, 1750). We mentioned earlier that the purpose of finance is to act as a conduit of funding for business activity. The consequence of this line of thinking is that one need not accumulate wealth before putting it to productive use; money can be borrowed, or created as a reflection of the wealth of society, as a consequence of optimism and confidence in the rise of this wealth. Money, in other words, is not a quantity of gold or silver but in essence a reflection of the potential for wealth creation.

How is money being created, if it is not borrowed from someone who previously gained it? We mentioned above that central banks can create money by 'printing it'. In modern times central banks do not 'print' money, but they create it, for example, by purchasing government bonds or treasury bills and crediting the government's account with a number representing money. This is the essence behind the process of quantitative easing that the Bank of England has employed since the crisis (Joyce et al., 2011). In fact, central banks are not limited to doing this via crediting government accounts through the purchase of treasury bills, but can also do it by purchasing securities issued by private parties, like banks and corporates. The European Central Bank has employed a rather different tool (long-term refinancing operations) that injects liquidity into the market by accepting lower-quality collateral for loans by the Bank (Linzert et al., 2004). Both actions represent an expansion of the central bank's balance sheet which pumps money into the economy or state coffers. These funds are in theory repaid to the central bank when the state or a private party redeems the securities in question, but the expansion in the central bank's balance sheet can be permanent, unless the bank then raises interest rates to reabsorb the excess liquidity. The main check on this process of money creation, or liquidity enhancing (as it is called), is of course inflation. If a central bank infuses funds into the economy through such liquidity enhancing operations constantly at large volumes, there is concern that inflationary pressures will build up in the economy bringing the value of the currency down, putting a stop to the process of expansion. In the current deflationary environment, on the other hand, quantitative easing has helped keep inflation to target and avoid the recessionary effects of falling prices. The 'creation' of money, however, is not a function limited to central banks. When a commercial bank lends money, it can lend in excess of its assets (within the limits set by law) (Schlichter, 2011: 52). This means that a bank can extend loans that are multiples of the funds it has in its vaults (or electronic balance sheets). Every time the bank lends money it therefore 'creates' money, it increases the total amount of money in circulation. This is the core of the notion of fractional reserve banking, and also an explanation for the confusion between the terms money and credit. If money is created via the extension of credit, are not then money and credit the same thing?

The de-materialisation of money and the severance of the link between what is perceived to be inherently valuable (e.g. gold) and what is valuable because it represents a commonly accepted exercise of authority (paper money) is not an automatic process but entails the involvement of law to baptise 'money' and make it acceptable. In that sense, it is a misrepresentation of historical process to argue, as Detlev Schlichter (2011: 35) does, that money has evolved organically and spontaneously from the voluntary actions of trading individuals. But, if the law brings about changes in the uses and functions of things like money, what motivates changes in the law? In seeking to answer this question we need to go deeper into the process of law creation, to peer behind the economic rationalisations and assumptions offered as prima facie explanations for legal changes and conduct an analysis of motivations for reform. We turn therefore to a study of the ideological foundations of legal and economic organisation.

2.4 Ideas in economic governance

The preceding section has discussed the artificiality of finance and the legally constituted and therefore 'constructed' nature of the arrangements behind financial capitalism as it operates today. This discussion, however, leaves us with the question, how do systems evolve and why do specific legal pathways lead to the results we have? Answering this question involves an assessment of the power ideas have to influence policy outcomes. This part of the chapter therefore discusses ideas in economic governance and their means of dissemination.

This work argues throughout that insufficient attention is paid to the role politics should have in economic governance. Integral to any discussion of politics is a discussion about the power of ideas. Indeed, in a dynamic policy environment, as in the one opened by the financial crisis, it is inevitable that ideas and political platforms based on specific ideologies will determine the shape of capitalism for the future. Slavoj Žižek (2008) noted that when the normal run of things is traumatically interrupted, the field is open for a 'discursive' ideological competition. The reason why ideology is presented here as 'inevitable' can be found in exposing the fallacy of the argument that the current orthodoxy is apolitical and non-ideological. As demonstrated in *Neoliberalism and the Law* (Glinavos, 2010a) our current institutional structures are the product of the dominance of free market ideology. Such dominance permeates economic and legal structures that underpin modern capitalism. Beginning from the realisation that the status quo is not apolitical, we can conclude that there should be space, even within the mainstream literature, for a model that uses ideas as a motivating factor of change. Ideology of course features prominently in Marxist thinking, but the usefulness of unearthing the role of ideas is not limited to Marxist critique. Even the purest of free market think tanks, the Institute of Economic Affairs (IEA), believes that there is a role for ideas. In an IEA publication (Blundell, 2007) its authors proclaimed that ideas have consequences and claimed that individuals who argue from principle and with persistence can change the policy debates and, ultimately, the history of their country.

Ideas can be defined as 'common beliefs about the cause-and-effect relationships in the world' (Haas, 1990: xviii) and ideology is the systematic ordering of these ideas into a worldview and a guide to action. The link between ideology and the law owes a lot to Marxist thinkers. Harris (1997: 271), explaining the Marxist use of the term ideology, describes it as an interpretive tool whereby the social theorist can explain the filtering of power and the demarcation of roles within a society without necessarily teasing out mechanistic causal connections but by pointing to the belief sets of social actors. The hope is that a framework for understanding the role of ideas, can lead to a technique for understanding the functions of law. Renner (1976) argued that the changing ideological background to law creation and enforcement explains how the functions of law may change while the form remains the same. For example, both feudal Europe and capitalist states employ the same Roman Law concept of ownership, but while in feudal times it suggested an institutionalised form of servitude to landlords, now it serves (in the view of Marxists) as a vehicle for command over the working class. Pashukanis (1987) went further in arguing that the essence of a juridical interpretation of human relations is that it regards human action as an exchangeable (economic) commodity, not as something intrinsic to human personality. As a consequence, it has been claimed that the very essence of law is capitalist. Even without going that far in identifying law itself as capitalist, it is still important to identify the degree to which law creation is an ideological exercise as opposed to a technical one. However, what influence can one have over the dissemination of ideology?

A possible result of using an ideas-based model of policy change and, by extension, law reform is to empower epistemic communities as agents of change. An epistemic community can be defined as a knowledge-based group of experts and specialists who share common beliefs about the cause-and-effect relationships in the world and have common political values concerning the ends to which policies should be addressed (Haas, 1990). Epistemic communities can help popularise ideas and make them guides to change. King (2005) argues that epistemic communities are most important during periods of uncertainty when they are able to influence a key politician by providing a road map to a politically salient solution. It is important to note here that while epistemic communities are conduits of ideas to political formations that can put them to the electoral test, they are not the authors of policies themselves. An epistemic community therefore is not to be equated with a technocracy that directly determines issues of economic governance, something that this book argues against.

As the authors mentioned above point out, ideas are most important during periods of uncertainty or in complex and technical areas. The reason for this is that fluid situations obscure the distributional effects of a given institutional arrangement or policy choice, making it difficult for interest groups to identify where their interests lie. When a policy cross-cuts prevailing material interests and party lines, interest groups find it difficult to adopt a position one way or the other (Parsons, 2002). While uncertainty may obscure distributional effects, it provides politicians with greater room to manoeuvre due to the difficulty in monitoring policy results under these conditions. In these circumstances, ideas are important precisely because they reduce uncertainty, give content to interests and make institutional construction possible (Blyth, 2001). McNamara (1998) explains that there are three distinct phases that allow ideas to shape events. First, a period of policy failure leads to the collapse of the old paradigm and the search for new solutions. While this policy failure may be accompanied by a crisis, the main feature is a period of greater uncertainty. Second, a new paradigm emerges offering a clear policy solution that is advocated by an epistemic community and implemented by politicians in a few states. Politicians in other states monitor the results of these test cases to judge whether the policy is effective or not. Third, politicians in other states proceed to emulate this policy, embedding the new paradigm in their own institutional framework.

Marrier (2008) offers a contemporary example of the power of epistemic communities to effect change. He examines pension reforms in Sweden and argues that a significant change came about, not as a result of Sweden's corporatist structures, but as a result of the penetration of ideas into the policy space through the creation of an epistemic community comprised of academics and politicians. This epistemic community provided a pathway through a multitude of barriers to change. According to this analysis, barriers to the transition of ideas from academia to policy include, as stressed by Zito (2001), entrenched interests and pre-existing institutional arrangements, a type of path-dependency, in other words, that results in national institutions being unwelcome to new ideas. Bureaucracies, for example, are inherently conservative with an entrenched organisational culture (Peters, 1995). For instance, the lack of substantive pension reform in Greece since the country's entry to the Economic and Monetary Union (EMU) and prior to the policy reversals brought about by impending bankruptcy in 2010 illustrates these difficulties. In the case of Greece, Featherstone (2005) argues that the governing party had difficulty proposing reforms in an intelligible way because, in part, it faced a complex and inefficient state apparatus and it could not circumvent powerful interests which benefited greatly from the status quo.

Further, the technical nature of a policy problem also plays a key role in the level of influence an epistemic community is likely to have on domestic jurisdictions (Ruggie, 1975). This suggests that when a policy problem is highly technical, experts tend to dominate the policy process making it difficult for political actors to play a potent role (Peters, 2005: 360). However, as this section seeks to demonstrate, regardless of the nature of policy issues, they 'are seldom purely technical or purely political' (Majone, 1989: 3) and 'scientists' – if one can call economists scientists – cannot really avoid the politicisation of 'science'. It is a belief in the power of technocracy, however, that can lead epistemic communities to determine policy responses. In a comparative survey of senior civil servants presented by Putnam (1977: 408) several natural scientists stated that 'they are not really very good at politics'. When the 'not good at politics' technocrats combine forces with an ideologically motivated group, however, then an epistemic community can be created that can shape policy directions. In other words, a successful epistemic community is likely to integrate politicians if it wants to have tangible policy results. We will test this theory, that epistemic communities can offer a transmission mechanism from theory to policy change, linking ideas and law reform, in the following section where we use the adoption of monetarism and central bank independence as an example of the successful seeding of an idea with global consequences.

2.4.1 The ideology of central bank independence

As the preceding discussion shows, there are a number of ways to test the power of ideas to influence policy outcomes in times of uncertainty. This section begins to test such a model of change based on the power of ideas by examining the very powerful concept of institutional independence as a feature of modern capitalism. As analysed extensively in *Neoliberalism and the Law* (Glinavos, 2010a), and also presented earlier in this book, an integral part of the way the market–state relationship is balanced today is the idea of institutional independence from political control. However, how did institutional independence come to be accepted as best practice in the design of regulatory frameworks? Finding answers to questions like this one can help us explain some contemporary paradoxes of pro-market policy agendas, like for instance the contradiction between arguments for significant law-making activity assumed by proposals to reform regulatory frameworks, and resistance to abandoning the idea of minimal state intervention which lies at the core of orthodox economic thinking. Further, the example of institutional independence offers an answer to the question: how is it possible to empower the state in economic decision-making (via improving regulatory frameworks as proposed by the G20 for instance) without risking a return to the era of political control over the economy? This section will attempt to answer these questions, starting with a presentation of the genesis of the idea that there are social-wide benefits to be had from the de-politicisation of economic governance. King (2005) makes the argument that if institutional reform is viewed as a two-level game where politicians first respond to pressure from international financial markets and second react to lobbying by domestic interest groups, then explaining motivations for reform can be based on structural factors or material interests rather than ideas. However, it can be hypothesised that ideas have a more powerful role as motivators of policy change, especially at times of crisis. In examining this claim, King assessed the ascendency of the idea in the 1990s that monetary policy ought to be determined on technocratic criteria by independent central banks. We will start by considering the provenance of the doctrine of central bank independence.

Historically, attempts to de-politicise banking rested on distrust of the capacity both of politicians and of the public to behave in a way conducive to a nation's best interests. Thomas Hutchinson, an eighteenth-century governor of Massachusetts, for instance, declared that 'the great cause of paper money evil was democratic government. The ignorant majority, when unrestrained by a superior class, always sought to temper with sound money' (Coggan, 2011: 36). The very concept of central banking is, perhaps as a result of beliefs such as Hutchinson's, associated with secrecy and intrigue. According to Chernow (1994: 132–40) the idea of an American central bank was formulated in a secret meeting in 1910 on Jekyll island, where participants travelled pretending to be taking part in a duck hunt. As a result of processes starting at that meeting, the Federal Reserve was created in 1913 to implement banking and currency reforms with the aim to prevent periodic banking crises, such as the panic of 1907. According to Das (2011: 130) central bank authority focused on ensuring that the value of money was not undermined by inflation, an idea consistent with Hayek's argument that mechanistic rules ought to limit the central bank's discretion (and as a consequence the influence of political processes over central bank policies).

King, focusing on the purported de-politicising effects of independence, claims that New Labour's decision to give the Bank of England operational independence was a decision responding to a change of belief system, not an economic one. It established New Labour's anti-inflationary credentials and delivered on the party's campaign promise to de-politicise the setting of interest rates (King, 2005: 94). In fact, Bank of England independence forms part of a global trend during the 1990s, when more than 30 countries passed legislation increasing the legal independence of their central banks (Maxfield, 1997) and represents one of the most dramatic changes in monetary frameworks since the collapse of the Bretton Woods regime. Bank of England reform came a decade after the start of the trend in central bank independence, which began with the 1989 reform of the Reserve Bank of New Zealand. The British decision, however, was not linked to changes in Britain's exchange rate regime, the collapse of the former Soviet Union, the adoption of an IMF programme, the decision to join the Euro area – explanations that cover most cases of central bank reform in the 1990s (Cukierman, 1994: 1446) – but it was motivated by the internalisation of the idea of independence by the labour leadership (King, 2005: 95–6). A similar ideas-based explanation can be found for the German Bundesbank's independent structure. According to Bernhard (1998: 322), the Bundesbank's independence resulted from the balance of power politics in Western Germany that could only be maintained by detaching government from the setting of monetary policy. The power of ideas can be used then to explain the current schizophrenic behaviour of the ECB which on the one hand does whatever it can to support liquidity in the Eurozone (as we saw in the first part of this chapter) while refusing to 'create' money in any significant volume (like its British and US equivalents) or (still at the time of writing) offer a Eurozone-wide bond. Within this inconsistency one can see clearly the ideological preoccupations of the Bundesbank and the conflict between Germany's view of the role of the central bank and the beliefs of Germany's Eurozone counterparts (Dyson and Marcussen, 2009).

The ideas-based model presented earlier can be used to argue that central bank independence resulted from the active involvement of an epistemic community that influenced a key political group to adopt this reform. As mentioned above, epistemic communities play a key role in articulating the cause-and-effect relationships of complex problems, helping states identify their interests, framing the issues for collective debate, proposing specific policies and identifying salient points for negotiation (Haas, 1997: 2). The potential influence of an epistemic community is increased when policy-makers are faced with a complex problem that must be addressed quickly, such as in response to a crisis. In order to translate its 'knowledge-based' power into effective influence, an epistemic community must hold a shared set of causative beliefs and must agree on a policy prescription (Goldstein, 1993). Expanding on McNamara's model presented earlier, King argues that policy failure and paradigm innovation are not on their own sufficient conditions for the adoption of new ideas by politicians. Even though an epistemic community may be united behind a new paradigm such as central bank independence, their proposals must be politically salient in order to be adopted. For politicians academic discussions of economic gains are not enough, there also needs to be clear electoral gains for the party in question, in order for them to champion such an institutional change. In a similar fashion, when the electoral costs exceed the electoral gains, politicians will have an incentive to stick with the status quo. In this case, Bank of England independence provided electoral gains for New Labour by making the party more attractive to voters. In particular, this policy was designed to win the support of homeowners that represent the median voter in the British context. By contrast, the Conservatives saw only electoral costs from this reform as it limited their ability to set interest rates strategically. In short, the political salience of the reform proposals put forward by the epistemic communities explains to a great degree the pattern of adoption and non-adoption (King, 2005: 115).

The core of the intellectual case for central bank independence revolves around the assumption of a persistent inflationary bias built into politicians' monetary policy preferences. It is argued that this bias can only be negated by vesting authority in policy-makers who can be trusted to choose a policy rule that is non-accommodating of inflationary tendencies, namely central bankers. Central bankers are assumed to be better placed than politicians to enforce such a rule, since there is no clear symmetry of interest between the central bank and the labour market in the way that there is between the government and the labour market (Watson, 2002: 184). Put in a simpler way, there is an assumption that political control over monetary policy makes the business cycle dependent on the political election timetable, with politicians trying to manipulate economic performance for short-term political gain. King certainly finds that the Conservative governments that preceded Labour prior to 1997 engaged actively in trying to manipulate economic indicators for political purposes. Accepting this argument as to the perverse incentives of politicians and their effects on distorting the economic cycle is a key precondition to allowing the idea of independence as a beneficial change to take root. The de-politicisation of central banking and the transfer of control over interest rates to independent central banks was also a key consequence of the success of the argument that Keynesian demand management was illegitimate. This was largely achieved by Friedman (Brittan, 1982) when he sought to demonstrate that a market economy would tend to gravitate towards a natural state of unemployment determined crucially by the cost of productivity and the distribution of labour (Callinicos, 2010: 15). For this reason, governments, Friedman and Schwartz (1963) argued, could not affect the rate of unemployment in the long term, unless they increased spending and cut taxes, which would result in an expansion of the money supply and thus inflation. Friedman's imperative to maintain monetary and fiscal stability could only be sustained therefore if the economy was run on an 'autopilot' for regulating the quantity of money. This autopilot was achieved via the ploy of institutionally independent central banks and inadvertently led to a re-naturalisation of economic relations. Such re-naturalisation of economic relations suggests a return to the view that market processes need no state direction that last held sway prior to the Great Depression.

While a methodology that allows ideas central place in policy formation can be challenged within the dominant neoclassical framework as placing undue reliance on a single set of agents within a larger institutional structure, it can also be suggested that the orthodox account of economic justifications for central bank independence miss-specified the whole nature of monetary relations within contemporary capitalism. In their examination of justifications for central bank independence Debelle and Fischer (1994) appear unconvinced with what they see as the three foundations of this idea. The three foundations, they argue, are the success of the Bundesbank and the German economy, the academic literature on the assumed inflationary bias of politicians and the literature on the effects of central bank independence. They found that the Bundesbank's unwavering inflation targeting has been very costly on German growth and sparked a number of serious recessions. Also they note that inflation targeting, as a goal of monetary policy, does not automatically require the independence of the central bank, and further that the causal relationship between strict monetary policies and independence is not one-directional. It could be, for instance, that countries have independent banks because they have chosen monetarist policies and not the other way around as commonly assumed.

This presentation of the reasons for the proliferation of the idea that institutional independence (in general and central bank independence in particular) is beneficial allows us to return to a consideration of the place of technocracy in modern economic governance. For Blinder (1999), the politics of macro-economics is not so much the struggle for the authority to impose efficient institutions as it is the struggle to legitimise self-appointed authority on the basis of technical expertise. The most important question to ask about the process of central banking therefore is who defines the social welfare function that acts as the guide for central bank interventions in the economy? Yet this question cannot be asked within an orthodox intellectual framework that essentially denies the constitutive role of politics in the economy. Within orthodox macro-economic analyses, the social welfare function is said to approximate the policy preferences of the 'representative' individual within society. However, those models conceptualise the representative individual as one who adopts the same cognitive approach to the question of monetary policy-making as that of orthodox macro-economists. By little more than a definitional trick, it seems, orthodox macro-economists are thus able to elevate themselves to the position of legitimate intellectual guardians of society's concerns for the key settings of economic management. Stiglitz offers a summary of his critique of the idea of the 'rational' individual in *Freefall* (2010: 248) and concludes that *homo economicus* is just a useful fiction that has been mistaken by economists as a description of reality. This fiction is then used to assess policy and to predict behaviour leading to patently unrealistic results. Such a result is similar to the one discussed above, of mistaking consumer choices with citizen choices, of a democracy of means with a democracy of votes.

The intellectual case for central bank independence is therefore less clear than its current political appeal would seem to suggest. It is undeniable, however, that financial markets have a significant impact on the way in which society is organised, since the allocation of credit is the *sine qua non* of distributional politics. Consequently, when the decision to cede operational autonomy to central bankers is justified in terms of the need for market-sensitive policies, it is equally clear that a particular way of organising society is being simultaneously constructed and defended against possible redefinition. As a result, the social basis of financial trading has changed markedly in recent years in a way which is selective of a social structure of accumulation grounded in the monetary orthodoxy that central bank independence was designed to deliver (Watson, 2002: 192). Exactly due to the intellectually suspect supports for the idea of central bank independence we can see the power of both ideas and epistemic communities to effect large-scale change on the basis of ideology. This realisation in turn allows us to re-access the ability of academic commentators to influence legal and political outcomes in the current period of uncertainty and crisis.

2.4.2 De-politicisation or dis-information?

At times of crisis one would expect scholars to show us a path to recovery, or at least to illuminate the past. In order to begin a journey towards this direction, towards solutions based in sound theory backed by evidence as opposed to solutions dictated by propaganda masquerading as science, we need to deconstruct the orthodoxies that surround us. Let us attempt to do this, beginning with the orthodoxy we have just been discussing, the sacred idea of institutional independence. Is it true that institutional independence, and more specifically central bank independence, results in apolitical economic governance, especially in the area of monetary policy? Could it be said that independence does not in fact 'de-politicise', but it only cements a particular ideology as the perpetual background to economic decision-making? McNamara argues (2002) that the advocacy of central bank independence relies on a series of contestable arguments including its purported de-politicising effects. The delegation of economic decision-making to politically independent institutions, however, does not eliminate partisan politics and interests, and monetary policy of any type (especially one with a strong anti-inflationary bias) has specific distributional consequences that raise important questions about legitimacy and accountability. While control of inflation is currently the standard priority of most central banks (for example the Federal Reserve, the Bank of England, the European Central Bank) this does not mean that inflation targeting has become an aim devoid of political content. There is indeed a trade-off between low inflation, growth and employment outcomes (Bernanke and Mishkin, 1997), which leads one to ask why is it branded political meddling to allow higher inflation as part of a policy aiming to promote employment and growth, or as part of a policy to erode the burden of public debt, while it is not political interference to maintain a strict low-inflation targeting regime in an economic climate (like the one post credit crunch) where the target is shown to do little to spur growth and employment (Krugman, 2012)? Why is it political to run monetary policy with an eye on social consequences for the worse off while it is apolitical and technically sound to run such a policy with price stability as an imperative to the benefit of the already well-off?

These questions help reveal that what passes as technically competent advice may in fact be pro-market bias dressed up as science. Joseph Stiglitz noted in an article in *The Economist* (1998) that decisions made by central bankers are not just technical decisions, they involve trade-offs, judgments about whether the risks of inflation are worth the benefits of lower unemployment, and these trade-offs involve value judgments. Stiglitz returned to this theme in fact in *Freefall* (2010) by arguing that it is not so much the details of regulatory policy that we ought to be considering in the wake of the financial crisis, but the ultimate goals: what is the role of regulation and what type of economy do we want? These are the most important of political questions and cannot be answered by institutions independent from democratic legitimacy. In the words of McNamara (2002: 53), severing the direct institutional ties to elected officials appears to create an apolitical environment for policy-making, while central banks continue to make policies which have important, identifiable distributional effects, which means that banks remain resolutely political and therefore partisan institutions. This observation is true without even beginning to consider substantive issues of macro-economic policy and the wealth of literature suggesting that inflation targeting in itself has dubious beneficial consequences on the economy (Bruno and Easterly, 1996).

At this point again, we can turn to Marxist scholars for some uncomfortable truths. Callinicos (2010) argues that the effect of the financial crisis has been to broaden our horizons and to allow us to question a distinctive feature of economic orthodoxy, what he calls the 'naturalisation' of economic relations. State intervention in the economy in the form of Keynesian policies or bailouts re-legitimises the idea of political control over the economy and dispels the fog of so-called de-politicisation. The lesson of the Phillips curve which posited a trade-off between inflation and unemployment (Callinicos, 2010: 14) was that governments could choose the mix of inflation and unemployment that best suited their values and priorities. Governments are largely denied the ability to make these choices when monetary policy is run by independent institutions fortified behind the high walls of economic orthodoxy. Giving governments the ability to determine balances of interests on the basis of political values that reflect a popular mandate is based on a recognition that economic relations are not governed by autonomous mechanisms, resembling those driving physical processes. Accepting the de-naturalisation of economic relations therefore allows states and their people to regain control of their destiny, to make choices on the basis of a shared vision of the public good.

As mentioned earlier, the discussion in this section can explain the great paradox of economic policy during the crisis: how is it possible to argue for significant law-making activity (assumed by proposals to reform regulatory frameworks) without abandoning the idea of minimal state intervention which lies at the core of free-market thinking; how is it possible to empower the state in this way without risking a return to political control over the economy? The currently technically competent solution to this conundrum is to entrust the regulatory functions of government to independent institutions, free from political influence and control. This is consistent with an ideology that serves market interests under a technocratic, scientific cloak. In this way the theory of a free market safe from political interference is maintained while all the necessary detail is filled in without upsetting a neoclassical theoretical structure that sees the separation of the economic from the political as central to the success of capitalism. In other words the orthodox mindset survives the reintroduction of regulation in the economy because more and more non-state institutions are being employed in regulatory roles (Glinavos, 2010a). Despite this argument, however, this discussion has demonstrated that appeals to 'technocracy' are little more than a cowardly attempt to avoid recognition of underlying power relations in society. Willing something apolitical does not make it so. When thinking about the nature of the state–market relationship post crisis, it would be helpful to stop thinking that neoliberalism dressed up as science is anything more than a pretence.

2.5 Conclusion

Mattei and Nader (2008) in their provocative book *Plunder* take issue with the sacred notion of the 'rule of law' and challenge its central place in western legal tradition. They highlight (Mattei and Nader, 2008: 12) the highly symbolic moment in which law and politics divorced, bringing to humankind the miracle of a government of law and not of men. The present book talks about the separation between politics and economics, and the consequence of law being relegated to the position of servant of economics, dragged down from its pinnacle as the expression of democratically determined values and goals. Why are these divides a problem? Why should we not take the view that apolitical law is the best kind of law? Why argue with the illustrious procession of scholars that praised the 'rule of law' and align ourselves with radicals like Mattei and Nader? The reason is that what passes as apolitical law is not devoid of political content. As explained in *Neoliberalism and the Law*, arguing for law separate from politics often means arguing for law that supports a certain type of politics: the politics of inequality and marginalisation. We are not arguing here for a complete abandonment of western notions of legality and of the value of courts independent from political masters. What we are arguing instead is for the ability to choose, to select what the law is for and what type of economic organisation best reflects the interests and choices of the people. We are arguing for a re-democratisation of capitalism and, in doing so, we need to ask ourselves anew some old questions, plus pose some entirely novel ones, like for instance what do we need financial markets for and how ought they be constructed?

The book in general and this chapter in particular have addressed the artificial, constituted nature of finance and link the virtual world that forms the commanding heights of the economy with legal fictions at the basis of a superstructure of constructs. This is done in an effort to counter the orthodox fallacy of the 'naturalness' of markets and to show the intellectual poverty of many market-promoting theories. In his excellent book *Extreme Money* (2011: 438) Satyajit Das relates a discussion he had with a French semiotician who suggested that the financial crisis is at its core a crisis of postmodernism. It is possible to argue that the financial crisis, in its soul a crisis of money and financial markets, manifests a modern anxiety about the nature of reality. Modern finance represents a high art of abstraction, things that are images of representations of real things. What are derivatives if not new forms of money abstracted from real things? Das's discussant argued that in postmodernity the meta-level eventually dominates the primary level it emanated from, virtual wealth overwhelms real wealth, leading to circularity and self-reference. Via this process value becomes driven by itself, prices become a function of what you can borrow against the collateral, driving up a 'value' feeding on itself. The speculative bubble that collapsed in 2008 was based on a bet that served as its own foundation. The financial bubble, piling credit on top of credit, got rich on self-affirmation. It was contained in its self-relation, which is what made it a bubble. It gradually eliminated the principle of reality: nothing counted but the financial products invented through people's investments (Glucksmann, 2009). Key to this process of disentanglement from reality is, as we saw in this chapter, the concept of liquidity and the uses it serves in modern capitalism. This chapter also demonstrated how the functions of the state are being subcontracted out to various allegedly 'independent', 'apolitical' institutions, such as central banks. It cannot be automatically assumed, however, that self-regulation and independence ensure accountability and serve the public interest, and there is a great need for explaining the distancing of economic management from the democratic process. If the running of the economy is a scientific matter best tackled by technocrats, independent central banks and independent judiciaries, in what ways (if any) can the public participate in the process? Indeed, why is there a need for a democratic state at all, if governing the economy does not need to be consonant with the popular will (Glinavos, 2010a)?

Reality cannot be defined in abstractions indefinitely, however, without at some point touching base with the way people live and what they experience. The perceived legitimacy and viability of institutions that rest at the basis of our capitalist settlement, such as private property, is ultimately dependent upon perceptions at the grass-roots level rather than upon exogenous decisions or top-down processes (Sindzingre, 2003). The people through the democratic process need to revalidate our assumptions as to the goals and institutions of finance. Without reconnecting with citizens, the functions of finance that sparked the crisis will continue to lose legitimacy, dragging down with them the whole belief in free markets and capitalism. Does this sound fantastical? It did until the European sovereign debt crisis (and the way in which it has been (mis)managed) showed the fragility of democratic politics in their contemporary constrained, castrated, technically competent interpretation. Despite this, as we will see in following chapters, most efforts to address the financial crisis are focusing on creating more independent institutions – stronger independent regulators, fiscal monitoring agencies, etc. – severed from political control and influence. Whatever the formal structure of these entities, the legitimacy of their operations depends on complex perceptions of the behaviour of political elites. Formally independent institutions cannot acquire legitimacy separately from the rest of the political system. Additionally, even if this were possible, it may not be desirable from a democratic perspective. As I noted when reflecting on legal reforms in the post-communist setting in *Neoliberalism and the Law* (Glinavos, 2010a), reforms originating from elites or foreign lenders that are not considered legitimate do not generate independent reasons for the public to accept new institutions. Consequently, law reform that ignores political factors does not address existing political difficulties. Reform that is widely seen as favouring specific interests has limited chances of success in changing social norms and practices – indeed it has little chance of carving a way out of crisis.

So far as the inclusion of elements of public accountability and participation is concerned, the commitment to the institutional devices of independent central banks and financial stability mechanisms is distinctive for preventing macro-economic policy from being determined in 'too democratic' a manner. This worrying trend finds its legal expression through the inclusion of distinctions between economic policy-making and democratic choice even in constitutional structures. As Teivanen (2002: 16) noted:

> In a capitalist context, democratic advances have often been constrained through the creation of constitutional constraints that protect, among other issues, the principle of private property. Constitutionalism helps to construct boundaries of an economic sphere within which property rights are more valid than democratic rights.

Add to this the modern practice of elevating legal norms pertaining to the protection of private property rights to supra-national structures and granting adjudicating powers to international investment tribunals (Glinavos, 2011) and you have de-politicisation of economic decision-making fortified behind a wall of laws, blocking democracy from translating popular choices into state actions.

In discussing regulatory reform therefore it is imperative to recognise that the regulation of the economy is not just a matter for law and economics. Regulatory interventions, or the lack thereof, can have severe consequences on the political economy of a state and changing popular perceptions of the functions of law can have direct effects on the democratic legitimacy of institutions. The substitution of state regulation by independent regulators is an example of the negative effects of de-politicisation on perceptions of legitimacy. Independent, non-state regulators are meant to achieve the aims of market support without abandoning the still dominant perception of the market as primarily self-regulating. The creation of allegedly non-political, independent institutions, however, means institutions isolated from the political and – by extension – democratic process. The European Central Bank (ECB), for example, prides itself in not seeking or taking instructions from European Union institutions or bodies, from any government of an EU member state or from any other body in determining its price stability policies. Considering, however, the effect on the economy that the setting of interest rates has, some degree of political input into the Bank's decision-making would be at least desirable, if not required. It is no wonder that the institutional independence of the ECB does not improve public perceptions of the EU as a democratically deficient structure (Glinavos, 2010b).

As we will see in Chapter 6, at times of severe economic crisis and recession, selecting types of self-regulation over political control can be a particularly politically dangerous route to follow. As suggested above, using the example of the ECB, central bank independence ensures that monetary policy is determined solely by 'economic' concerns. This ensures the pursuit of policies deemed good for the 'investment climate'. It also, however, disempowers governments; they are less able to control the economy or to pursue expansionary economic policies necessary to achieve wider social objectives (Watson, 2002). When elected representatives are unwilling or unable to deal with fundamental economic issues, there can often seem to be little difference between democratic and authoritarian government. De-politicisation creates a legitimacy vacuum which can damage people's belief in democracy. Is it really beyond explanation that the Greeks, faced with the longest depression the world has ever seen, abandon traditional politics in favour of extreme, even fascist alternatives? Further reforms aimed at addressing these problems often create a new set of difficulties, not least because they usually seek to build on structures which are little respected. This risks a downward spiral that affects legal and institutional structures alike (Glinavos, 2010a). If the traditional parties of power have become transmission mechanisms for policies demanded by international lenders, would you vote for someone so anti-systemic as to be against democracy itself? In 2012 in two successive elections 7 per cent of Greeks voted for the neo-Nazi group 'Golden Dawn', with opinion polls showing its surging popularity in 2013. Have we come to a point where the institutional structures of financialised capitalism point to an abandonment of democracy?

One consequence of the de-politicisation of economic decisions is to make many citizens today quietly contemptuous of democracy. Either one considers that others are not competent to be consulted as to how a country should be run, or one thinks that whatever people think is irrelevant, as the political system is captured by an 'establishment' that renders democratic processes a sham. This nihilism is a very dangerous aspect of our times. Being disinterested in democracy is a threat to the survival of the only workable idea of government we have left today. After having tried different versions of authoritarianism, from paternalist dictatorship to self-interested oligarchy, the world seems – by a process of elimination – to be left with liberal democracy. This has been claimed to signify a so-called 'end of history' according to authors like Francis Fukuyama (1992). While talk of an end to history is of course nonsensical, the question nevertheless remains: is there an alternative to democratic capitalism available? The opposing doctrine of course is not theocratic dictatorship as implied by easy to digest yet empirically false claims of a clash of civilisations (Huntington, 2002), but an evolution of liberal democracy along a different path. Such a path cannot open, however, unless we are willing to re-examine how we got here and whether we want to use our democratic institutions to determine where we want to get to. The following chapter will deal with how we got here, while the latter parts of the book help us along the way to a different, hopefully better, debate about our future.

Part 2

Crises

A lot of what we think we know about the state–market relationship is a result of perception and propaganda that does not correspond with evidence or the historical record. This book began in Part 1 by setting the framework for our discussion, defending the methodological use of the state–market dichotomy and by unpacking many notions we think we recognise but in fact know little about. The nature of markets, the role of the state in economic management, the meaning of finance, credit, money, are all contestable notions resting on sometimes weak legal foundations. By exposing where these foundations lie, we can begin to understand what this book attempts to prove: that our political economy is a matter of choice, a matter of a political consensus that was crafted at a particular point in time. Our political economy, the balance we currently have between states and markets, is not the result of automatic, natural, scientific processes. We may have forgotten the social contract that gave birth to capitalism, but this does not mean that democratic choice has become obsolete, that it has become supplanted by an orthodoxy peddled by 'experts'.

The second part of this book continues the myth-breaking we have already commenced. Part 2 begins with Chapter 3 by offering a historical exploration of different balance points achieved between states and markets. This journey takes us from the Industrial Revolution to the roaring laissez-faire 1920s, to the shock of the Great Depression, the Golden Era of embedded capitalism and then finally to the neoliberal revolution of the 1980s. Such historical background allows us to view anew what the role of law has been and what market freedom has meant in the past. It is through this historical reflection that we can rediscover the place of notions of public utility in the law, and how those became lost in the resurgence of laissez-faire over the last three decades. Our historical journey then reaches in Chapter 4 the current crisis. The latter section of this part of the book presents the key features of the financial crisis that began in the USA in 2007 and follows its evolution to the European debt crisis that still rages at the time of writing in 2013. The latter part of this presentation takes on the example of Greece, explaining in some detail the calamities created by the inability to envisage a different balance in the state–market relationship and a consequent path out of crisis.

Our reflection ends with a presentation of the consequences of institutional rigidity, arguing that the structures of the European Union exacerbate the crisis, exactly by doing what this book is cautioning against: embedding the de-politicisation of economic decision-making. At the end of this part of the book, we will be fully equipped to begin an evaluation of policy changes post crisis, and we will be able to glimpse possibilities for a rebalancing of the market–state relationship in the future.

3 History and deregulation

A focus on law creation as an exercise in protecting economic fundamentals limits the purposes of law and relegates it to the role of market supporter, instead of a tool to achieve social justice.

3.1 Introduction

As we have already highlighted in this book, one of the central questions underlying a lot of commentary on the financial crisis is to what extent should the state intervene in the economy, and what form should any such intervention take? In Chapter 1 we presented an outline of arguments relevant to the legitimacy of state intrusion into markets which reflect the main thrust of the 'public interest' and the 'capture' theories of state intervention. The conclusion of Chapter 1 was that more market freedom may mean less choice for citizens. We highlighted that choices given to consumers are not necessarily the same thing as choices on how society is organised and about how the popular will is reflected in economic governance. Robert Hale (Ireland, 2003), writing about the nature of markets, captured exactly the fallacy of considering market relations as free of coercion. He suggested that a free market is a legal construct that allows choices within a specified framework that is inevitably characterised by coercion. This coercion is exercised via the exclusionary and relational nature of property rights. Markets, according to Hale (structures of rights that are constituted in particular ways), are therefore sites in which power is exercised (structures of mutual coercion). From this perspective, securing existing rights merely serves to secure very particular structures of power rather than to maximise some notion of economic 'efficiency' (Ireland, 2003: 489). In *Freedom Through Law: Public Control of Private Governing Power* (1952), Hale argued that concentrations of private economic power were slowly taking on many of the attributes formerly thought of as the exclusive prerogative of public sovereignty. Hale (1923) held that these new forms of 'private government' were just as capable of exercising social force and coercion and destroying liberty as 'public government' itself. The consequence of this realisation is that to preserve capitalism and to safeguard 'freedom' we may well need to accept more state involvement in market processes. This is because a stronger hand of the state in market regulation allows for higher participation of the public (through the democratic process) in economic governance. The current chapter examines in more detail the nature of state intervention. This is achieved via a historical presentation of phases through which the relationship of the state to the market has passed. Before we begin on our historical journey, however, it is worth briefly expanding our background of knowledge on the theoretical justifications for regulation, building on the material presented in Chapter 1.

It is commonly suggested that the rationale for state action in a political economy rests on the assumption that such action presents an adequate response to an identified problem. No solution to a problem, especially if the solution implies regulation, can, however, be without wider consequences. To that effect, an economist would argue, if active intervention in markets is pursued through the adoption of any particular regulatory initiative, policy-makers must be aware that the adoption of the initiative in question, as well as having potential benefits, also imposes costs on all members of society. This is consistent with a neoclassical view of regulation which focuses on market failure and the role of government in mitigating such failure (or alternatively, in the absence of inefficiencies, on the design of the least-costly methods of redistributing resources) (Trebing, 1987: 1716). Regulatory initiatives designed to enhance the efficiency of private markets therefore need to ensure that the costs imposed by regulation do not eliminate the intended benefits (Nickerson and Phillips, 2003: 445). In other words, state intervention is the result of the positive conclusion of a cost-benefit analysis. If state intervention is likely to make things better (usually interpreted with an economic yardstick as making things more efficient), then its costs are justified. This reduction of the issue of balance between state and market to a cost-benefit analysis has been a crucial methodological tool in understanding regulatory interventions. This tool has inadvertently allowed, however, the advance of technocratic (scientific) and non-political approaches to law reform.

From this perspective, both regulation and deregulation are state actions with a diminished political content, merely imposing costs (or alleviating burdens produced by market interactions). The latter point is consistent with an institutionalist approach to regulation (we came across this literature in Chapter 1 when we briefly referred to the work of institutional economists) which rests on the need for government intervention to combat concentrations of power, high uncertainty, performance failures, uncompensated costs and adverse distributional effects. The role afforded to regulation from this viewpoint is then to promote public interest or social values that cannot be derived exclusively from monetary or market-oriented measures. This is all good, but even institutionalist theories do not envisage regulation as a method of pursuing a political agenda consonant with the popular will (to the extent that what is good is defined in contrary ways to what is perceived as efficient). The basic idea behind intervention is that regulation should seek to promote higher levels of efficiency while at the same time promoting greater individual choice by guiding allocative decisions to better reflect social needs (Trebing, 1987: 1714–15). This can be achieved by regulation or at times deregulation, and it is for this reason that Amato and Fantacci in their book *The End of Finance* (2012) present regulation and deregulation as two sides of the same coin.

The words efficiency and choice, however, can be and are frequently taken outside a social context to mean things solely economically defined. Yet if state intervention is to be justifiable, it is only because it places emphasis on the fulfilment of social needs in an effort to achieve something more than mere profit facilitation. Intervention should therefore be judged by criteria independent of economic efficiency. Inevitably, a discussion of social needs and how to meet them leads to consideration of issues like fairness in society, and this is why we spent some time in the opening chapter of this book discussing regulation (and its absence) from an ethical point of view. Indeed, as many commentators observe, the objectives of efficiency and equity may often be mutually incompatible in practice. It is exactly for this reason that this book claims that economic governance is at its core a question of political consensus. Thus a traditional conception of regulation that focuses on how objectives can be attained through government intervention within an economically deterministic framework can be too narrow. Can state initiatives pursue efficiency and equity (or justice) while avoiding the potential conflict between government discretion and the rule of law as explained by Hayek as we saw in Chapter 1? Or could it be that this conflict between efficiency and justice is illusory, as suggested by a closer look at the historical record?

This chapter follows the evolution of economic and legal theory on how to balance the market–state relationship from the era of the Industrial Revolution to the resurgence of liberalism in the latter part of the twentieth century. The aim is to show how law and regulation have been used as buffers (in accordance with theoretical innovations borrowing from both neoclassical and institutional economics) against the potential of the market to self-destruct. This function of law, as a mechanism for restraining markets from spinning out of control, is consistent with Minsky's analysis (mentioned frequently in this book) suggesting an evolution of capitalism through stages of ever increasing instability (from hedge to speculative and finally to Ponzi finance structures). The chapter also attempts to explore the consequences of various incarnations of the balance between state control and market freedom on the wider political economy. This analysis allows an evaluation in this part of the book of the links between deregulation and financial crisis to take place. This part will also consider how the tendency towards de-politicisation (exemplified by deregulation from the early 1980s to the latest financial crisis) is responsible for a degrading of the role of the state and politics, leading to a sub-optimal balance of market vis-à-vis social interests.

3.2 The nineteenth century

3.2.1 A paradise of laissez-faire?

> ... good society, floated on gossamer wings of light irony, is of very expensive production, requiring nothing less than a wide and arduous national life condensed in unfragrant deafening factories, cramping itself in mines, sweating at furnaces, grinding, hammering, weaving under more or less oppression of carbonic acid. (Eliot, 1860)

The concept of controls on market activity is as old as the concept of the market itself, but the modern view of regulation as a limited function of government with the purpose to correct market distortions and socially unwelcome outcomes is largely a late nineteenth-century creation. We saw in Chapter 1 a summary of how modern theory seeks to justify state interventions into the market. This chapter traces the evolution of these ideas historically, seeking to unpack our understanding of the function of law in economic governance. This section discusses the presence (or absence) of laws and regulations on market activities during the period of the Industrial Revolution (defined as spanning the period from the end of the eighteenth to the end of the nineteenth centuries). This presentation is necessary in setting a framework to subsequent perceptions of the function of law. The key question explored here is whether the industrial era was, as is famed to be, a golden age of laissez-faire.

In fact, the very notion of regulation is one that can be traced to the late nineteenth century, even though that era itself is perceived to be the golden age of free enterprise. Karl Polanyi has described the eighteenth and early nineteenth centuries in *The Great Transformation* (1957) as heralding an era of self-regulating free markets. This is seen as a world where markets are uninhibited, characterised by mostly privately owned property, where economic decisions are determined in a manner unfettered by state interference and where profit is the goal. This was an era described by John Higham as an 'age of boundlessness' (Bruchey, 1988). According to Germain (2010: 21) the late 1800s were an era of self-governance, particularly in finance, which was dominated by a small number of key players (such as Baring Brothers and Rothchild & Sons). Describing arrangements pertaining to financial governance in that era, he notes that there were close links between these firms and the Bank of England (established in 1694), which itself was rather like a private member's club whose original purpose was to provide long-term funding to the government, and later came to control monetary policy in order to ensure Britain adhered to the gold standard (Dickson, 1967). The governance, however, that the Bank oversaw in the financial sector was very much self-regulatory, with no easily identifiable mandatory rules. The road to more formal lines of control was opened from the point at which state institutions, like the Bank of England, came to play a pivotal role in rescuing private actors, like the troubled Barings, from the 1890s onwards.

Before we reach the end of the nineteenth century, however, we can consider what was the nature of legal intervention in the operation of markets? One of the oldest examples of financial regulation is that of laws preventing usury, the practice of lending money at extortionate interest rates. Such prohibition may sound novel to the modern reader used to seeing on the screen promotions for short-term loans with interest rates reaching into the thousands of percentage points. The online provider wonga.com, for instance, proudly announced in early 2012 a loan service with a representative APR of 4,214 per cent. Usury laws in America, for example, date back to at least 1641 when Massachusetts set the maximum legal rate of interest for loans at 8 per cent. The rest of the original 13 colonies enacted their usury laws during the eighteenth century and the remaining states adopted their usury laws in the nineteenth century, all with rates around that of Massachusetts. In addition to regulating the maximum legal rate for borrowing, these provisions also set penalties for charging usurious rates. The penalty typically made a distinction between 'loss' and 'forfeiture'. Lenders that violated the law could lose the legal interest and/or the principal if the law denied the collection of the debt from the borrower. Moreover, in some states, lenders were subject to forfeiture of up to triple the amount of the principal (as in Maryland until 1860), or triple the illegal interest as in Illinois, Massachusetts and New Hampshire in 1850 (Benmelech and Moskowitz, 2007: 11). If a modern scholar was looking for the reasons behind these laws, she could utilise the theoretical justification for regulatory interventions on the basis of the public interest and capture theories discussed in Chapter 1, with the core argument against usury being that it is a socially corrosive and economically harmful practice. Alternatively, if one is religious, one could consider the theological explanation behind most usury laws, which is that money-lending was limited by Godly command. It would be interesting to see what the author of this passage in the Bible (Leviticus 25: 35–7) would make of the modern pay-day loan industry

> If your brother becomes poor and cannot maintain himself with you, you shall support him as though he were a stranger and a sojourner, and he shall live with you. Take no interest from him or profit, but fear your God, that your brother may live beside you. You shall not lend him your money at interest, nor give him your food for profit.

Religious-based prohibitions on interest, however, do not alter the perception of this era as synonymous with laissez-faire. The common perception of the nineteenth century as the pinnacle of free markets is perhaps enhanced when one looks at the attitudes of courts in relation to issues of liability. The treatment of worker's rights (especially for legal responsibility for workplace incidents) is illustrative of a general distaste for legal intervention in market processes. For instance, the English law doctrine of 'common employment', deriving from the judgment of Lord Abinger in *Priestley* v. *Fowler* [1837] 3 M&W, ensured that employers were not liable for the personal injuries of their workers when caused by the negligence of another worker, especially in cases such as Priestley, where the employer had no means of knowing about his worker's negligent actions. The judicial fear was of the famed slippery slope variety, suggesting that the imposition of liability on employers in such circumstances would lead to a proliferation of similar claims, a resultant loss of control by businesses and an increase in the costs of production, which would (in turn) adversely affect economic progress. Implicit in the doctrine of common employment was the assumption that when workers contracted to work they knew, or ought to have known, what risks they were exposing themselves to. This belief may remind the reader of the proclamations of financiers during the crisis suggesting that sophisticated counterparties in derivatives transactions can assess risks and are therefore responsible for any losses resulting from bad investment decisions. This judicial approach was reflected in the fact that up until the late nineteenth century employers could raise the defence of consent (known as *volenti non fit injuria*) to claims brought by workers injured as a result of negligence in the workplace. In addition, workers who were found to be contributory negligent in failing to have sufficient regard to their own safety even in a small way were denied any compensation from their employer (Open University, 2011: 79).

The above suggests that there was little or no recognition of the economic reality that in most cases workers had no practical alternative but to continue to work and to subject themselves to the risk of unsafe workplace practices. Thus employers were effectively immune from liability for industrial incidents and there was little or no incentive for employers to develop safe industrial practices. This is a handsome parallel as suggested above with the financial industry where, in the absence of 'stifling' regulation, investors were continually subjecting themselves to risks of huge losses, while financial firms were immune from liability for selling them products designed to fail. For example, in 2007 Goldman Sachs sold to its clients a product known as Abacus. It was suggested that this collateralised debt obligation (CDO) was specifically built to fail so that its creator, investment firm Paulson & Co., could collect on a related insurance policy. Goldman allegedly knew, but did not disclose to its clients, that the product had been designed to be 'shorted' in this way and was duly charged with fraud by the US Securities and Exchange Commission (SEC) in 2010. The firm has since settled for a $300 million fine and $250 million restitution payment to its clients (SEC, 2010a, 2010b). The protected position of employers in the 1800s did not last, however, and was slowly eroded during the latter part of the nineteenth century as judicial opinion veered more in favour of workers and as Parliament took action, bringing in statutes controlling labour relations. For example, the impact of the doctrine of common employment was reduced by the Employer's Liability Act of 1880. In 1891, the House of Lords in *Smith* v. *Baker & Sons* [1891] AC 325 determined that a worker's consent could not be inferred from their awareness of the risk of harm they may suffer as a result of their employer's negligence (Open University, 2011: 80).

What is the explanation, however, for the lack of earlier state intervention during the industrial era, even in areas with such observable problems as health and safety in industrial production? One explanation for the anti-statist stance of courts during that period is that a conservative bench saw itself as the guardian of class privilege rather than a supporter of progressive causes (Geary et al., 2008). Lord Halsbury, for instance, immediately after his appointment in 1885, sought to influence the composition of the bar along ideological lines, expressed as antipathy to trade unions and to parliamentary encroachment upon the common law (Geary et al., 2008: 126). While the courts were reluctant to enact regulatory measures, Parliament was more willing, but not because it suddenly saw the plight of the workers. One could argue that legislative initiative was hardly motivated by a desire to fuel progressive causes, rather it was responding to market pressures for the rationalisation of legal regimes. The German civil code of 1896 is an example of a great codification undertaken by a large political entity to facilitate a growing market (Marciano, 2009: 252). The multitude of laws governing bills of exchange (there were 56 different legal systems involved in their operation in Germany) in 1848, for instance, was seen by the majority of scholars of this period as an impediment to the development of a market economy. Increased regulation over the operation of the market therefore, according to this view, was more a by-product of the modernisation of the legal system than a conscious effort to limit socially harmful (yet profitable) endeavours.

The above discussion suggests agreement with the widely held view that the early part of the Industrial Revolution – and in any event the era up till the end of the nineteenth century – was a period of market self-ordering. Are we right, however, to treat this view as applicable to the whole of the industrialising world?

3.2.2 Laissez-faire as historical misinterpretation?

Not everyone concedes that this era was anti-statist and anti-regulation for the Anglo-Saxon world as a whole. Novak (1993), after an analysis of nineteenth-century product and inspection laws, licensing cases and controls on urban marketplaces, argues that economic regulation was deeply rooted in American life, even before the Civil War (1861–5). He argues that the existence of multiple restrictions on economic and social life passed by state and local authorities suggests that 'a regulated economy' is a better description for this era than 'freedom of contract' or laissez-faire (Novak, 1993: 2). The reason behind this argument is the realisation that the notion of a 'well-regulated society' and of a 'public economy' functioned as a central philosophy of American public law. While a laissez-faire revolution may have been true for England at the beginning of the nineteenth century, it had been less successful in the US where political and legal institutions resisted change in the period between 1776 and the mid-1800s. The explanation for this inability of laissez-faire to take root lies in the decentralised nature of policy-making and the fractured legal system that existed in America at the time. This decentralisation helped maintain the conception that the economy ought to be embedded in society and be subject to various social constraints (Novak, 1993: 8), with the usury laws described above being just one example. Beyond restrictions on lending, product control laws proliferated. In *Mayor and Alderman of Mobil* v. *Yuille* (1841) 3 Ala. 137, 159–43, the Supreme Court of Alabama, for instance, upheld the assize (statute) of bread declaring that:

> Whatever doubts have been thrown over the question by the theories of political economists, it would seem that this great end (the urban supply of bread) is better secured by licensing a sufficient number of bakers and by an assize of bread, than by leaving it to the voluntary acts of individuals.

Similarly, there was no freedom to trade without licence and obtaining one was not a mere bureaucratic requirement. In *French* v. *Baker* (1856) 36 Tenn. 193, the Tennessee Supreme Court held that the occupation of merchant was a privilege sanctioned by government and not a natural right of individuals. In *Wartman* v. *City of Philadelphia* (1859) 33 Pa. 202, 209, the Pennsylvania Supreme Court defended the power of local government to control the market by arguing:

> The necessity of a public market … is very apparent. There is nothing which more imperatively requires the constant supervision of some authority which can regulate it and control it. Such authority is seldom, if ever vested in individuals.

Therefore any activity 'affected with a public interest' was deemed an appropriate target for regulation. The phrase 'affected with a public interest' itself was first used by the Supreme Court in *Munn* v. *Illinois* (1877) 94 US 113. Munn was one of nine owners of 14 grain elevators in Chicago who had set themselves up (unofficially) in a price-fixing cartel. Grain elevator businesses did not have or need a franchise or charter from the state in order to operate. Yet Midwestern farmers transporting their grain to Chicago for shipment to more distant markets had to use the elevators in Chicago, and had no choice but to pay the steep fees. The state government intervened and established lower maximum prices by statute. Munn challenged the state's right to regulate in the courts. In its decision, the court noted that Munn stood in the very gateway of commerce and took a toll from all who passed, and as such his business was a legitimate target for regulation. It referred to English common law, quoted Lord Hale and established what has come to be recognised as the public utility principle (Melody, 1997: 12).

> When, therefore, one devotes his property to a use in which the public has an interest, he, in effect, grants to the public an interest in that use, and must submit to be controlled by the public for the common good, to the extent of the interest he has thus created. (p. 126)

The court noted (p. 132) that the right to regulate 'may not be made so by the Constitution of Illinois or this statute, but it is by the facts'. Implicit in this judgment is a view of law as something more than a dispute settling mechanism. Law came to be seen as a dynamic tool of social control and a facilitator of economic progress (Horwitz, 1974: 917). *Dicta*, such as those from Munn, also suggest that the idea of laissez-faire as a synonym for growth is an intellectual construct that does not fit very well with historical data. And it was not only American courts that expressed reservations about allowing markets to self-control. In nineteenth-century France, the 1804 Napoleonic Civil Code recognised property rights and rights of alienation in a forceful way, but treated them both as creations of civil law and thus subject to limitations in the public interest (Halpérin, 2011).

If scholars are looking for a better match between the historical record and modern impressions of an unregulated free-market utopia, they would be better served by looking at the next historical period – the beginning of the twentieth century. The coming section presents perceptions of the role of law in markets up to the stock market crash of 1929.

3.3 Early twentieth century

While the nineteenth century was a great incubator of ideas and the first testing ground for modern versions of the balance between the market and the state, the beginning of the twentieth century heralded both the supposed peak of laissez-faire and its swift demise in the 1930s. A significant part of the debate as to the appropriate reach of the state into market activity took place in the courts as we have already seen. Indeed, one could say (as we will see in Chapter 6) that the courts seem like a better contender (as opposed to legislative process) for the title of appropriate venue where a balance between state and market should be struck. As a result, a great deal of the debate on the role of law and its place in economic processes has focused on the merits of litigation (as opposed to legislation) as the most efficient way to direct markets to producing socially acceptable outcomes. Richard Posner, who we came across in Chapter 1, was not the first American to consider the merits of private litigation versus state-mandated regulation. At the beginning of the century, the American President Woodrow Wilson repeatedly complained about the failure of the courts to stand up to large corporations because, he said, 'the laws of this country do not prevent the strong from crushing the weak' (Pestritto, 2005). He articulated his vision of government regulation in his New Freedom programme, noting:

> It was no business of the law in the time of Jefferson to come into my house and to see how I kept house. But when my house, when my so-called private property, became a great mine, and men went along dark corridors amidst every kind of danger in order to dig out of the bowels of the earth things necessary for the industries of a whole nation, and when it came about that no individual owned these mines, that they were owned by great stock companies, then all the old analogies absolutely collapsed and it became the right of the government to go down into these mines to see whether human beings were properly treated in them or not; to see whether accidents were properly safeguarded against; to see whether modern economical methods of using these inestimable riches of the earth were followed or were not followed. If somebody puts a derrick improperly secured on top of a building or overtopping the street, then the government of the city has the right to see that that derrick is so secured that you and I can walk under it and not be afraid that heavens are going to fall on us. Likewise, in these great beehives where in every corridor swarm men of flesh and blood, it is the privilege of the government, whether of the State or of the United States, as the case may be, to see that human life is protected, that human lungs have something to breathe. (Pestritto, 2005: 113)

French courts in this period seemed also to interpret their role as protectors of private, as opposed to public, interests. Armed with the belief that rights over property and that provisions for compensation for takings were based in the 1789 Declaration on the Rights of Man, French courts at the turn of the twentieth century became protectors of private enterprise and bulwarks against the creation of state providers (and what was seen as dangerous municipal socialism). In the Bac d'Eloka case (Tribunal des conflits, 22.1.1921, Société Commerciale de l'Ouest Africain), the court confirmed that state enterprises were subject to civil law (and thus subject to the requirement to pay compensation) like private businesses. In the interwar period, in fact, courts treated enterprise like a prerogative of the private sector with only limited tolerance for state provision in exceptional cases. When in 1937, for example, the bankrupt railways were nationalised (essentially bailed out, to use the modern term), great care was taken to protect the interests of private investors and shareholders. This little appreciated tradition (in Anglo-Saxon scholarship) of the French courts was echoed on 16 January 1982 when the Conseil Constitutionnel struck down President Mitterand's nationalisation statute on the issue of calculating compensation for takings, noting that private property rested at the basis of the Constitution since 1789, and that a complete suppression of the free market would be unconstitutional

(Halpérin, 2011). One could even see parallels between that decision and the move of the Conseil Constitutionnel in December 2012 to delay the implementation of President Holland's 75 per cent tax rate for the super rich (Carnegy, 2012), a tax which incensed a number of prominent business and media figures enough to head for tax exile, most notably film star Gérard Depardieu, who sought refuge from Mr Holland's clutching hands in the loving embrace of Mr Putin of Russia.

However, as we saw in the previous section, Novak (1993) argues that the notions of a 'well-regulated society' and of a 'public economy' continued to be central principles guiding the development of legal norms in the United States during the early twentieth century. In *Nebbia* v. *New York* (1934) 291 US 502, for instance, the Supreme Court in the spirit of *Munn* v. *Illinois* (discussed above) argued in favour of a wide scope for legitimate government intervention in the market, stating that even in industries that are not public utilities, the public interest still dictates their behaviour:

> The phrase 'affected with a public interest' can, in the nature of things, mean no more than that an industry, for adequate reason, is subject to control for the public good. So far as the requirement of due process is concerned, and in the absence of other constitutional restriction, a state is free to adopt whatever economic policy may reasonably be deemed to promote public welfare, and to enforce that policy by legislation adapted to its purpose. (p. 536)

Nonetheless, in response to public dissatisfaction with legal provisions deemed inadequate to protect the public from potentially harmful activities, political actors in the United States sought a range of remedies against social harm beyond reliance on litigation. Glaeser and Shleifer (2003) argue that these remedies were not just aimed at changing the behaviour of courts in relation to corporations, but rather also to change the form of social control of business. Starting with Charles Francis Adams and the Massachusetts Railroad Commission, regulatory agencies became a complement to judicial action. The reforms started with states and municipalities but eventually moved to the federal level, in part because the increase in the scale of firms made state regulation inadequate. In 1887, the Interstate Commerce Act created the Interstate Commerce Commission which, using powers granted by subsequent legislation, had the power to stop railway companies from exploiting their customers and, under the Hepburn Act of 1906, to set maximum freight charges.

The real growth of regulatory activity, however, occurred after the turn of the century, during the presidencies of Theodore Roosevelt and Woodrow Wilson. In 1906, Congress passed the Pure Foods and Drugs Act which aimed to control the distribution of medicines, as well as a federal meat inspection law. Under Wilson, the regulation of both banking (under the Federal Reserve Act of 1913) and competition (under the Clayton Act in 1914) became commonplace. Further legislative initiatives, following legislative activity in Britain at the end of the nineteenth century, led to the adoption of workers' compensation laws by several US states around the 1900s, a move seen as a response to the failure of courts to address the problems of workers being injured in industrial incidents (Fishback and Kantor, 2000). The new laws replaced the negligence standard used in courts with a combination of regulation and strict liability (Glaeser and Shleifer, 2003: 12). We see therefore a mixed picture on attitudes to regulation, even during a period that most associate with the peak of laissez-faire.

The process of increasing regulatory intervention via the legislative process (and away from court-made law) was to accelerate rapidly during the period marked by the Great Depression. The next section offers a summary of the seismic changes brought about by the 1929 crash and the ensuing Great Depression.

3.4 Reacting to the Great Depression

The 1929 stock market crash in the United States and the subsequent Great Depression on the one hand solidified in the eyes of the leadership of the Democratic Party the need to protect states from the dangers of market failure and, on the other, created among the population at large a massive fear of unemployment and its consequences (Aman, 2004). Franklin Delano Roosevelt was elected President in the fall of 1932 and inaugurated in March 1933. This was at the height of the Great Depression, when the short-term nominal interest rate was close to zero and deflation was accelerating (Eggertsson, 2005). This meant that the government had to address a situation where, while prices were falling, the debt burden was actually increasing since the purchasing power of the dollar went down, making debts more difficult to repay. The outgoing Hoover administration contributed to this disastrous outcome because it encouraged the Federal Reserve to aim for price stability while at the same time the Treasury tried to balance the budget (failing to support demand in the economy). One way the federal government could have arguably kept up demand would be by significantly increasing government spending, which was of course anathema to the market loyalists of the Hoover administration. Famously, Hoover's Treasury Secretary Andrew Mellon advised him to liquidate labour, liquidate stocks, liquidate the farmers, liquidate real estate, suggesting that this would purge the rottenness out of the system.

Such policies made a collapse inevitable as the Federal Reserve could not lower interest rates enough to accommodate deflationary shocks and, to make matters worse, the political will to directly intervene in a range of economic sectors was lacking. The reader will note the worrisome parallel between these attitudes and the insistence of Germany on austerity in Europe during the European debt crisis (a theme we will return to in later chapters). Eggertsson notes (2005: 2) that this 'deflation bias' of policy before Roosevelt took over helps explain the severity of the Great Depression (and the way money was sucked out of the economy) because real interest rates were excessively high in 1929–33 due to double-digit deflation. This situation led to diminished spending and investment as nobody was interested in investing when the returns from holding on to cash were 10–15 per cent in real terms. Roubini (2011) concurs that the failure to deal with deflation was the trigger that turned the depression to a Great Depression.

The lessons from this catastrophic instance of 'market failure' that the Great Depression represents, Aman (2004) argues, led the government and the courts in the United States to coordinate in erecting a significant institutional framework of economic management, aimed at protecting the public from further crises. This institutional framework, constructed under Roosevelt, became known as the 'New Deal' and has been described as the cornerstone of the American version of 'embedded liberalism', a term first formulated by John Ruggie (1982) as an elaboration of the distinction drawn by Karl Polanyi (1957) between embedded and disembedded economic orders. For Polanyi, as we saw in Chapter 1, embedded economic orders were inextricably linked to and inseparable from their social environment. Disembedded orders, on the other hand, were an alleged creation of the nineteenth century and were based on the idea of an independent, universal, market-based, economic rationality. Modern economic orthodoxy can be interpreted therefore as an extreme descendant of this intellectual history that advocates a radical separation or disembedding of the economic from the political (Ruggie, 1982: 385). Embedded liberalism, David Harvey (2005: 10) suggests, also represented a class compromise between capital and labour, forged for the sake of social tranquillity and peace, and manifested in a web of political and social constraints on market activities imposed through a regulatory environment guiding economic and industrial strategy. Ruggie argues that this compromise was (politically) inevitable due to the almost universal (outside the USA) opposition to economic liberalism (especially in the postwar period) stemming from the terrible experiences of the Great Depression.

Roosevelt, immediately upon coming into office, implemented several radical policies, including an aggressive fiscal expansion and a change in monetary policy. These policy changes violated three policy dogmas of the time, followed religiously by the previous administration: (1) the gold standard; (2) the belief that the budget should remain balanced; and (3) the belief that real government spending should not be used to increase demand. Roosevelt embraced therefore what was unthinkable before 1929, the need to reign in markets to protect capitalism from itself. This last point is worth repeating: Roosevelt was not a closet socialist (nor was Keynes for that matter), they were trying to protect markets from the excesses that bred instability and risked social disintegration. As Keynes put it in *The End of Laissez-Faire* (1926: 40):

> It is not true that individuals possess a prescriptive 'natural liberty' in their economic activities. There is no 'compact' conferring perpetual

> rights on those who Have or on those who Acquire. The world is not so governed from above that private and social interest always coincide. It is not so managed here below that in practice they coincide. It is not a correct deduction from the principles of economics that enlightened self-interest always operates in the public interest. Nor is it true that self-interest generally is enlightened; more often individuals acting separately to promote their own ends are too ignorant or too weak to attain even these. Experience does not show that individuals, when they make up a social unit, are always less clear-sighted than when they act separately. We cannot therefore settle on abstract grounds, but must handle on its merits in detail what Burke termed 'one of the finest problems in legislation,' namely, to determine 'what the State ought to take upon itself to direct by the public wisdom, and what it ought to leave, with as little interference as possible, to individual exertion.'

In the view of traditional Pigouvian (1952) welfare economics, extensive government regulation is perfectly compatible with a successful market. Markets fail, as Pigou would say, because of externalities, asymmetric information and lack of competition, and governments need to intervene via regulation to counter these failures. This suggestion implies that if regulation is ubiquitous, this is only because market failures are so (Kessler, 2010). In a stark message to our own era, the events of the 1920s offer considerable evidence to suggest that under-regulation of markets (and financial services in particular) creates opportunities and preconditions for speculative bubbles. John Kenneth Galbraith (1992) has noted that, in the aftermath of most historical bubbles, the focus of attention tends to shift to new instruments and techniques and the role they played in the process of the bubble's formation, while the key factor (leveraged speculation) is commonly ignored. The power of speculation to cause crises was not lost on Minsky (2008), however. Evidently though, it is more comfortable for all concerned with the behaviour of markets to blame the supposedly unpredictable side effects of 'innovation' than to admit to having failed to acknowledge the build-up of all too common exposures. Also, the focus on 'new' causes for a collapse helps mask structural defects in the way the state–market relationship is balanced. According to White (2008: 308), in virtually every previous financial collapse, the crisis was preceded by very rapid credit expansion, which manifested itself (in part) in higher asset prices. Profits from initial successes provided the collateral to justify even more lending and euphoria generated by gains also seemed to both lower perceptions of risk and increase the appetite for risk-taking for both lenders and borrowers. As a result, leverage increased even as the general quality of credits deteriorated, although this was commonly not appreciated at the time. At a certain point, usually when earlier expectations about profits or future income growth began to look unrealistic, the whole process went into reverse turning boom to bust. Even though not every episode unrolled in every way corresponding to the model described by White, the general description of what happened seems appropriate to the crisis that began in 2007.

The experience of the United States in the 1920s and 1930s provides a great illustration of the links between inadequate regulation and financial instability. The absence of regulatory restrictions on the operation of financial firms and the sale of financial products led to the explosion in the price of securities in 1927–8 as it has contributed to every subsequent asset bubble. During the 1920s the desire of banks to circumvent statutory restrictions by organising affiliated corporations which engaged in a full range of underwriting, selling and dealing activities (involving both bonds and stocks) greatly reduced their borrowing within the banking sector and made the securities markets the prime source for financing (Benton, 2003: 101). The reason for this preference for markets over customers can be found in the decline in banks' traditional corporate lending business. This decline made real estate and securities markets attractive new profit sources and offered incentives to push for and take advantage of lax regulation (Glinavos, 2010b). The consequence of the subsequent explosion in the price of real estate and asset prices led to the speculative bubble that exploded in 1929, marking the beginning of the Great Depression, a phenomenon with catastrophic global consequences, if one considers the links between the depression and the rise of fascism in Europe.

3.4.1 *The New Deal*

In trying to get a feel for the scale of the changes to economic governance brought about by the Great Depression, it would be helpful to look into the New Deal in some more detail. Crisis can be (and many argue, indeed, it should be) a catalyst in developments in policy that can at times lead to rapid and wholesale reversals of policy directions. One such reversal was the expansion of regulation in the United States after the 1929 crash and the initiation of the New Deal by the Roosevelt administration. As a product of pressure from various sources, the New Deal was grounded in no single coherent or systemic theory (Glinavos, 2010b: 543). Perhaps the most prominent unifying theme was the popular conviction that an unregulated free market guided solely by the invisible hand of private interest could lead only to the dispossession associated with the depression. The Roosevelt administration responded to this popular perception (in synch with Keynes' ideas) by offering the countervailing power of government, administered by disinterested expert regulators, in order to discipline the market and stabilise an economy that laissez-faire had all but destroyed. The result was a stunning expansion of administrative authority both within and independent of the executive branch (Tomlins and Grossberg, 2008: 284). What is particularly interesting is that the state sought to set in place a regulatory framework that would prevent the re-emergence of circumstances that could lead to another bubble and subsequent catastrophic crash.

One of the most important legislative responses to the failures of the Depression (particularly in the banking sector) was the work of Senator Carter Glass, Representative Henry Steagall and other proponents of the Banking Act of 1933, known as the Glass Steagall Act. The Act's backers were convinced that the banks had played a significant role in promoting unsustainable booms in the real estate and securities markets during the 1920s. As a solution to this problem it was suggested that commercial banks should restrict their operations to the acceptance of demand deposits and the extension of short-term, self-liquidating loans to finance the production and sale of goods by businesses. Banks therefore should be prevented from making unsound loans and investments that encouraged an overbuilt real estate market and an immense overexpansion of real estate values (Glinavos, 2010b: 544). The banks should also be discouraged from making investments in securities that undermined their solvency during stock market downturns and they should be restricted in making loans to finance the purchase of securities. Liberalisation that removes the above restrictions has since been shown to produce a banking system that is more vulnerable to systemic risk. Admittedly, deregulated financial markets generally promote faster growth rates by providing more extensive financing to consumers and businesses during economic expansions. However, by encouraging greater reliance on external funding, deregulation creates a higher risk that consumers and firms will become overextended and end up insolvent if external funding sources shut down during economic contractions (Benton, 2003: 79). An example of this happening was the credit crunch of 2008. As Amato and Fantacci explain in their book *The End of Finance* (2012), the reliance of the economy on ever-increasing availability of funding (known as liquidity, which we discussed in Chapter 2) propels what is a market economy to its turbo-charged, crisis-prone financialised version, something the aforementioned authors equate with modern capitalism.

The experience of the evolution of finance after the 1930s shows that the problem is not so much enacting legislation immediately after a financial collapse, but ensuring that safeguards are maintained when memories of the collapse fade and an appetite for risk returns. It could be said that regulation following the 1929 crash sought to protect against a non-existent danger, as the appetite for risk that had fuelled the bubble was entirely dissipated after the crash and did not return for some 30 years (Glinavos, 2010b: 544). What the use of law after 1929 failed to achieve, however, was to implement lasting safeguards that could outlive memories of the crash, safeguards that could protect future generations (far removed from the Great Depression) from repeating the mistakes of the 1920s. Nonetheless, it is difficult to overestimate the importance of the New Deal as a watershed in twentieth-century American constitutional development that also had far reaching global consequences. Cushman (in Tomlins and Grossberg, 2008: 268) notes that the profound economic crisis that gripped the nation during the Great Depression inspired a period of extraordinary legislative activity, generating a series of strikingly wide-ranging and far-reaching changes in the American legal and constitutional order. Consequently, by the time the US entered the Second World War, Congress had gained an unprecedented degree of authority over economic governance. Legislative activity during this period included a vast array of spending programmes to relieve distress and to stimulate economic growth coupled with a remarkable succession of regulatory programmes designed to return the economy to stability. The administration of these new programmes rested on the creation of several federal agencies and the significant expansion of existing ones, resulting in an explosive growth in the size and power of the federal bureaucracy. Such activity is interpreted as having resulted in the creation of an administrative state, with the office of the presidency at the top of a structure actively engaged in managing various aspects of the American economy.

A consequent development in the 1930s was the evolution of the role of the Supreme Court from being the guardian of vested rights to the promoter of civil liberties. The expansion of the role of the state over economic management meant that the Supreme Court had to assume a more active role to legitimise government action, sometimes struggling against the confines of the established constitutional order. While the court was resistant to the underlying notions of state expansion contained in the New Deal originally, as its membership gradually changed with appointments made by Roosevelt between 1937 and 1941 (Tomlins and Grossberg, 2008: 270), it accepted the role of guarantor of the new 'embedded' economic order. A new balance to the state–market relationship was found therefore where the government felt empowered to steer markets to the production of social goods, drawing legitimacy from the ballot box, as well as from court interpretations of constitutional freedoms. The era of a 'regulated economy' seemingly widely accepted in the US in the nineteenth century had made a come-back after the laissez-faire interlude of the 1920s.

3.4.2 The 'golden' era

Keynesian economic policies which represent the theoretical reflection of New Deal practices take an approach to economic affairs which grants a significant interventionist role to the state. The state thus attains an active role in economic affairs alongside a freely operating market. In such a political economy, the political and the economic are seen as inextricably entwined, forming part of the wider social whole. The recognition of such close links between these areas of social interaction is known (as mentioned above) as 'embedded liberalism', or in the words of Karl Polanyi (1957) 'embedded economic order'. This growing entanglement of state and market, of the legal and political with the economic, is also associated with the rise of social democracy. Following the economic, political and social upheavals of the Great Depression of the 1930s (and the disruption of the two world wars), development of policies that promoted economic stability, tempered unemployment and alleviated poverty rose to the top of the political agenda in all industrialised countries. It was in this context that Keynesianism emerged as the dominant feature of economic policy in the period following the Second World War, continuing until the late 1970s (Glinavos, 2010a).

According to Keynes, the important thing for government is not to do things which individuals are doing already, and to do them a little better or a little worse, but to do those things which at present are not done at all (Keynes, 1926: 47). Keynesianism, in short, advocated the maintenance of a vibrant market economy alongside a strong state with a significant presence in the economy and considerable influence over economic management in pursuit of full employment and growth. Keynes' ideas thus came to provide a general policy framework for governments to follow in the difficult process of postwar restoration. Thus emerged the postwar era of 'embedded liberalism' and social democracy, during which most developed economies in the West enjoyed low levels of unemployment and modest inflation, as well as steady growth. The influence of Keynes' theories can consequently be seen as having contributed to the rapid and controlled rebuilding of postwar Europe and to a long period of economic prosperity thereafter. An important element in postwar economic restoration was the creation of the Bretton Woods system, whose introduction incorporated some, yet not the totality, of Keynes' proposals, to try to stabilise the operations of the currency and capital markets. In trying to use currency and capital controls to temper destabilising market fluctuations, the Bretton Woods system represented recognition at the highest level of the need for market regulation. Among its guiding ideas was the belief that governments should be able to cushion their domestic economies (at least to some extent) from the strictures of the currency and capital markets and from potential balance of payments problems. The latter was crucial in reigniting international trade after the breakdown caused by the war (Glinavos, 2010a).

According to Amato and Fantacci (2012: 134) the weakness of the Bretton Woods compromise (one that Keynes cautioned against) was that it created a monetary system but it did not create an international currency. In fact, the reason why the US occupies such a central role in international finance can be traced to the decisions taken in the Bretton Woods conference and the move not to create an international unit of account or international currency. By deciding to use national currencies, contrary to Keynes' suggestions, the currency of the country that at the time was a creditor to the world (the US dollar) became the *de facto* international currency. (One could argue it also become the *de jure* international currency, as the Articles of Agreement of the IMF in 1944 specified – Article 31.2 – that contributions to the fund could be made in gold or US dollars which was to have a fixed convertibility to gold, an arrangement later amended and finally abandoned by Nixon in 1971.) This allowed, according to many, the US to exercise seigniorage over the world economy (Amato and Fantacci, 2012). As Valéry Giscard d'Estaing, French Finance Minister at the time (1960s), noted, it granted the US an exorbitant privilege (Reinert et al., 2009: 396).

Bretton Woods required therefore the denomination and payment of debts in one of the established national currencies. As the whole point of the system was the facilitation of trade, such reliance on bilateral payments in national currencies to settle trade accounts was a big potential problem. If each country sought equilibrium on a bilateral basis, this would lead to severe imbalances on a multilateral level, as not all accounts could be settled with all counterparties in a satisfactory manner using different currencies. The way around this problem was the creation of multilateral lending institutions that would offer loans in the currencies needed to allow countries to settle their trade accounts (as best as possible) with all their counterparties. The institution charged with this task was the International Monetary Fund (IMF). A corollary to this arrangement, was the ability to maintain some capital controls alongside the creation of the IMF to provide short-term assistance to finance current account deficits. Indeed, this model was used in the reconstruction of Europe and Japan after the Second World War and was subsequently applied to the emerging economies of South East Asia. While Amato and Fantacci claim that the creation of an international monetary system without an international currency (to go with it) led to increasing pressures that made capitalism more crisis-prone, this system can be credited with the remarkable recovery in Europe from the 1950s, which led to long periods of growth thereafter, and with the rise of the 'Asian Tigers' later in the century.

Gradually though, Keynesian models for economic management and development that had been so successful across the globe since the end of the Second World War (and in which the state played such a key role) fell into disrepute. This was in part because of the perceived inability of supposedly 'Keynesian' policies to deal with the economic crises that (as a consequence of the institutional inadequacies of the Bretton Woods system) began to afflict the developed western economies in the 1970s. The immediate cause of these crises was the inability of capitalist states to balance public finances, due in part to increases in prices for natural resources (oil) and in part to the growing competitive pressures placed on established industrial powers by emerging economies in Asia. These material factors, combined with important changes in ideas powering economic thinking (we have explored the power of ideas to influence our understanding of the role of the state in economic governance in Chapter 2) led many policy-makers to question the capacity of the Keynesian model to make sense of contemporary economic patterns and to provide ways of maintaining growth. What replaced the Keynesian model was an ideologically fuelled belief in the superiority of unrestrained markets and unrestrained competition, accompanied by minimal state intervention: what has come to be known as neoliberalism (Glinavos, 2010a). The 1980s represent therefore an attempt to return to the alleged era of laissez-faire (the 1920s) that had been forsaken after the Great Depression due to the (then) return of the idea that markets served a social purpose determined by forces external to the markets themselves.

3.5 The neoliberal era

Neoliberalism has become a distasteful word that proponents of the market shy away from. Its use is limited therefore to the critical literature and implies hostility to laissez-faire. This book uses neoliberalism occasionally as shorthand for 'free market economics', and while the author is no admirer of financialised capitalism and laissez-faire, the use of the term is not meant to be derogatory. A thorough disposition of the term and its meaning in relation to the law can be found in *Neoliberalism and the Law* (Glinavos, 2010a). In its general use, the term neoliberalism denotes the backlash against the social welfare state as developed from the end of the Second World War till the 1970s. It also represents a revival of individualistic liberalism and a return to laissez-faire as supposedly experienced in the first decades of the twentieth century. This new theory of liberalism (neoliberalism) represents a return to the original liberal project of asserting society against the state, the market against planning and regulation, the right of the individual against authorities and collectives. In this, neoliberalism claims to follow the spirit of the American and French revolutions of the eighteenth century in emphasising liberty under the law. There is a continuum in the literature from liberal authors of the era of the French Revolution to authors like Milton Friedman for whom individual liberty is more important than government acting in the general good. Friedman, and to a great degree Hayek (Wapshott, 2011: 44), who argued that it is the natural laws of economics that govern human behaviour, not governments, have actually defended the idea that government is usually contrary to the interests of the people (either because it is not truly representative or because it acts against economic rationality). This is supported by legal scholars like Robert Nozick who has made a strong case in favour of a minimal state (Newman et al., 2002).

David Harvey (2005) defines neoliberalism as a theory that sees individual entrepreneurial freedom as the best means to realise human potential. This goal is best achieved, it is claimed, in an environment characterised by strong property rights, free markets and free trade. The role of the state in this model is essentially to provide a framework in which existing markets can operate with as few impediments as possible and on which new markets can be created in areas where they do not yet exist. However, in the economic sphere at least, the state should not generally venture beyond these strictly defined, market-facilitating limits. These limitations should be maintained in part for the technical reason that the state purportedly lacks sufficient information to determine prices adequately and in part for the practical reason that states are very vulnerable to capture by special interests which provide motivations other than the promotion of economic efficiency (Harvey, 2005: 2). We saw in Chapter 1 how discussions of economic efficiency tend to morph into theses on the ethics of wealth creation and the good of society. Affected by the powerful ideas of neoliberalism's proponents, during the 1980s and 1990s in the United States both Democrat and Republican administrations proceeded to gradually dismantle most of the institutions of the New Deal that many saw as having had injected an element of wealth redistribution and social justice into the American economic system, opening the way for the expansion of what some call neoliberal globalisation at home and abroad. A parallel process took place in the UK during the 1980s under Margaret Thatcher and continued in the 1990s under John Major and Tony Blair's New Labour (Glinavos, 2010a). Similar efforts to dismantle certain parts of the traditional welfare state that were under way in continental Europe gained new momentum as a result of the financial crisis due to the fact that fiscal consolidation and a headlong surge towards balanced budgets was interpreted as a suitable solution to the debt crisis (as we will explore in more detail in Chapter 4).

Changes in economic policy reveal important shifts in perceptions as to the nature of the state and the purpose of law. While the state was seen in the postwar period as an agent of progress and as a central and positive player in reconstruction, the political and economic shocks of the 1970s brought with them a crisis of confidence in Keynesianism and social democracy, one expression of which was a growing discontent with political actors and state bureaucracies. What this meant for law is that the use of law has been greatly restricted in what was considered the domain of the market since the early 1980s. The reason for this 'lack of law', evidenced in worldwide efforts at deregulation and privatisation, has been the dominance of free-market ideology. The reader may disbelieve this argument regarding a 'lack of law' when everyone presumably is faced with constant talk of a deluge of regulations and rules. While one may question whether such a 'deluge' is fact or useful propaganda, an argument can be validly made that there is no contradiction between a lack of law and a system characterised by a wealth of rules. In Chapter 1 we addressed the issue of rule creation through a debate on the meaning of law and the purpose of regulation. If one considers law the result of the legitimate creation of rules via a political process, then we can see that a great deal of the rules and regulations that are stemming from the industries themselves in the form of codes of conduct and self-regulation should not be considered as one and the same with 'law'. It is true that as regulation stemming from the state retreated, it got replaced by 'standards' set by market participants. The argument as to a lack of law here therefore suggests a lack of law seeking to shape the market, as opposed to a lack of technical instructions according to which the market operates, or claims to operate.

Such distinctions, however, between law, rules, principles and standards (light touch or self-regulation being the best examples of the latter) are often obscured by the righteous anger of 'entrepreneurs' seeking to rid themselves of the shackles of regulation. According to Robert Wade (2008: 34) the prevailing ideological climate that created the conditions for the expansion of the bubble that deflated in 2007–8 resulting in the credit crunch and subsequent financial calamities was characterised by hostility to regulation as a concept. Antipathy to any sort of state involvement in market processes stemmed from a laissez-faire ideology that celebrated the unregulated areas of finance as demonstrating the validity of the efficient market theory of markets, suggesting that markets are self-adjusting and that competition plus light-touch regulation produces efficient, innovative and stable financial markets. Aiming at the withdrawal of the state from the economy, a worldwide consensus in favour of liberalisation (bearing the traits described above: minimal state, reliance on self-regulation, etc.) became common sense in both developed and developing economies, displacing the political economy that as we described above largely characterised the postwar era. Remarkably, as Thomas Frank eloquently relates in his book *Pity the Billionaire* (2012), even the dislocation brought about by the crisis served to reinforce an orthodoxy that sees the state as the enemy.

The preponderance of a market liberalisation agenda, throughout the 1980s in the US and the UK and from the 1990s globally, identified as key roles for law the definition, allocation and protection of private property and the enforcement of contractual agreements. Law was seen as having the central aim of being the guarantor of private property rights, for the market mechanisms and economic processes which lie at the heart of liberal democracy are premised upon the existence of private property. Policy discussions as a result tended to translate all human activity to transactions of property rights and reduced the aims of economic governance to the pursuit of 'economic efficiency'. Such focus on law creation as a function of protecting economic fundamentals limits the purposes of law reform and relegates law to the role of market supporter instead of a tool to achieve social justice. This disconnection between law and justice (which we explored in Chapter 1) is, however, completely in agreement with Hayekian notions of the rule of law as a base for market transactions (distinct from political aims such as wealth distribution).

A state that used law in a facilitative manner, absconding itself from any pretensions of achieving social outcomes, was deemed a 'capable state' by international economic institutions. The notion of a 'capable state' so prevalent in World Bank publications starting with the 1997 World Development Report implies a state that is not a direct provider of growth, but a partner, catalyst and facilitator. In order to keep an eye on social fundamentals (without doing overtly political things, like encouraging redistributions of wealth), this capable state has, according to the World Bank, tasks additional to the usual list of market fundamentals. These tasks include the establishment of a foundation of law (Craig and Porter, 2006: 99). However, a definition of the state as a 'facilitator' does not necessarily imply a greater acceptance of the state as a regulator. Commentators like David Kennedy note that the minimal state/deregulating paradigm so central to neoliberalism means that laissez-faire remains a potent default proposal when governments are thought inept (Trubek and Santos, 2006: 151). The persistent desire to set outer limits to legal regulation has shifted focus away from the state to non-regulatory and so-called mixed modes of governance, so far as the achievement of social objectives is concerned. This is reflected in the emphasis on non-governmental organisations, civil society and 'soft' forms of regulation.

Even after the onset of the financial crisis, the World Bank, like other international financial institutions, has not altered its default position that the state ought to intervene as little as possible in the market and that market inefficiencies are more easily dealt with than state capture and corruption. This view serves to place limits on both the reach and purposes of legal reform, as the presumption of government failure often undercuts the case for state intervention even where it might otherwise be warranted in order to enhance efficiency. Consequently, even though there appears to be a shift in attitudes towards the role of law, this shift is limited by continuing scepticism about the state's capacity to intervene effectively and a continuing belief that state interventions should be kept to a minimum. After all, the position of international organisations still is that growth is more likely to result from deregulation and liberalisation that encourage foreign investment rather than from government sponsored development policies, despite all the evidence to the contrary (Rittich, 2004) and despite the historical link between deregulation and financial instability. The IMF, for its part, used the excuse of the sovereign debt crisis in Europe from 2010 to revert to form and demand once more adherence to its well-known (and mistaken) policies of austerity and fiscal consolidation, starting with Greece in May 2010 and moving to Ireland in November 2010 and Portugal in May 2011. This explains why it is difficult to resist those like Mattei and Nader (2008) that now deny the usefulness of terms such as 'the rule of law' in their entirety, rejecting them as nothing more than a cloak for the promotion of policies that sustain the domination of the strong over the weak.

3.6 Conclusion

The aim of this chapter has been to challenge commonly held assumptions about the shape the state–market relationship had in the past. We often forget that economic power is a source of coercion regardless of the origin of that power, be it private or public. What Robert Hale was writing in the 1920s is very much of relevance today, in an era when we seem to trick ourselves into believing capitalism offers freedom and choice when in fact it may only deliver servitude and constraints. We seem to make the mistake to equate markets with liberty and states with oppression. Yet the state and the law have often been used as mechanisms set to break the markets' headlong lunge towards disaster. It is imperative to state again that the purpose of this reflection is not to discredit capitalism, but to raise a consciousness that will lead us to take the steps necessary to save it, lest we suffer another great crisis before we had the chance to recover from the current one. In a way, shattering the often repeated myths of free-marketeers is what this chapter has mostly been about. Our historical journey has demonstrated that once we look behind the labels, we can discover a different, more complex picture about past perceptions of what the public interest requires of markets. Our presentation of the industrial era demonstrated, for instance, that laissez-faire is not an accurate label for the political economy of the whole western world in the nineteenth century, and perhaps surprisingly we find the notions of a well-regulated society and of a public economy deeply embedded in US jurisprudence.

We also saw how the previous major instance of market failure, the Great Depression, scared policy-makers out of their complacency and led them to abandon the sacred tenets of that era: the gold standard, trust in balanced budgets and a determination to contain government spending. Why, may we ask, hasn't the current crisis brought about a reversal in thinking such as that expressed by the Roosevelt administration and the courts in the 1930s? Why aren't we seeing a return to an era accepting of a regulated economy, such as the one prevalent in the US in the nineteenth century and again after the New Deal? Perhaps even see a return of the idea that markets serve a social purpose determined by forces external to the market itself? The answer can perhaps be found in the presentation we offered here of neoliberalism and its hold over contemporary thinking. We argued that neoliberal thinking has pushed the law into the corner of market facilitator. This is true to such an extent that even politicians themselves are unable to envisage state intervention in anything other than negative terms. Consequently, this book has argued that we have let law retreat while the gap was filled by the market itself, with its codes and alleged self-discipline. The law became, and remains as Chapter 5 will show, a tool to support the market and constrain democratic choice, with the state seeming capable when it ensures the protection of market fundamentals. Is this ideological hold so great that not even a crisis akin to that of the Great Depression fails to displace it? Perhaps this crisis is not quite 'bad' enough, one may think. The next chapter delves directly into a presentation of what the crisis that enveloped the world in 2008 is like. In short, it is time to discuss what happened and to begin to explain why, so that we can make a comparison of substance between our troubled era and the ones that we described earlier in this chapter.

4 The crisis of 2008

If it is the move from speculative to Ponzi finance that unravels financial capitalism, then the function of law could be to prevent one state from morphing into the other.

4.1 Introduction

There is already a wealth of literature seeking to present the timeline of the brewing crisis that became noticeable in the residential property market in the US in 2007 and then spread to banks, financial institutions and, ultimately, states. This literature tries to pinpoint key stages in the chain of events and to explain causal flows as the sub-prime mortgage crisis morphed into a general financial crisis, then a series of domestic recessions and then a global crisis enveloping the majority of developed economies. There are many terms with which these unfolding events have been described, with the most apt being the characterisation of a 'Great Recession', a term whose paternity is too multiple to reference adequately. It has become commonplace to argue that while everyone can offer an accurate timeline of events, there is no agreement as to the causes of the crisis. I disagree with this view. Contributing factors to the crisis have been well identified and the way different institutional characteristics have combined with the actions of individuals to create a cascading economic collapse are well documented. What is not obvious is the formation of a consensus on what to do to prevent future crises, and what remains unanswered is the question of whether instability in capitalism is inherent, and if it is, whether it is worth doing something to ameliorate the incidence or extent of crises. As this book is one about the law, the discussion in this chapter will present the key characteristics of the Great Recession as they relate to the relationship between law and economics. Rather than rehashing existing debates and re-documenting what is widely available, this chapter seeks to offer some insights that will be of interest to those seeking to identify the role of law in a capitalist economy. In this way, this chapter paves the way to understand the legal and institutional responses to some select aspects of the crisis discussed next in Chapter 5.

This chapter is divided into two main sections, the first dealing with the so-called credit crunch that resulted from the collapse of structured finance built around the US residential property market. The second part deals with the sovereign debt crisis that arose as a significant problem in Europe after the effects of the recession were felt and after efforts to address the credit crunch impacted on state finances.

4.2 The credit shortage

As mentioned above, the events that led to the Great Recession are well documented. There are already plenty of books on the crisis, its key events and attempts to bring all this knowledge together in order to form a coherent narrative that carries some message for the future organisation of finance. For these reasons, this book will not offer a detailed account of the events that we are all aware of, apart from the short summary present below. What this book will focus on is the role law reform (usually in the form of deregulation) has played in these events and will debate whether it was a lack of or an excess of law that has contributed to the crisis as it unfolded. The important issue to remember throughout this discussion is that law is perceived here as fashioning a link between the popular will and the organisation of our economy. It is via the law, as explained in the introductory chapter to this work, that we – the citizens – can influence the structures of the economy that govern our lives. Citizens yield such influence through the democratic process and it is through the political process therefore that we can change what our world looks like. This simple yet important point is often missed in the plentiful analyses of the crisis that focus on blaming one thing or another. It is crucial therefore to remember that perhaps it matters less what institutional arrangement existed prior to 2008 or how they contributed to the crisis. What should matter is whether the institutional structure in place was the result of a process whereby the people who suffer the consequences of the crisis had a say in its creation. The suggestion in this book is that they did not, and therein lies the problem. The key point, in other words, is that we need a discussion as to the input the democratic political process needs to have in the process of creating regulatory frameworks and rules, a function that can only be fulfilled if we are allowed to ask, as we discussed in Part 1 of the book, fundamental questions about the nature of law and the purpose of finance.

4.2.1 The sub-prime mortgage market

The workings of the sub-prime mortgage market have been well documented in a series of books on the financial crisis written over the last five years. I would recommend to the reader Munchau's *The Meltdown Years* (2009) and McLean and Nocera's *All the Devils Are Here* (2010) among the many who are mentioned in the pages of this book. The meaning of 'sub-prime' is a relatively uncontested term that is generally taken to refer to a section of the housing market in the US that consisted of people purchasing properties with questionable ability to repay the associated loans. The reason why a paradoxical phenomenon like banks lending money to people who cannot repay them came into existence is explained by two factors we consider in turn below: one is the ability of mortgage originators to sell onwards the debt they create; the second is the move of the entire financial system to a structure Minski (2008) called Ponzi finance. What is important to understand about the sub-prime mortgage market and associated areas of housing loans (like expensive second mortgages taken by otherwise prime borrowers) is its role in sparking the financial crisis, not due to the size of the finances involved directly in the housing market, but due to the size of the financial leviathan that took housing as the starting point for ever increasing leverage. Before we get to the role of leveraged finance, however, we will start at the beginning, looking at the trigger for the crash, so it is the housing market in the US that we need to turn to.

The downturn in the US housing market became noticeable by most commentators in 2007 (Posner, 2009). In fact 2007 was the first tumultuous year of what has been an unrelenting procession of bad news to the time of writing in mid-2013. This six-year period has provided enough time and misery to newspapers to provide plenty of parallels with the era of the Great Depression. It all seemed to begin to go badly wrong in the summer of 2007 when two Bear Stearns hedge funds collapsed alongside three hedge funds owned by BNP Paribas and the US sub-prime provider American Home Mortgage Corporation. At the same time things were also deteriorating rapidly for Countrywide Financial Corporation, one of the biggest mortgage originators in the US. In March 2008, Bear Stearns itself collapsed followed in September by the bankruptcy of Lehman Brothers, the sale of Merrill Lynch, the Freddie Mac/Fannie Mae nationalisation and the massive bailout of AIG. The events in September 2008 led to a sharp drop in world stock markets in the autumn of that year and the now famous credit crunch commenced. In October, the US announced the $700 billion TARP programme, but that did not stop terrifying events unfolding. At the end of 2008, US automakers found themselves in deep trouble and there were significant drops in share prices and strong deflationary pressures across the American economy. According to Posner (2009), these events combined to create the first US depression since the 1930s.

While there exists no commonly agreed definition of what an economic depression is, a contraction of real GDP that exceeds 10 per cent or a continuous contraction for more than three years will qualify as a depression (*Economist*, 2008). Posner (2009) classes the events of 2007–8 as a US depression by considering the gravity of the downturn, the radical nature of the policy response, a sense of deep crisis, the threat of deflation and the costs of remediation. Taking these factors into account, it is difficult to find a better candidate than the title 'depression' to characterise the situation in the US in 2008, and while this depression never became global, the global effects have been so severe as to define economic policy everywhere in the world in the last six years. One country of course where the title depression fails to actually capture the apocalyptic nature of economic events is Greece where the cumulative drop in GDP from 2008 to 2013 has been in excess of 24 per cent (Bank of Greece, 2012).

4.2.2 Leverage and the monster called securitisation

How it came to this is a question that has occupied everyone since the credit crunch took hold. While of course there are competing explanations and a lot of finger pointing (market advocates blame the government, while everyone else blames financiers), there is some consensus on a single key fact. The crisis of 2007 would not have spread so fast across finance, and would not have impacted so much on the real economy, if it were not for the proliferation of financial products and the vast scale of the liabilities resting on the shaky foundations of loans made to US homeowners and consumers. The core role of debt in financialised capitalism has been explained in our discussion of the operation of finance and liquidity in Chapter 2. Here, we have the opportunity to see in more depth the legal background to the changes that unleashed the dynamic that led to the crisis, changes that we described in the latter pages of Chapter 3 (where we saw the effects of neoliberal thinking on the role of law in the economy) as the expanding phenomenon of deregulation.

While deregulation has been a dominant trend in the USA since the mid-1980s, it came properly into its stride in the latter part of the 1990s. By 1998 regulators and the courts in the United States had allowed banks to make substantial inroads into the securities and insurance sectors by exploiting loopholes in the Glass Steagall Act and the Bank Holding Company Act of 1956, both enacted with the memories of the Great Depression present in people's minds and considered strong legal barriers to bank entry into the securities and insurance fields. The model of finance to emerge after the repeal of the Glass Steagall Act was based on securitisation and became known as the 'originate and distribute' model. A securitisation is a financial transaction in which assets are pooled together and securities representing interests in the pool are issued. Under the originate and distribute model, financial institutions would create assets (such as loans) then repackage these and sell them to investors. The resulting funds would be used to originate more assets which in turn would be re-repackaged and sold, recommencing the cycle. This model of banking recreated in a way the institutional framework that had led to the crash of 1929 (Glinavos, 2010b). By allowing the banks to lend not on the basis of deposits but on the strength of the money markets, the way was opened for the financial sector to depart from the fundamentals of the real economy, creating fictional wealth. It is this fictional world where the concepts of value and liquidity are intermingled that we discussed in Chapter 2, coming to the conclusion that the ethereal nature of modern finance is due to the inherent contradictions of its core concepts. While these contradictions, between assets and money, liquidity and risk, were a fertile ground for academic commentary, they were not benign. They had some very real-life consequences: they made a few people very rich, and have plunged very many into poverty since 2008.

In confirming the return of universal banking powers to the financial holding companies, allowing the combination of commercial with investment banking, the Gramm-Leach-Bliley Financial Modernization Act repealed several Depression era safeguards in 1999. Unlike the system of finance established in the United States in the 1930s, the new model of finance allowed competition between commercial banks and investment banks for securities business. As a result, opportunities for profit increased dramatically, encouraging investment banks to engage in ever more risky proprietary trading – speculating with their own capital to increase returns (Glinavos, 2010b). A key boost to the trade of derivative financial products via the process of securitisation we just described was given by another major step in deregulation in the form of the Commodity Futures Modernization Act of 2000. Lynn Stout (2011) writes that the legal framework was not merely reflecting innovations in financial markets, but that changes in the law spawned the so-called innovations. In other words, it was not changes to the markets that brought about the conditions that created the credit crisis but, crucially, changes in the law. Stout argues that the Commodity Futures Act suddenly and totally removed century-old legal constraints on speculative trading in over-the-counter (OTC) derivative financial products.

It is useful to remember that derivatives were not always seen as a clever way to speculate but rather as a risk limitation technique. Derivatives were considered in US jurisprudence to be valid methods of dealing with risks of future events, and while hedging was legal, speculation in OTC derivatives was not and courts would not allow enforcement of financial bets whose sole purpose was speculation (as opposed to risk diversification). One way that the pre-2000 system dealt with speculative derivative trading was by moving it to clearing houses which assumed the risks associated with such transactions and kept the volume of trading low in order to minimise the exposures of the clearing houses themselves. This system operated fairly consistently on the basis of the common law (eventually codified by the Commodity Exchange Act of 1936), which retained the prohibition of speculative trading outside regulated exchanges. The Commodity Futures Act of 2000 represented the final blow to this system of controlled derivative trading (Stout, 2011). After the Act, speculative trading in derivatives was in effect legalised in the US with the result that a massive market in OTC products grew without anyone being able to assess the systemic risk effects of ever expanding volumes of trading. According to the Bank for International Settlements (2008) notional amounts of all types of OTC contracts stood at $683.7 trillion at the end of June 2008 – for comparison the amount for June 2011 stood at $440 trillion (ISDA, 2012). The response, post credit crunch, at least in the US as we will see in Chapter 5, has been to try and reverse the tide by restoring legal limits to derivatives trading outside clearing houses in the Dodd-Frank Wall Street Reform and Consumer Protection Act of 2010.

Why were financial markets so keen to escape the confines of the legal framework established during the Great Depression? From the standpoint of financial institutions, the originate and distribute model had two benefits. First, it increased profitability by generating income from fees charged for origination rather than relying on interest repayments – something that would keep profitability modest in the low-interest environment maintained by the Federal Reserve post the dot-com bubble and then after 9/11. Second, the originate and distribute model gave the appearance of reducing risks (as it turned out mistakenly) of any potential defaults because the originators did not remain the owners of the assets originated; instead the resulting securities were widely distributed in the markets. From the standpoint of regulators, this model likewise had two benefits. First, banks were deemed less risky because they were holding fewer loans and hence were exposed less to default risk in any future economic downturn. Second, by repackaging and distributing credit risks widely into the market, this brought down the charges which lenders had to charge borrowers, increasing opportunities for home ownership through cheaper mortgages and supposedly generally enhancing economic activity (Glinavos, 2010b). Unfortunately, as Arner (2009) points out, these alleged benefits, when taken to excess, also turned out to be the greatest weakness of the new model.

In fact, the weaknesses of the new financial model were evident long before the credit crunch. The dot-com bubble and its subsequent collapse (and short US recession at the beginning of the new century) were based on much the same correlation between deregulation and excessive risk-taking. In his book *The Roaring Nineties* (2003), Joseph Stiglitz argues that the dot-com collapse and ensuing recession should have been a final warning that deregulation had gone too far. He suggests that the state-withdrawal policies of Reagan and the first Bush administration created an environment where the spread of financial services came to substitute investment in the real economy as a source of innovation and growth. Even the earlier recession in 1991–3, he notes, was a direct result of overexposure and weakness in the financial sector. However, lax regulation and opportunities for quick profits returned in the 1990s and fuelled the technology bubble resulting in immense waste and record losses when the market realised that the magical profitability of new technologies would not materialise. The important point to note here is that changes in the markets that produced a systemically much riskier environment were brought about largely by excessive deregulation. The successes of the Clinton administration in restoring balance in the budget after 1993 (which helped release capital in the economy due to a combination of low interest rates and other incentives) helped mask vulnerabilities. The Bush administration then continued on the deregulating path which led to overexposure in the sub-prime mortgage market that started off the current crisis: a crisis in which market participants and regulators were equally complicit, by exhibiting the remarkable lack of foresight and even modesty that had also defined the great crash of 1929 (Glinavos, 2010b).

4.2.3 Interconnectedness and globalisation

Perhaps at this point of our discussion it would be useful to offer an explanation of the international dynamics powering this process of debt inflation in the US at the beginning of the new century. In an area where a lot has been written, I would recommend Robert Reich's *Supercapitalism* (2009) as an excellent summary of the global trade dynamics behind the crisis. A central question to confront in this area of study is how did the process of debt creation and expansion operate, from the sub-prime originators to the investment banks and then on to other banks and financial institutions all over the world? So far in this discussion we have addressed how securitisation operates and presented the key reasons why banks were incentivised to enter into this game. What we will do in the rest of this section is to explain the global dynamic behind this process. While it may be understandable why an American citizen would want to purchase a house through a mortgage, or why a loan originator may entice – or con – people into taking their loans, it is less immediately obvious why a financial firm would want to securitise the resulting financial obligations and why anyone would want to buy them. Furthermore, even if we understand the basic features of the demand and supply for these assets, we still need an explanation as to why there was such a high demand for 'synthetic' financial products so as to lead to runaway inflation in asset prices for all sorts of derivative products.

We can advance two broad explanations for these phenomena. One addresses the supply side and one deals with the demand side. The supply side explanation is a classic Marxist explanation based on diminishing returns. One could argue that as opportunities to make profits decline, capitalists turn to more and more risky bets in an effort to maintain profits (Callinicos, 2010). For example, when the prime segment of the housing market was saturated, there were not many places mortgage originators could turn for profits, beyond extending loans at punitive rates to those who could ill afford them. Also, the rates of interest in high-rated loans were very modest in a low interest-rate environment as the one operating in the majority of developed jurisdictions in the 2000s. Packaging diversified portfolios of mortgages, consumer loans and credit card and student debts allowed the creation of segmented products that offered attractive rates (for the more risky tranches) and a range of credit ratings. A series of asset-backed securities (ABS) could be bundled together into a collateralised debt obligation (CDO) that had a series of tranches which investors could buy. Each tranche had a rating representing an assessment as to its risk of default and offered interest at a corresponding level. The more products (or tranches of products) with higher risks one could produce, the higher the price these could command in an environment where higher returns were desperately sought by investors. Hence the phenomenon of lower quality products being turned out in increasingly higher volumes. But while the above explains how these products came to be, does it fully explain the demand? Is it sufficient to say there was a desire for products with better yields due to the generally low-interest environment investors were operating in?

The explanation that people were buying these assets only because they were chasing profits is only part of the picture. It is of course true of the supplier and the buyer of the products that a demand for yield pushed the volume of lower-rated tranches to an extreme, but there were also legal reasons pushing demand. Regulatory requirements for diversified portfolios effectively demanded that financial institutions bought a variety of different risk-absorbing products. This diversification provided the illusion of security while other measures indicating the stability of enterprises such as leverage ratios were downplayed. For example, the SEC's Basel II-based rules permitted the top five major investment banks to achieve leverage of over 30 to 1. Insufficient capital held against such significant exposures proved a major cause of the failure of Lehman Brothers and Bear Stearns, and also played a major role in forcing Merrill Lynch to sell itself to Bank of America (Scott, 2010: 776). The risks involved in holding these securities were seriously underestimated. The illusion of security inherent in diversified investment portfolios was enhanced via the presumed ability to hedge risks through insurance arrangements. However, due to over-optimism and an excessive reliance on the assessments of credit rating agencies, for most securities, the hedges covered only a fraction of the exposure. Regardless of that fact, once the credit risk of a position was hedged, this risk was deemed to have been neutralised and did not appear any more in the quantitative risk analysis of the banks holding the securities. Moreover, no attention was paid to the possibility that counterparties to the hedges might themselves be in trouble and that this was most likely to happen at the very time when they would be called upon to step in and replace losses from borrower defaults (Hellwig, 2009: 160).

There is another more interesting question on the demand side, however. How could the buyers of derivative products afford to buy them – where was all the money coming from? To answer this question, we need to move into a short discussion of geopolitics and international trade relations as they existed at the beginning of the new century. It is often said that America has become the debtor of the world, with a significant trade deficit that needs to be financed through a current account surplus (Jackson, 2012). The reason why this has come to pass is well documented in the literature on globalisation that emerged since the 1980s. The process of de-industrialisation in the West that followed its transformation into a set of primarily services-oriented economies (this is more true of the US than of Europe, but the trend is overall consistent) was met by a process of rapid industrialisation primarily in South East Asia, but also in India. Since the 1980s therefore China became, as is commonly said, the workshop of the world (Fung and Lau, 2003). The widening gap between what the US economy exported (capital goods, technology) and what it imported (consumer products of gradually increasing sophistication) needed to be funded somehow. How was it funded? One way that US consumers could maintain their purchase power would be through increases in real wages in the US. This, however, did not happen, and since the 1990s real wages in the US have been stagnant, if not falling (Reich, 2009). American consumers managed to maintain their ability to buy through increased lending, both personal and that based on home equity. The fact that manufactured goods from China were flooding the US market at very low prices helped mask the fact that wages for all but the richest of workers were not keeping up with inflation. Where did the money that went into loans to American consumers come from though?

As the trade gap increased and commodity prices were pushed up, many countries around the world that we perceive to be poor or developing began accumulating significant foreign exchange reserves (Jackson, 2012). Those reserves joined the race for yield that we described above. The consumer and home loan market in the US provided an obvious opportunity for dollar-rich foreigners to invest. Hence we arrived at the situation in the new century where increased spending on imports in the US made companies and sovereigns in developing countries rich, who in turn invested the money in US financial institutions who then lent them to consumers to allow them to continue their spending. It all seemed like a virtuous spiral till it got out of hand, because there is a maximum point beyond which underlying asset values could not support the level of lending at hand. The party could go on in other words while US house prices were increasing, which allowed home owners to release new equity from their properties to spend on Made-in-China consumables. Once house prices reached levels that houses became unaffordable to many who were far from being called sub-prime borrowers, it was obvious that further increases were not possible. It was also at that point (2005–6) that the Federal Reserve began raising interest rates to dampen strengthening inflation (Nautz and Schmidt, 2009). Once house prices flatlined and then began their long decline, no more spending could be based on borrowing. When asset values started falling, no more financial products could be generated and amassing defaults starting showing the real risks accumulated in the system. This forced the process into reverse, with asset prices falling, homes de-leveraging, spending contracting. It was this dynamic that brought a crisis of finance out into the real economy, a crisis that ultimately caused what Posner (2009) describes as a new depression. Why were these processes allowed to unfold, however, and is such uncontrolled boom and bust part and parcel of capitalism? The following presentation of the work of Hyman Minsky helps shed some light on these questions.

4.2.4 Financial instability and the role of law

In Chapter 3 we noted that the current crisis shares many characteristics with previous historical cycles and we argued that in virtually every previous financial collapse, the crisis was preceded by very rapid credit expansion, which manifested itself in part in higher asset prices fuelling an appetite for risk-taking

(White, 2008: 308). As the quality of credits deteriorated when earlier expectations about profits or future income growth began to look unrealistic, the whole process went into reverse, turning boom to bust. This analysis seems to suggest that a crisis-prone dynamic is inherent in capitalism. There is indeed strong evidence to support such a view. One of the most important insights into the workings of capitalism was offered by Hyman Minsky (2008) in his 'financial instability hypothesis'. His thesis posits that there are three types of finance: hedge, speculative and Ponzi finance. Hedge finance suggests a situation where financial investments are fully supported by deposits (no relation to hedge funds). Speculative finance denotes a situation where investments can cover repayments of interest but not of the principal amount offered by depositors without attracting new funds. Ponzi finance denotes a situation where the income generated by the investment can cover neither the interest nor repayments of the principal amount deposited; such schemes operate only so long as new deposits come in that exceed repayables. It is needless to say that the move from hedge to speculative to Ponzi finance involves an escalation of risk to the point where the fund (and the economy if this behaviour is systemic) collapses. According to Minsky, in good times the economy generates Ponzi finance structures as investors seek better returns. This race to sustain profitability in turn becomes the cause of a crash. This is an important insight to the operations of capitalism as it demonstrates the instability dynamic to be endogenous. This means that crashes and recessions occur not due to external events, but due to internal dynamics in capitalist structures. For a crisis to occur, one does not need commodity prices to go up or wars or earthquakes. Minsky teaches us that even if everything is plain sailing, the crash will always come in the end.

What is the message of the financial instability hypothesis for the role of law in economic governance? If it is the move from speculative to Ponzi finance that unravels financial capitalism, then the function of law could be to prevent one state from morphing into the other. One way to achieve this would be to limit debt inflation, in other words leverage, from increasing beyond some commonly accepted level. Such suggestions abound in the literature (see, for example, Sullivan, 2009). In order to prevent leverage from exceeding 'safe' levels, regulatory policy would need to have adequate countercyclical weapons and the ability to constrain bubbles at the early stages of their creation. According to this view, equity and leverage ratios are sufficient, even in the absence of tools to micromanage the economy. A further assessment of these ideas is offered in Part 3 of the book where we look into what the future role of law should be and how a system could be structured in order either to avoid crises or to enhance participation in both the benefits and the costs of financialised capitalism.

One of the key underlying themes of this work is the idea that our entire political economy has degenerated into being a machine that supports, protects and promotes the market. This phenomenon is reflected in the law, with legal frameworks having being reduced to the role of market foundations.

Within this situation we have lost a view of law and law reform as a mechanism for translating the popular will into economic action. In our efforts (internationally, and specifically in Europe) to 'modernise' and embed market friendliness into state institutions, we have created a rigid institutional framework that can only deal with the incidence of crisis through a 'scientific' orthodox viewpoint. The book argues that when this viewpoint diverges from a social contract about what the economy should be like and what its structures are for, then we are in trouble politically and economically. For this reason we now turn to examine an example of rigidity and neoclassical orthodoxy par excellence, the structures of economic governance of the EU. This analysis is of immediate concern due to the European debt crisis. The following section offers an exploration of the idea that legal inflexibility (stemming from the constitutionalisation of market-friendly legal frameworks) hampers states' ability to deal with crises, limiting policy options and marginalising democratic choice.

4.3 The sovereign debt crisis

The previous section demonstrated how, in a system reliant on leverage and liquidity, a downturn in one corner of the financial universe spelled catastrophe for the whole. We also offered some reflections on the mechanisms that allowed the crisis to spread from a subsection of the US economy and become a calamity of global proportions in the space of a couple of years. This section presents what is often described as the follow-on act of the Great Recession, the predominately European sovereign debt crisis. It is at this part of the discussion that conceptualising the role of law becomes a discourse on the nature of institutional design. The debt crisis that has plagued Europe since 2010, placing question marks over the survival of the Eurozone and the European Union as a whole, brings to the fore one of the key themes of this book: the propensity of market-friendly reforms to restrict policy options when they are most needed. In seeking to show the consequences institutional design can have on the political economy of a country and of the continent (in the case of Europe) this part of the chapter will present a short history of the sovereign debt crisis in Europe and then will go into some detail in the case of Greece, which at the time of writing and perhaps for the foreseeable future serves as the focal point of the crisis.

4.3.1 Transmission mechanisms: from financial to sovereign crisis

One of the primary topics to consider when discussing the calamities that Europe faces at the beginning of the second decade of the new century is how the crisis moved from being a crisis of financial markets to a crisis in the real economy and simultaneously to a crisis of state indebtedness. How did we get to where we are today, and what is likely to follow? Crucially, why has this transmission taken place considering the allegedly sophisticated understanding policy-makers (internationally) have of the features of economic crises and their consequences? Ben Bernanke, Chairman of the American Federal Reserve, is after all a scholar of the Great Depression. Asking why do we move from one phase of a crisis to another reminds one of the question that Susan Strange (1994) sought to answer (and for that matter the question the whole research field of international political economy in general is geared towards answering): why do states fail to act to regulate and stabilise an international financial system which is known to be vitally necessary to the 'real' economy, indeed a financial system which most experts in and out of government since 2007 agreed is in serious need of more regulation for its own safety?

One answer for inactivity or ineptitude is provided by Paul Krugman (2008). He argues that policy-makers know that Keynesian expansionary policies are needed in recessions to boost demand and rebalance the economy. Governments have demonstrated their knowledge historically, after digesting the lessons of the Great Depression, by acting decisively when markets fell into crises. A recent example is the expansionary policies pursued during the first stage of the global crisis from 2007 to 2010. However, why have they failed to act since 2011 and why has the IMF consistently argued in favour of pro-cyclical fiscal policies when theory and practice both demonstrate that their effect is to deepen recessions? Why do the EU and the IMF insist on contractionary policies and fiscal consolidation in Greece, Italy, Spain, everywhere in the Eurozone in fact, when it is every day demonstrated that such pro-cyclicality is creating a debt spiral? Are they blind to the effects of their policies due to an ideological commitment to neoliberalism, or is there a conspiracy of interests that insists on policies that harm the many for the benefit of the few?

Krugman's answer is that policy choices nowadays are motivated by fear of the market. It is what we could call a 'market confidence' game that restrains political choices and prevents demand-side economic proscriptions from paving a way out of crises. If this is true, the question then becomes: why do markets demand recessionary policies, ignoring the fact that they are bad for the economy? Isn't what is bad for the economy also bad for the market? Unfortunately such correlation is not necessary. The handling of the current crisis had certain investors win both when states propped up their banking sectors to keep them from collapse and when subsequently states tried to radically reduce their (recently exploded) debt burden. We find ourselves therefore in the peculiar situation of doing the 'wrong' thing to appease a market that wins all the time. An additional reason (to money making) why markets insist on contractionary fiscal policies is indeed an ideological obsession with a minimal state, brought about by the neoliberal domination of thinking about the state–market relationship. The issue of how ideology can define policy responses and why this happens was addressed in Chapter 2. It is not the book's aim to point the finger at a conspiracy of markets and finance against the people. Such explanations exist of course, but they fail to capture the extent of the problem. No conspiracy can achieve the level of damage that ideological hangups can deliver, something true whether the ideology appeals to free-marketeers or Marxists. *Neoliberalism and the Law* (Glinavos, 2010a) explained how a neoliberal ideological straitjacket led even well-meaning policy-makers in post-communist states to contribute to the creation of a legal system that undermined both economic recovery and political normalisation (towards democratic governance). A similar process is under way in Europe at the moment with policy-makers consistently failing to address problems, caught as they are between the Scylla of the markets and the Charybdis of their own ideological blindfolds.

However, we also have to concede that markets cannot play a dominant role in the way in which a political economy functions unless allowed to do so by whoever yields power and possesses authority (Strange, 1994: 23). It is important therefore to determine first who has power and secondly to assess where they get this power from. As indicated in other parts of this book already, a great part of the power to control modern economies comes from finance. As our reflection on liquidity shows, however, finance should not only be understood as accumulated wealth or money, but crucially as credit. Whoever can gain the confidence of others in their ability to create credit will control the economy (Strange, 1994: 30). The scale of economic activity nowadays (in advanced capitalism) is such that accumulation of wealth (on a traditional Marxist analysis) is not enough to power the system. What does power the system is the capacity to attract credit and to accumulate debt. This realisation stems from the analysis of the concept of liquidity and the role it plays in modern capitalism that we came across in Chapter 2. As we saw, a complex system of legal instruments results in a make-believe world where money is credit, credit is wealth and wealth is (as has always been) power.

Neoliberalism and the Law highlighted the paradox of the expectation that international outcomes are borne of national policies. This by-product of globalisation handicaps governments who are on the one hand expected to react to international market imperatives but on the other can only influence directly national policies. This is why, for example, reform proposals of a liberal trajectory are meant to be national in origin but international in effect, determining a country's comparative advantages over the rest of the world. Strange's assessment of finance as a national and simultaneously global phenomenon offers support to the explanation above. For Strange (1994: 90) the financial structure has two inseparable aspects: it comprises political economy structures through which credit is created and the monetary system that determines the relative values of moneys in which credit is denominated. The first power is generated by the dynamic between states and banks, the second between states and markets. A financial structure therefore is the sum of all the arrangements governing the availability of credit plus all the factors determining the terms on which currencies are exchanged. It is through these interconnected mechanisms that crisis can spread from one aspect of economic activity to the others, like the infamous contagion that poisons sovereign debt markets in Europe.

And yet none of this answers the question as to why policy-makers in their totality (at least in Europe) have been so ineffectual in dealing with calamities that are in fact the return of old problems. The sovereign debt problems of the 1980s for example, while not a novel situation even then, came about in an institutional environment where state debts were perceived to be a problem for banks when states faced bankruptcy, yet the risk of increased interest rates was a problem for the borrowing nations in an environment that not much could be done to directly control the behaviour of states (for instance by military intervention). Banks and creditors made super-profits from speculation as interest rates shot up during monetary and fiscal crises, only to lose everything if states defaulted. Such an imbalance between the opportunity of profits and the risks of total loss presented a danger for creditors. The solution to this power vacuum for creditors was filled by the IMF and its structural adjustment lending (along with the World Bank), which sought to direct state policy-making in the interests of avoiding default. The results of dealing with this problem via IMF-mandated austerity programmes, especially in Latin America in the 1980s, are well documented. A new era began where creditors enjoyed the upside from increasing rates but did not suffer the risk of losses from unstructured state defaults. It is in the context of this new era that the European debt crisis is currently playing out.

The above discussion demonstrates that the sovereign debt problems of today, while not that dissimilar to those of the 1980s follow a novel pattern: private interests are protected while borrowing nations have to undertake painful restructuring under the direction of the IMF. The best way to explain how and why this happens is the case of Greece that unfortunately has become ground zero of this new phase of the crisis. A study of Greece allows us to delve deeper into the question of why the crisis has evolved in the way it has, and why policy responses have failed to address spreading disasters.

4.3.2 *The case of Greece*

4.3.2.1 *Background: Greece up to the first bailout in 2010*

Shortly after a national election in 2009 which resulted in a change of government in Athens, Greece announced that its national debt and budget deficit had been mis-stated in the 2009 budget. In fact, the deficit shot up to 12.7 per cent of GDP in 2009, while the national debt, according to the government's own estimates, amounted in January 2010 to 125 per cent of GDP (Reuters, 2010). What followed these announcements was a crisis in the Greek bond market as investors lost confidence in the country's ability to stay solvent, fearing that the banking crisis of 2008 was developing into a sovereign debt crisis in 2010. The practical failure of Dubai World in 2010 gave basis to these fears. This part of the chapter will focus on Greece as an example of the political, legal and economic issues that the sovereign debt crisis has brought forward, marking a new stage in the world financial crisis.

Greece in 2013 is still a member of the European Union (EU) and of Economic and Monetary Union (EMU), having entered the Eurozone (as it is commonly referred to in the literature) on 1 January 2001. As such, the powers of the Greek government are restricted in economic management in the same way as for other euro participating EU member states. As a result of entry to the EMU macro-economic policy is severely restricted as the Greek government has no control over monetary policy. Faced with the legal restrictions on sovereignty imposed by the framework of the EMU, when presented with a loss of confidence in the markets Greece had very little room for manoeuvre. Countries with command of their monetary policy can deal with market pressures by devaluing their currency in order to maintain their export competitiveness. Such action is not open to members of the Eurozone who trade in the single currently, the euro. The only way a country can deal with a loss of competitiveness, without devaluing its currency, is by producing more efficiently or more cheaply. As efficiencies are difficult to achieve and time-consuming to implement, Greece has been pressured by its partners in the Eurozone to 'reform' its economy via cost savings. This means that Greece has to reduce wage spending which inevitably means that it has to lower the population's standard of living. Such internal devaluation, it was hoped, would allow Greece to retain or to regain some of its lost comparative advantages and mimic the effects of currency devaluation (which of course was not an option).

According to George Soros (Soros, 2010), the risk premium on Greek government bonds (over the rates at which Germany borrows, for example, known as 'spreads') hovered around 3 per cent in February 2010, depriving Greece of much of the benefit of Eurozone membership. Soros warned that a continuation of this phenomenon meant that there was a real danger that Greece would not be able to extricate itself from its predicament whatever measures it took. Further budget cuts would further depress economic activity, reducing tax revenues and worsening the debt-to-GDP ratio. Given these dangers, the risk premium could not revert to its previous level in the absence of outside assistance. This view was shared within Greece in the spring of 2010. Debt repayment levels were expected to outstrip earnings forecast on the basis of GDP growth for years to come. This meant that domestic capacity would not be enough to refinance the debt and Greece would need to keep coming back to the markets to raise finance. Indeed, in the absence of external assistance either from EU countries or the IMF, Greece was set to continue on a path of domestic recession and market punishment for years to come. Even with such assistance, duly offered in May 2010, the future for Greece looked bleak even before the endless depression that ensued.

Greece's formerly dominant (self-proclaimed socialist) PASOK party had argued (successfully) in the 2009 election that a package of severe cuts and an enforced recession along the advice of international financial institutions

(EU Commission, IMF) would damage long-term prospects of growth and cause avoidable suffering. It proposed instead a phased reduction of state spending and a gradual recalibration of the macro-economic situation, cushioning the more vulnerable sections of the population. If this message sounds familiar to readers in the UK it is because it mirrors almost exactly the argument presented by the ailing Brown government in London on route to its own 2010 electoral Rubicon. The British Labour government in the spring of 2010 was trying to forestall the opposition by suggesting that the 'tough love' policy of the Conservatives of immediate and deep cuts to state spending was likely to do more long-term damage than good. In Greece, unlike in the UK, no one seriously proposed a programme of harsh austerity and the suggestion of one at the eve of the election by Prime Minister Karamanlis was not taken seriously by anyone. However, despite its original intentions, as a result of the ballooning costs of borrowing, the new PASOK government performed a volte-face, declared a national emergency, and proceeded to announce (if not actually fully implement) a punishing programme of fiscal discipline sharply reducing expenditure across the public sector.

It could be argued that Greece did not have to go to the IMF – indeed it did not even have to formally request its European partners for help in order to be forced to implement what looks like the standard package of austerity and macro-economic stabilisation so familiar from the years of World Bank/IMF structural adjustment. It had to implement a partly home-grown, partly EcoFin (Economic and Financial Affairs Council, part of the Council of the European Union) recommended austerity package to appease 'the market' if it were to maintain its ability to borrow from private investors. It looked in the spring of 2010 very close to a situation of jumping before being pushed. In fact in the face of unabating pressure from the markets that brought the interest rates on Greek debt to unacceptable and unsustainable levels, the Greek government requested the activation of a rescue package drawn up by the IMF/EU, promising to sacrifice yet more sections of its vulnerable population hoping in the end to appease the unsettled markets.

4.3.2.2 Greece between 2010 and 2012

As was predictable, and indeed predicted, the 'assistance' offered by the troika of the EU, IMF and ECB did not improve Greece's fiscal position, both because the enforced retrenchment deepened the recession, and because the measures required were beyond the willingness and capacity of the Greek political establishment to implement. Greek society was equally unwilling to accept austerity and who can blame them? In the words of Keynes (1984: 64)

> There has never been in modern or ancient history a community that has been prepared to accept without intense struggle a reduction in the general level of money income.

The result was that Greece needed another bailout. The second bailout was indeed agreed at the end of 2011, but this time it also required the participation of the private sector in an effort to reduce Greece's unsustainable level of debt. Bond holders of Greek debt were offered a swap of Greek bonds to new bonds issued by Greece having a face value equal to 31.5 per cent of the face amount of the exchanged bonds; in addition, investors were offered European Finance Stability Facility (EFSF) notes with a maturity date of two years or less from the Private Sector Involvement (PSI) settlement date and having a face value equal to 15 per cent of the face amount of their exchanged bonds. The detachable GDP-linked securities issued by Greece have a notional amount equal to the face amount of each holder's new bonds (Greek Ministry of Finance, 2012a). As a result of the terms of the offer, the notional haircut is 53.5 per cent (Reuters, 2012a). It is held that a restructuring is deemed successful when 90 per cent or more of bond holders participate in an offering that is no less than 50 per cent of the net present value of the debt (Hornbeck, 2010). On 9 March 2012 (Greek Ministry of Finance, 2012b) 152 billion euros worth of bonds had accepted the offer out of a total outstanding obligation of 177 billion.

After this deal went through with a lot of fanfare, the realisation dawned that the reduction in the debt burden achieved was nowhere near enough to bring the debt to GDP ratio close to the 120 per cent level the IMF considers the threshold for affordability. Data for 2011 showed Greek debt at 170.6 per cent of GDP even though Greece reduced its deficit to 9.4 per cent from 10.7 per cent in 2010 and (re-estimated at) 15.6 per cent in 2009 (Reuters, 2012b). Faced with the prospect of the IMF withdrawing from the Greek rescue plans, the Europeans agreed on November 2012 yet another deal to cut Greece's debt by €40 bn, projecting a drop in debt to 124 per cent of GDP by 2020 (involving cuts in the interest rate on official loans, extending their maturity by 15 years to 30 years and granting Athens a ten-year interest repayment deferral). It was also agreed that €11 bn of profits accrued through the European Central Bank's purchase of distressed Greek government bonds would be returned and that Greece would engage in a debt-buyback scheme in order to bring privately held debt down (Wearden and Fletcher, 2012). This debt buyback involved repurchases of the debt restructured in March 2012 as part of the PSI haircut and amounted to €31.9 bn, which would (if all the other projections are correct) reduce the Greek debt-to-GDP ratio by 9.5 percentage points by 2020. However, this is far from the end of the Greek debt saga. Already the projections for debt reduction are claimed to make inadequate allowances for the continuing depression. For example, Greek forecasts of debt levels for 2013 rose from 167 per cent to 189 per cent of GDP within a period of six months alone (Mackintosh, 2012). Even if projections were not wildly optimistic when the plans for new Greek debt-reduction steps were agreed among Eurozone finance ministers on 27 November 2012, the expectation was that the buyback would reduce the debt by 11 per cent of GDP. This means that even if everything does go to plan, there is still the need for a new haircut or an extension of the buyback to PSI holdouts (Reuters, 2012c).

As mentioned earlier, anyone familiar with the history of sovereign defaults will be having an acute sense of déjà vu. Greece's troubles mirror to an extent the situation in Argentina a decade ago. Since Argentina fell victim to a debt crisis at the beginning of the century its policy-makers attempted to negotiate a restructuring under the supervision of the IMF. After years of unsuccessful efforts, in 2004, Argentina announced that it would open a one-time bond exchange and passed domestic legislation mandating that it would never hold a future swap with a better offer. In January 2005, the country opened an exchange on over $100 billion in principal and interest on a diverse number of bond issuances whereby the bond holders were to receive a 67 per cent haircut. In the end it restructured just over $62 billion with a 76 per cent participation rate (Cohen, 2011). As we will see in Chapter 6, Argentina is still working its way through the consequences of this restructuring in the markets and in the legal arena. We will also have the chance to reflect on the opportunities for litigation generated by forcing bond holders to take losses and on how the decisions of courts and international arbitral tribunals affect states' capacity to determine economic policy that benefits its population as opposed to policy that aims to protect creditor interests.

What have we learned from the detail on Greece presented so far in this chapter? Why is this presentation of Greece and its troubles necessary as part of a discussion on the global financial crisis and what does it tell us about economic policy and the role of law? One of the key themes of this book is the propensity of market-friendly legal frameworks to reduce policy discretion when it is most needed. At times of crisis, policy-makers have the difficult task of addressing economic calamities while continuing to carry popular consent and to act for the benefit of their citizens. Institutional structures that prioritise the interests of investors, however, or proclaim the superiority of market mechanisms in the distribution of benefits and costs of economic activities, create the risk that policy-making becomes disconnected from the popular will. Such disconnection is not an abstract evil, it carries a very real risk of the disintegration of the body politic and threatens the survival of democracy and the maintenance of peace. It is exactly this descent into chaos that we are witnessing in Greece and this is why being familiar with the progress of Greece through this crisis can help us appreciate deficiencies in legal frameworks. This discussion assists therefore in explaining how constitutionalising market superiority risks everything, including the survival of the market itself. The next section deals with the notion of institutional deficiency by looking into the structures of the EU that play a central role in the growing sovereign debt crisis.

4.3.3 Institutional inflexibility as a doomsday machine

One of the key issues in addressing the financial crisis has been Europe's institutional capacity (or incapacity) to respond to economic shocks. The argument here is that if legal structures lack flexibility, they are unable to soften the blows dealt by crises. As we have shown elsewhere in the book, the construction of legal frameworks on the basis of market-friendly requirements means that less flexibility is left to policy-makers in order to ensure that market expectations are met. This constitutionalisation of pro-market economic decision-making renders the legal frameworks inflexible. When stress is applied, as for example by the European sovereign debt crisis, these inflexible structures risk breaking under intense political pressures. Politics inevitably can be constrained by legal frameworks only for certain periods of time and under certain circumstances; their resilience reaches its limits when the disconnect between economic decision-making and democratic choice becomes too wide. In the tumultuous economic climate of the last few years, perhaps the best test for institutional resilience is to consider the legal framework governing disentanglement from the Eurozone. The following discussion therefore presents a summary of the literature on the legal framework governing exit from the Eurozone, seeking to show how a legal framework built to be market friendly and predictable becomes inefficient, unpredictable and, crucially, undemocratic.

The underlying hypothesis of the following discussion is that the legal framework bringing together the European Union and the Eurozone is deficient in that it fails to be flexible enough to accommodate policy changes required to deal with significant shocks. A central example is the capacity of member states to leave the EU as a whole, or the Eurozone in particular. A related issue is the ability of the EU, or the Eurozone, to expel members that are no longer considered able to remain within the groups. This is no longer a purely academic discussion. As analysts for Nomura noted in a research paper in 2011 (Nordvig and St-Arnaud, 2011), escalating tensions in the Eurozone, around Greece as well as core Eurozone countries, mean that the risk of a break-up has sharply increased. The nature of the European project as a forward-only moving locomotive is to blame for the lack of flexibility. As mentioned above, it is argued here that institutional and legal inadequacies do not prevent situations from occurring, but lacking the tools to deal with them, tend to make things worse. As the old axiom goes, there are no dead-ends in politics. The problem is, however, that solutions outside the legal framework and institutional arrangements, even if politically negotiated, risk further deconstruction of the European project. It is for this reason that the institutional framework should accommodate the possibility of both a multi-speed Europe and of withdrawal from the various spheres of integration. As Charles Proctor noted with reference to the need to prepare for unwelcome situations arising from the euro debt crisis, the best that a lawyer can do is to seek to understand the problems which might confront him in such a situation, and to hope that the availability of legally rigorous solutions might at least help to mitigate some of the chaos which would undoubtedly descend on the financial markets (Proctor, 2010: 7). The link of this discussion with the wider themes of the book is that institutional frameworks should allow space for democratic politics to determine the future for each political entity. A permanent institutional structure, like the EMU for instance, constitutes a violation of the key democratic principle of self-determination. What if the Greeks, as a sovereign polity, decide that they would rather seek a future outside the euro? Would this be possible, and if not, what does that tell us about the role of legal structures in a democracy?

In the opening part of this book we posited the question of what would be the result of continuing in the de-politicising path of previous decades if not a negation of democracy in its entirety? The more we elevate market protective structures onto unalterable legal mechanisms beyond the reach of normal politics, the more we limit the scope and importance of a democratic polity. The more we allow this distance between the economic and the political to widen, the more we risk that the people themselves will exercise whatever choice they have left to oust the inept and economically shackled political system, handing the reigns to a new breed of fascists, in Greece, in Italy, in Spain. Is it so shocking to wonder whether by hiding the European unification project behind an armour of law, we have created in Europe the legal foundations for a dictatorship of finance? The following discussion explores the strength of this armour and enquires into the possibility that the European locomotive can change speeds. This is done through an evaluation of the possibility of a member state stepping off the European locomotive, or even of being thrown out.

The obvious place to begin a discussion of departures from the process of European unification is Greece. The year 2012 was replete with talk about a possible 'Grexit' (a term beloved of the press, denoting a Greek exit from the Eurozone). In our presentation of Greece's troubles above we have hinted at the reasons why continued participation in the Eurozone may no longer be guaranteed or indeed desirable for Greece. Before considering in more detail the technical feasibility of an exit, however, we need to look into the issue more directly. Why would Greece want to leave the Eurozone? Wouldn't such a move make its situation a lot worse than it is now? Greece may not in fact have the choice to remain in the Eurozone if its economic situation continues to deteriorate. Greece has had a prolonged recession, five years and counting by most estimates (Geoghegan, 2012), during which it has been subject to a harsh austerity programme aimed to bring about an internal devaluation to improve competitiveness. This programme is both unlikely to succeed and lacking in political support. An exit from the Eurozone would allow the Greeks to devalue their currency instead of lowering wages, so some of the pressure would be lifted from wage earners. Having said that, it is important to realise the extent to which the trade imbalance in Greece would decimate consumer spending if a devaluation of 30–40 per cent were to happen to a newly introduced drachma. It is also highly questionable whether the political establishment could handle the stress of a Grexit without resorting to short-lived and calamitous measures like the unchecked printing of money to compensate for high inflationary pressures resulting initially from devaluation.

Athanassiou (2009) summarises the legal challenges presented by withdrawal from EMU. Withdrawal would entail (among a large variety of more detailed measures) creating a new currency or re-establishing the old currency of the withdrawing member state, refunding the departing national central bank's contribution to the European Central Bank's capital (including reimbursing its foreign reserve assets) and transferring full monetary sovereignty back to the seceding national central bank, with all the practical difficulties and legal uncertainties that this would involve for outstanding monetary policy operations, especially in the case of unilateral withdrawal. All this is a technical challenge of immense proportions, even before one considers the possible unwinding of assistance packages offered to member states (and their banking sectors) suffering from the debt crisis. As for a member state's withdrawal from the EU, the complexities surrounding it are legion, affecting the rights and obligations of every natural or legal person inside or outside the territory of the withdrawing member state who is or who may be affected by it (Athanassiou, 2009: 10).

Whatever the economic argument in favour of or against a return to the national currency, assuming the legal difficulties could be overcome (see below for further information), the political situation is one that could swiftly result in poor economic decisions on purely political criteria divorced from the interests of citizens (the Greek body politic has an illustrious tradition of opting for self-preservation instead of selecting what is best for the country). In the two elections of 2012 a pro-European (presumably pro-austerity) coalition of parties narrowly prevailed because the population feared the consequences of a Grexit more than they hate the austerity programme. During the latter part of 2013 with further evidence of unending recession (and money running out for hard-hit consumers) perhaps people began to feel they have less to lose from a Grexit than initially thought. The main beneficiary of such despair will be the populist left-wing Syriza coalition which pledges an end to austerity funded via endless support from the EU, obtained apparently through blackmailing the European institutions with the threat of a disorderly exit from the Eurozone. It is against this background that a discussion needs to be had concerning both the possibility of a unilateral exit from the Eurozone and of a possible expulsion. It is to this analysis that we now turn, starting with a presentation of the European institutional framework before the introduction of an EU exit clause in the Lisbon Treaty.

4.3.3.1 Before Lisbon

It has often been argued that Treaty provisions for withdrawal from the EU would be incompatible with the nature of the Union, which involves the intention of the member states to work towards an 'ever closer union'. Nonetheless, there is general consensus that all member states in agreement can decide to let a member state withdraw. The question about a legal right to withdraw therefore primarily concerns withdrawal without such a multilateral agreement. Negotiated withdrawals are, in principle, always possible. For example, in 1868 the US Supreme Court ruled in *Texas* v. *White* (74 US 700) that while the US Constitution prohibits unilateral secession (and by implication expulsion) one or more states may be allowed to leave the Union with the consent of their peers, an argument supported by Article 54 of the Vienna Convention on the Law of Treaties 1969, which states that the termination of a treaty or the withdrawal of a party may take place (a) in conformity with the provisions of the treaty; or (b) at any time by consent of all the parties after consultation with the other contracting states. Whether the Vienna provisions were considered sufficient or not, however, the European Treaties did not contain express provision for withdrawal either from the EU or EMU prior to the Lisbon Treaty.

The silence of EU primary law on the existence (or otherwise) of a legal right of withdrawal had led to two fundamentally opposed interpretations of the right to leave the Union. One was that a right of unilateral withdrawal existed (derived from the Vienna Convention as a matter of public international law) even in the absence of any explicit reference to it in the treaties, since sovereign states were, in any case, free to exercise their sovereign right to withdraw from their international commitments. This is an argument often raised in Britain by the Eurosceptic part of the political establishment that aims at disentanglement from the EU. The other argument is that the lack, until recently, of a formal exit clause in Community primary law must have been intentional, testifying to the member states' lasting commitment to the EU's objectives and to the irreversibility of the European unification process, which is irreconcilable with a unilateral right of withdrawal (Athanassiou, 2009: 11). Whether European integration can be 'undone' therefore depends to a large extent on determining whether powers from the member states are delegated or (instead) transferred to the EU. If member states have only delegated powers to the EU, retracting them should be legally possible. This interpretation would be consistent with Community legislative practice and rulings by the constitutional and supreme courts of the member states (Berglund, 2006: 149).

Regarding the views of the courts of the member states, two examples are often mentioned: the verdict of the German Constitutional Court on the accession of Germany to the Maastricht Treaty (*Brunner* v. *European Union Treaty* CMLR [1994] 57) and the opinion of the British House of Lords in the Factortame case (*R* v. *Secretary of State for Transport,* exp. *Factortame Ltd (No. 2)* [1990] UKHL 13). In the verdict of the German Constitutional Court, it was stated that the German Law of Accession was provisional in the sense that it depended on the development of the EU being consistent with the Basic Law. This leads to the conclusion that, according to the German Constitutional Court, Germany has not surrendered sovereign powers to the EU institutions but only delegated them. In the UK case, the derogation from sovereignty involved in being part of the EU was viewed neither as final nor irreversible. The argument was that since Parliament was ultimately sovereign, it could still repeal the European Communities Act 1972 that authorised accession to the EC, and that the United Kingdom could thus withdraw completely. Craig and De Búrca (2003: 307–8) mention that one of the Law Lords involved in the Factortame case declared that the supremacy of EC law does not stem from the Treaties but from the will of the British Parliament. This theoretical point may be about to be tested if the Conservatives in the UK get their wish and stage in 2017 a referendum on EU membership (announced by David Cameron in January 2013).

The concept of 'transfer' of powers, on the other hand, is accepted, if not by the courts of the member states, then at least by the European Court of Justice (ECJ), which has in several cases stated that the transfer of powers to the EU by the member states is irreversible. In *Costa* v. *ENEL* (Case 6/64, *Costa* v. *ENEL* [1964] ECR 585) the ECJ stated that:

> By creating a Community of unlimited duration, having its own institutions, its own personality, its own legal capacity and capacity of representation on the international plane and, more particularly, real powers stemming from a limitation of sovereignty or a transfer of powers from the States to Community, the Member States have limited their sovereign rights and have thus created a body of law which binds both their nationals and themselves. The transfer by the States from their domestic legal system to the Community legal system of the rights and obligations arising under the Treaty carries with it a permanent limitation of their sovereign rights.

As we will see below, the fact that an exit clause was introduced in the Lisbon Treaty indirectly confirms the validity of the proposition that such a right did not exist under Community law and that nothing short of a treaty agreement between the member states could bring it into being. On the other hand, as Hill (1982: 356) has observed, as a practical matter, if a member state were determined to withdraw, the EU has no sanctions that can be applied to compel lawful compliance with the Treaty. Thus, from this point of view, it really is of no consequence whether a legal right of withdrawal exists. In the same vein, referring to withdrawal from EMU and the possible deterrent effect of the Vienna Convention, other commentators have noted that a country contemplating withdrawing from EMU is not likely to be deterred by the Vienna Convention, nor would there be an effective enforcement mechanism to compel adherence to the Convention if a country was determined to withdraw (Scott, 1998: 214).

4.3.3.2 After Lisbon

The position regarding withdrawal from the EU has altered after the passing of the Lisbon Treaty which entered into force on 1 December 2009. Article 50 of the Lisbon Treaty explicitly makes provision for the voluntary secession of a member state from the EU. Specifically, the exit clause provides that a member state wishing to withdraw from the EU must inform the European Council of its intention; the Council is to produce guidelines on the basis of which a withdrawal agreement is to be negotiated with that member state; and the Council, acting by a qualified majority and after obtaining the consent of the European Parliament, will conclude the agreement on behalf of the EU. The withdrawing member state would cease to be bound by the treaties either from the date provided for in the withdrawal agreement or, failing that, two years after notification of its intention to withdraw.

On the basis of the above it appears that the right to withdraw from the Union introduced by the Lisbon Treaty is a genuinely unilateral right. The right to withdraw is not, for instance, preconditioned on adoption of a constitutional change that a member state cannot accept but exists independently. Athanassiou (2009: 24) also stresses that it is not the element of negotiation that would make a member state's withdrawal consensual (as opposed to unilateral), but the absence of restrictions on a member state's right to withdraw. This is perhaps because the exit clause represents recognition of a political reality. A sovereign member state cannot be coerced into honouring commitments it no longer has an interest in. If the UK, for instance, votes in a referendum to leave the EU, it would be nonsensical to require the manufacturing of an artificial excuse based on constitutional incompatibility to premise the right to leave on. However, and this is crucial for the purposes of our discussion in relation to the sovereign debt crisis, the exit clause in the Lisbon Treaty contains no special provisions on the requirements for the withdrawal of a member state which has adopted the euro. It is for this reason that we needed to consider above the position regarding withdrawal as a general matter in EU law before considering the Lisbon amendment. To return to the central reason for this discussion, the possibility of a Grexit, we can ask whether a state that is part of the EMU would be able to leave the Eurozone while remaining in the EU.

4.3.3.3 Leaving the EMU

The German Chancellor Angela Merkel said before the Bundestag in July 2011 that 'the euro is much, much more than a currency … the euro is the guarantee of a united Europe. If the euro fails, then Europe fails' (Mayer, 2011). One interpretation of the Lisbon withdrawal right is that withdrawal from EMU without a parallel withdrawal from the EU would be legally inconceivable. Unlike EU participation, EMU participation is a legal obligation for all its member states from the point of entry onwards. While a member state may be free to denounce its EU participation and repudiate its treaty obligations in their entirety, it would not be free to go back on its decision to join EMU without breaching a binding obligation under the EC Treaty, unless it were also to withdraw from the EU. Consequently, it seems the only way to withdraw from EMU is to withdraw from the EU using Article 50 of the Treaty and then try to rejoin the EU, but asking not to re-enter into the monetary union. The alternative would of course be to negotiate a EMU exit with the other member states, but this is not realistic considering the long negotiations it would entail and the need for ratification by all member states to any treaty amendment. Perhaps as a matter of urgency, a unanimous agreement by the European Council leading to the issue of a European regulation could be sufficient, despite the legal uncertainty that this could entail (Dor, 2011). The problem with this solution, however, is not so much theoretical, but practical. In the current political and international environment a speedy decision by all member states to any EU wide change, especially one allowing one of the Eurozone members to leave, is difficult to conceive.

Indeed, it could be argued that a genuinely unilateral right of withdrawal would be unthinkable in the context of EMU due to the incompatibility with the language of EU Treaty provisions and Protocol 24 on the Transition to the Third Stage of Monetary Union. It is difficult to envisage an agreement to withdraw in the face of the references in the legal instruments to the 'irrevocability' of the substitution by the euro of the currencies of the participating member states and to the 'irreversibility' of the monetary union process (Athanassiou, 2009: 28). Perhaps an exit from EMU was never properly theorised because of the complex network of rights and obligations that EMU entails for its participating member states and their central banks, which cannot easily (never mind automatically) be resolved through a withdrawal. We are left with the result therefore that only an agreed exit from the euro area is possible, yet in practical terms extremely unlikely for reasons already mentioned. EMU is a subset of the EU, which is why the Statute of the European System of Central Banks and of the European Central Bank – lying at the heart of the ESCB and the euro-system – is annexed as a Protocol to the EC Treaty. While after Lisbon the possibility of unilateral withdrawal from the EU also implicitly recognises the possibility of unilateral withdrawal from a subset of the EU (namely EMU), we cannot in conclusion argue that the European institutional framework can accommodate the secession of a member state from the Eurozone. This leads credence to the hypothesis posited in this chapter that the EU's institutional structures are inflexible and therefore deficient in the sense that they limit policy options, even when these options are necessary due to political or economic realities.

4.3.3.4 Expulsion from EU/EMU?

So far we have been discussing the feasibility of exit from the euro-system or the EU at the instigation of a member state battling a severe economic crisis (Greece) or has a change of heart about membership (for example the UK). There is another aspect of this discussion, however. What would be the institutional treatment of a member state that ceased to cooperate with

EU institutions to a degree that the other members wished to expel it from the Union or the Eurozone? There is no treaty provision at present for a member state to be expelled from the EU or EMU. The closest that Community law comes to recognising a right of expulsion is Article 7(2) and (3) TEU, allowing the Council to temporarily suspend some of a member state's rights (including its voting rights in the Council) for a 'serious and persistent breach by a Member State of the principles mentioned in Article 6(1)' of the EU Treaty (Athanassiou, 2009: 32). If a right to expel member states from the EU or EMU does not exist then, could such a right be asserted? Let us consider once more the current case of Greece. If the Greeks were to elect someone who proves less willing to deal with international lenders (the best candidate in the current political environment for this being Syriza) and reacts to a withdrawal of financial support by European institutions (and the subsequent economic collapse as money runs out) by introducing capital controls and other measures restricting freedom of movement for services, capital and people, we would have a situation where a member state is in breach of fundamental treaty obligations. We assume in this scenario that the Greek government seeks to remain in the Eurozone and the EU but does not wish to cooperate in implementing an austerity plan as a precondition to the re-commencement of assistance. Measures in violation of the treaties would in this case be borne out of necessity (dealing with the consequences of bankruptcy) rather than an act directed to provoke expulsion from the EU. If the EU moved to expel Greece regardless, this would then be done against the wishes of the Greeks to continue their membership of the EU. If then EU members (minus Greece) voted for a treaty amendment to expel Greece, they would fail as such action would necessarily entail an unauthorised treaty amendment, in breach of Article 48 TEU.

To make matters worse, any attempt to expel a member state would compound the complexities we discussed in relation to a state's voluntary withdrawal, because of the risk of legal challenges by disadvantaged natural persons, legal entities or even countries, objecting to the loss of the rights that they or their nationals may have acquired from membership of the EU (one could assert, on any reading of the treaties, a legitimate expectation of maintaining membership benefits in perpetuity). Participation in the European Union gives rise to a wide web of rights and obligations to citizens, companies and governments. To erase all those obligations at a stroke by expelling the member state would create huge confusion and (to select just a single example) would penalise ordinary citizens and businesses who rely on their rights of residence and free movement (Hansard, 1998). The position in summary is that the exhaustive list of sanctions provided for in the treaties does not include a right to withdraw 'in protest' against a fellow member state's failure to comply with its treaty obligations; the same is true of expulsion, which is not catered for in the treaties, however serious or repeated a member state's non-compliance may be and however much its departure may be desired by its partners (Athanassiou, 2009: 35).

The conclusion seems to be rather secure therefore that a member state cannot be expelled from the EU or the Eurozone. But if one cannot expel unwanted member states, can they be marginalised? One possibility would involve the extensive use by the errant member state's partners of the 'enhanced co-operation procedure', Article 20 of the TEU. If it were supplemented by additional measures including extra-EU treaties or other informal action, the enhanced cooperation procedure could represent a genuine alternative to the treaties' decision-making mechanisms, helping marginalise more 'minimalist', less 'integrationist' or otherwise 'uncooperative' member states. An alternative and somewhat more radical possibility would be for the mainstream member states to agree on a new, treaty-based partnership with an independent institutional structure outside the framework of the 'old EU' (effectively, a 'new Union') to be worked out, approved and ratified solely by the states participating in this new entity (Emmanouilidis, 2007: 4). Let us remember, however, that while the EU's institutional make-up does not allow for expulsions, EU institutions could make life for an intransigent member state impossible within the Union. Consider, for example, what we said above about what life would be like for Greece without continued financial support for its state finances and its banking system. Sovereign insolvency within the Eurozone is not a situation that can be maintained, as the suffering inflicted on the population would be unacceptable. If Greece, for example, were to go bankrupt in the absence of assistance, it would inevitably ask to leave the EMU utilising the mechanisms described above. Therefore anyone wishing to blackmail the Europeans to obtain improved terms for financial support better remember that the inability to expel a member state is no guarantee of economic survival within the euro-system. If any proof is needed of this point, one can look at the threat of the ECB to push Cyprus into a disorderly default by withdrawing liquidity support for Cypriot banks, unless the island were to accept an unprecedented haircut on the funds of all depositors as part of a rescue deal in March 2013 (Hope and Hadjipapas, 2013).

In concluding this discussion we should consider whether leaving the EU would mean an end to the use of the euro in the territory of the member state in question. While a member state's exit from the EU would entail its exit from the euro area, this does not necessarily mean that the euro as a currency could no longer circulate in its territory. Indeed, a distinction should be made between a member state's euro area participation, in an institutional sense, and the circulation of the euro in its territory (Athanassiou, 2009: 40). If Greece or another country were to introduce a new currency, a new drachma for example, and abandon the euro, this would continue to have value as a currency of other countries in the EMU. There is one main question, however: can the old contracts and debts in euros be automatically converted to the new currency (new drachma in this case) or will the receivers take payments only in euros seeing that it still exists? These matters become extremely difficult when it is forecast that the new national currency, as we noted earlier, would lose value quickly compared to the euro. Indeed, the borrowers would prefer to re-denominate debts in the new currency, while the lenders would demand to keep them in euros (Dor, 2011: 4).

In the Nomura note we mentioned above (Nordvig and St-Arnaud, 2011), the bank addressed the unspeakable: the consequences of a Eurozone break-up. The authors noted that even though there is no well-defined legal path towards Eurozone and EU exit, the recent political reality has demonstrated that the lack of legal framework for an exit/break-up is unlikely to preclude the possibility (Nordvig and St-Arnaud, 2011: 2). During its 2011 national congress Merkel's Christian Democratic Union party voted to allow Eurozone states to quit the currency area. Finance Minister Wolfgang Schaeuble said that the intention was not to kick any member state out of the Eurozone, 'but if a country can't carry the burden or doesn't want to carry the burden, and the Greek people have to carry a heavy load, then we have to respect the country's decision' (Parkin and Czuczka, 2011). While none of this changes EU rules or has the force of law, it is still indicative of trends in Europe. Nevertheless, whatever the trend may be the legal framework shows no obvious route out of the Eurozone. The only technically secure way to leave the Eurozone seems to be via unanimous agreement to treaty changes at the EU level, something logistically and politically challenging. The Greeks cannot choose to leave unilaterally, nor can their partners choose to expel them from the Eurozone. For Greece to leave, both the Greeks and their partners need to wish to terminate the relationship. Even then, the legal and institutional barriers remain significant.

4.4 Conclusion

This chapter has presented the key aspects of the crisis that demonstrate the need for law to regain its role as the link between the popular will and the organisation of the economy. We should heed perhaps the message of Minsky's work and use law as a buffer against market overconfidence, as a firewall preventing the evolution of finance into ever riskier forms. The dual crises we have presented here, the crisis in the financial markets and the European sovereign debt crisis, make re-empowering citizens a necessary step in ensuring the survival of democratic politics and in helping societies find an acceptable and legitimate way out of economic crises. This chapter has devoted some time to discussing the European debt crisis and the Greek problem, both because the literature on this topic is inadequate and because Greece's troubles illustrate exactly the key themes of the book. When legal structures are built around the need to support markets, as opposed to them being a reflection of a popular consensus, dangers lurk. In 2008 I wrote a paper entitled 'Neoliberal law: unintended consequences of market-friendly law reforms' (Glinavos, 2008). The main point made in that paper was that well intentioned policies can have significant adverse consequences on popular perceptions of legitimacy. A point at hand is the warped evolution of political and legal institutions in former soviet republics. This chapter has shown that the sclerotic structures of the EU threaten political disintegration and social conflict as they fail to envisage changes of speed or direction in the process of integration.

The discussion of a right to withdraw from the EU or the EMU therefore highlights where the dangers come from: de-politicisation. Once again we are faced with institutional structures created with the paternalist wish to shape a better future (be it for Europe or market development) that, when faced with crisis, end up harming the objectives they were built to promote. Lacking the ability to change speed to accommodate political sea changes in Europe, institutions like the EMU threaten political and economic chaos. Institutional structures that prioritise the interests of investors and foreign lenders (as mentioned earlier) proclaim the superiority of market mechanisms in the distribution of benefits and costs of economic activities, creating the risk that policy-making becomes disconnected from the popular will. Are we wrong to talk about this? Is it just scaremongering that plays into the hands of those who wish to withdraw from the EU for their own ideological agendas? Whatever the use someone may make of this information, the truth is that the problem exists, that political tensions that cannot find expression through the democratic process can break outside the frameworks of legality. To repeat a concern raised earlier in the book, do we wish to see a neo-fascist party (Golden Dawn for instance) gain power in Greece before we realise that there are worse alternatives to changing speeds in the European locomotive?

This chapter posed the questions why do states fail to stop crises from happening and why do policy-makers watch as disasters unfold despite allegedly having both the tools and the expertise to react in time? Perhaps the answer lies in the realisation that decades of pro-market reforms have in fact handicapped states, denying them the tools to react to crises, when the reaction needs to take a less market friendly character. The constitutionalisation of market-friendliness appears to have outlawed in many states the ability to say no to a neoliberal orthodoxy that demands 'scientific' solutions. I really do not believe that the IMF seeks to harm the countries it 'assists'. Neither do I think the German government enjoys the mayhem austerity is creating in Greece. As was mentioned earlier, conspiracy theories fail to capture the extent of the problem. What I do believe, however, is that we have spent decades building a monument to liberalism that now defines our institutions and policy responses. This monument seems to be able to continue to dictate solutions even when their result will probably be painful to all. Legal frameworks built to be market facilitating and predictable become inefficient, unpredictable and, crucially, undemocratic. Does the inflexibility that comes from the 'permanent' nature of EU structures threaten a 'doomsday' for European democracy? Our inability to discuss these issues openly adds insult to injury. Is it not better to reform EU structures now, to allow for options, rather than waiting for events to overtake our carefully constructed boundaries of legal and 'logical' solutions? To reiterate a point often made in this work, market friendly policies often deny policy options when they are most needed. This is a time when policy options are very much needed.

The final part of the book will discuss what options for a better future are being explored in reforms to counter the crisis on both sides of the Atlantic (Chapter 5). An evaluation of the thinking motivating post-crisis policies will then allow a reflection on the future of the state–market relationship in Chapter 6.

Part 3

Futures

This book has progressed from setting the methodological bases for an investigation of the market–state relationship and a discussion on the purpose of law in financialised capitalism in Part 1, to a reflection on the different balance points between market freedoms and state control, including a presentation of the challenges presented by the current crisis in Part 2, to the point that we can reach some conclusions and perhaps glimpse possible futures for the nature of the political economy of capitalist states in this Part 3. This final part of the book begins with Chapter 5 by offering a presentation of some illustrative policy responses to the financial crisis. The analysis takes us from Europe to the US in an effort to discern patterns in policy-making that may or may not suggest an ideological and cultural shift from the norms of pre-crisis liberalism. Particular attention is paid in this discussion to the topic of executive remuneration and efforts to control it, on both sides of the Atlantic. Chapter 6 then takes the lessons learned from the book thus far and explores the consequences adjudication mechanisms can have on the evolution of norms and their impacts on state policy discretion. We ask in Chapter 6 whether the challenges of the crisis could lead to an opposite suggestion to the one suggested in this book: a retreat from law, rather than a strengthening and redefinition of the role of law. This critical view of the messages of the book allows us to conclude this discussion by defending the book's thesis against two key challenges: the concern that greater discretion in policy-making is dangerous as the political classes are incapable of assuming the role envisaged by a reversal of de-politicisation; and a wider concern about the necessity of preserving capitalism. These concluding reflections bring the discussion in the book back into contact with the theoretical analysis we started off with in Part 1: a discussion as to the nature and purpose of law and the consequences of de-politicisation.

5 Responses to the credit crunch

Accepting the de-politicised nature of markets means that we cannot use our democratic structures to define what are social goods.

5.1 Introduction

The previous chapter presented the evolution of the crisis, from a crisis of the financial markets to a crisis of sovereign debt. In the process, Chapter 4 demonstrated how institutional inadequacies in the US financial markets, in the global banking system and in the structures of the EU have worked as a series of magnifying lenses that helped feed the fire that started in the residential sub-prime mortgage market in the US in 2007. The chapter also reflected on the transmission mechanisms through which the crisis spread, and considered the role of legal frameworks as conduits through which the crisis became embedded and progressively larger. In order to get a complete picture of the severity and evolution of the crisis, however, and also in order to appreciate the role of policy- and law-making in these processes, we need to address some key illustrations of remedial responses, at the national and international level. This chapter therefore aims to present a short selection of key examples of regulatory responses and use those to delve into the mindset and priorities of law-makers. The chapter aims to examine whether we see a change of tone and direction in post-crisis reforms that suggests a boundary is being revealed separating pre- and post-crisis thinking. Will we discover a continuum that seems to treat the Great Recession like a normal incidence of market disequilibrium that does not require anything radical as a response? We have spent a lot of time in this book already pointing out the ideological backgrounds to many allegedly 'technically competent' solutions to problems of economic governance; addressing some of the key responses to the challenges brought forward by the crisis will allow us to complete our investigation of the political nature of building regulatory regimes.

5.2 Regulatory wish-list

Initial regulatory responses to the credit crunch seemed to share, on the level of rhetoric at least, the rationale behind the post-1929 changes. There seemed to be an expectation that governments would use law as a shield against future collapses. A couple of years after the onset of the crisis, a series of priority issues had already emerged. One issue that became prominent was the use of tax havens as strongholds of finance beyond regulatory reach; diminishing their size and operations was a constant theme of G20 meetings. Also, foremost on the political agenda was an effort to create at an international level safeguards against repeats of the financial calamity of 2008. That meant that emerging regulation would aim to forestall conditions that gave rise to the excessive and irresponsible lending that led to the credit crunch. In this environment a rapid theoretical shift appeared to be taking place, as happened with the Roosevelt administration, away from market-led solutions and laissez-faire (Glinavos, 2010b). As the shock of the collapse in the autumn of 2008 faded, however, and developed economies prepared for a prolonged recession, public pronouncements in favour of concentrated changes to the way capitalism operates receded. While it was generally recognised that the financial crisis was caused by excessive borrowing, excessive lending and excessive investment incentivised by a series of significant economic and regulatory factors, it was not immediately evident how regulatory frameworks ought to change. Undoubtedly the systemic financial crisis in 2008 highlighted the need for significant changes in both domestic and global financial regulation to prevent future systemic financial crises (Arner, 2009: 8) and was interpreted as an opportunity to improve regulation and supervision. But which direction should regulatory reform take? For example, was this the time for the abandonment of voluntary codes, self-regulation and soft law in favour of 'harder' provisions? Maybe being cautious and doing nothing was the best solution?

Even in 2009, slowly but definitely, a chorus against mandatory law-based re-regulation was emerging. For example, the Organisation for Economic Cooperation and Development (OECD) argued that the financial crisis has shown the need to strengthen financial market regulation, while, however, resisting any temptation to revert to a too conservative banking system (Furceri and Mourougane, 2009: 41). The tendency was thus to address this crisis not by rethinking the purposes and reach of state power, but through the formal market-enhancing institutions of banking. But what about the place of finance in modern capitalism and the role of law as a break to corporate excess? By adopting, once again, the language of economic orthodoxy (efficiency, proportionality, engagement) emerging responses to the crisis ran the risk of failing to address the underlying social relations of power that shape changes to economic institutions (Marois, 2011). As Gerard Greenfeld argues (Panitch and Leys, 2004), there is a need to move beyond institutions and policy to examine underlying power relations and structures. The commitments made by world leaders in that seminal G20 meeting in London in the April of 2009 (to take whatever action is necessary to stabilise financial markets and enable families and businesses to get through the recession; to reform and strengthen the global financial and economic system; to restore confidence and trust; to put the global economy on track for sustainable growth) were intended to rescue global capitalism and the place of finance therein and did not constitute a radical rethink of the state–market relationship akin to the one represented by the New Deal in the 1930s.

What was the content of these 'non-radical' proposals? Principles aimed at reform of the global banking system agreed in the 2009 London G20 summit included bringing the shadow banking system, including hedge funds, within the global regulatory net, new international accounting standards, the regulation of credit rating agencies and a commitment to end tax havens that do not transfer information on request. The summit communiqué stated that strengthened regulation and supervision must promote propriety, integrity and transparency, guard against risk across the financial system, dampen rather than amplify the financial and economic cycle, reduce reliance on inappropriately risky sources of financing and discourage excessive risk-taking. Regulators and supervisors, it claimed, must protect consumers and investors, support market discipline, avoid adverse impacts on other countries, reduce the scope for regulatory arbitrage, support competition and dynamism, and keep pace with innovation in the marketplace (Glinavos, 2010b). How would all this be achieved? It was clear that more regulation was to be expected, at least to the extent that regulation and oversight would extend to all systemically important financial institutions, instruments and markets, including, for the first time, systemically important hedge funds. Also, some regulation over levels of pay was forthcoming and indeed endorsed via the Financial Stability Forum's (FSF) new principles on pay and compensation (Financial Stability Board, 2009). These principles were meant to be implemented by firms and would be reinforced through supervisory examination and intervention at the national level. Authorities working with the FSF were meant to ensure coordination and consistency of approach across jurisdictions. The principles were intended to reduce incentives towards excessive risk-taking that may arise from the structure of compensation schemes; they were not intended, however, to prescribe particular designs or levels of individual compensation.

We have branded the above as 'non-radical'. What would 'radical' look like and why should it be so? The problem with G20 pronouncements and specific initiatives like that of the FSF is that they seek to repair 'market imperfections' without altering market structures. As this book aims to show, altering market structures involves rethinking the relationship between the state and the market and the role of law as a constraint on market activity (as opposed to a facilitator of said activity). The rest of this chapter helps to highlight the deficiencies of this approach and the final Chapter 6 reflects on proposals for perhaps more 'radical' alternatives.

Let us take the example of the aforementioned FSF principles. While the principles aimed to prevent compensation packages that encourage dangerous risk-taking, they were not intended to address inequalities in compensation within and between firms and were not concerned about distributing corporate gains more equitably between employees. This is a small indication that responses to the causes of the credit crunch deal with making the existing system more efficient and stable, instead of addressing wider concerns touching on the legitimacy and equality effects of financial capitalism (Glinavos, 2010b). Perhaps more ominously, the 2009 G20 also agreed on the importance of resisting protectionism and promoting global trade and investment, arguing in favour of reinvigorating world trade and investment. The summit communiqué (London G20 Summit, 2009) explicitly mentioned that the world will not repeat the historic mistakes of protectionism of previous eras. Within a continuing system of openness for trade and capital, the role of the IMF would be crucial in the effort to restore growth by revising conditionality for its loans. We saw in the previous chapter how helpful IMF conditionality has been when dealing with the European debt crisis. Protecting, promoting and relying on markets somehow survived the best example to date of market failure. The desire of the governments of the developed world to resist nationalisation, even when large financial institutions failed spectacularly and had to be rescued with public money, suggests that the trend towards private sector solutions was not seriously undermined by the rhetorical embrace of better regulation. The unfortunate consequence, however, of using the public purse in supporting the private sector, while allowing the private sector to reap the benefits where they occur, is that we find ourselves in a situation where losses are socialised while gains remain private, otherwise known in the words of Gore Vidal as 'socialism for the rich and capitalism for the poor' (Reich, 2008).

Overall, initial regulatory responses in the UK and the United States following the credit crunch as well as the declarations of the G20 failed to give a clear picture regarding a shift away from the market-liberalising imperatives of the last two decades. Yes, regulation is meant to reach more areas of market activity. Yes, international financial institutions are meant to have regard to the social consequences of their actions. Yes, social responsiveness, sustainable development and legitimacy are buzzwords in policy communiqués. Did this suggest a return of the state as the centre of regulation? Did it signal an abandonment of the divide between politics and economics so carefully constructed during the de-politicisation decade of the 1990s and the 'independent institutions' era that began in the new century? The next section examines regulatory reforms in Europe and the US for evidence of a change in policy imperatives.

5.3 Regulatory reform initiatives in Europe

Once the dust from the initial financial shock started to settle, the European Union embarked on a major programme of institutional redesign, churning out new agencies to head a multitude of reform projects and to perform a series of reconceptualised regulatory tasks. This brought to the fore the usual tension between federal and national regulators and arguably risks attenuating the problems of political legitimacy that have plagued the EU for decades. While everyone can acknowledge the need to regulate and coordinate better, the problem of the democratic deficit of European supranational bodies is not likely to disappear on its own. The key underlying question in relation to European-wide reforms is why and how can sovereign powers over economic organisation be handed over to supra-national bodies? Is it correct to assume that what is supposedly more economically efficient is automatically politically acceptable? This section focuses on European reforms and seeks to reveal the rationale behind new policies by examining firstly the enhancement of 'independent' institutions tasked with determining economic governance, and secondly by using efforts to control remuneration for top executives as a proxy for Europe's understanding of equity vis-à-vis market operations.

We discussed in Chapter 2 the provenance of the idea of central bank independence and we saw in Chapter 3 how institutional independence was a key component of the neoliberal interpretation of the state–market relationship. Consistent with this intellectual tradition, one of the key responses to the challenges raised by the financial crisis has been the bolstering of the regulatory roles of independent central banks. The expansion of the role of the Federal Reserve in the US, the ECB and of the Bank of England are central examples. Indeed, a number of commentators have argued that central banks lacked the tools to intervene effectively in curbing the abuses that led to the crisis. In one sense therefore, enhancing the role of the banks is a sensible response to the crisis from an economist's point of view. In our discussion of the idea that politically independent central banks should have a central role in determining monetary policy, we concluded that it is a mistake to view the crisis as a legal/technical challenge. It was proposed that the crisis is, at its core, the result of de-politicisation and of the expanding domination of technical/orthodox economic views on policy-making. A response to the crisis that enhances de-politicising economic governance risks therefore heightening the disconnect between policy formation and public accountability. One of the themes of this book is indeed the suggestion that strengthening the barriers between regulation and the political process may have the unintended consequence of undermining (even in developed countries) a social consensus that continues to favour pro-market policies. In the previous Chapter 4 we saw how Greece serves as an example of an extreme situation where the distancing of economic priorities from political legitimacy is causing social disintegration and contributes to a deteriorating economic outlook.

The view of this book is that the de-politicisation of economic decision-making carries risks and may well endanger the future of democracy. This is far from a mainstream view. In fact, not only are the majority of commentators horrified at the prospect of more political input in economic decision-making, but they view the very expansion of regulation (regardless of whether the regulators are independent or not) as a threat to the proper functioning of free markets. Moloney (2010: 1344–5), for example, notes that a significant intensification of the wider EU rule book can lead to an increase in governance risks. For example, the evolution of European supervisory agencies, like the European Securities and Markets Authority and the European Banking Authority, presents an uneasy fit within the EU's traditional legitimacy and accountability structures. The agencies' direct decision-making powers over individual actors, particularly with respect to operational supervision and their related ability to make decisions binding on market actors and on national supervisory authorities, is likely to augment the considerable accountability, legitimacy, independence and constitutional problems which supranational agencies already raise in Europe. This concern is heightened due to the impression that the new institutional structure is empowered and incentivised to produce a massive rule book (Moloney, 2010: 1355–6). The new institutional architecture for law-making makes it more likely, it is alleged, that regulatory interventions become the subject of detailed and potentially error-prone and costly rules. The expansion of regulatory authority is a concern therefore for those who fear the 'politicisation' of regulation. There are plenty examples of this regulatory overreach indicated in the literature, most prominent being moves at various points during the crisis towards a prohibition on 'naked' short sales and transactions in CDSs related to sovereign debt which demonstrate a strong political steer from France and Germany, reflecting in part local political interests as well as a concern to protect the euro sovereign debt markets from speculation.

How do we resolve this paradox? How can we argue for more state intervention in the form of expanding regulatory frameworks and yet deny political input and distrust the motives of regulators? Here of course we have a contemporary illustration of the tension between a public interest view of regulation as opposed to a capture view of regulation as we discussed in Chapter 1, but what are we left with and where do such discussions on regulatory reform finally take us? Can it be that after noting the need for regulation and the necessity of reform, we return to a distrust of the capacity of regulators to perform the task? The scale of the regulatory task also suggests that room should be made for a range of disciplining tools, including market discipline, we are told. The chorus of opinions endlessly repeats that reform should be 'mindful of the usefulness of self-regulation by the private sector' (De Larosiere, 2009: 15). In a conference on Regulation and Corporate Governance in Cambridge in September 2012, I sat through a number of paper presentations all detailing the vastness of the regulatory task and reaffirming the need to avoid over-regulation. The mantra that self-regulation and voluntary codes offer the necessary flexibility to allow for economic recovery was repeated by almost all speakers. Few, however, spoke of democratic legitimacy and the need to link a democratic vision of economic governance with our regulatory frameworks. The question has to be asked again: are we so distrustful of democracy and so cynical about the ability of the people to influence economic governance that we prefer the decisions of lofty technocrats? Do we prefer a dictatorship of finance or the paternalism of those 'in the know', rather than the democratically expressed will of our compatriots?

Everyone seems to be wondering: despite the crisis, the failures, the hubris, isn't after all self-regulation the most appropriate way to deal with corporate behaviour? According to some observers of the European scene, a move to more intensive regulation suggests that market discipline is being pushed to the back of the EU's toolbox. Soft law has been largely eschewed, it is claimed, even in the corporate governance sphere, where the merits of a uniform approach are highly contested (Moloney, 2010: 1357–8). These arguments presuppose a conflation of the notions of regulation and politicisation. However, what is wrong with politicisation if politics channel the popular will? Why should market regulation be apolitical, and isn't this a way of avoiding a discussion with regard to the direction of regulation? Does apolitical mean market-friendly, while political means anti-liberal or anti-capitalist? A good example to use in exploring whether regulatory intervention equals politicisation is the EU's treatment of the issue of executive pay which has allegedly evolved to an increasingly interventionist logic. It is to this that we turn in the next part of our discussion.

5.4 The issue of compensation

In our discussion of the ethics of regulation in Chapter 1 we presented reactions to proposals for the regulation of executive compensation as an entry point to the mindset of capitalists in contemporary finance. Executive compensation has become a headline topic in the wake of the financial crisis. One can easily see how the continuation of high rewards in the financial industry, especially bonuses, seems out of line with austerity and contraction in the rest of the economy. Things become especially heated when commentators make the connection between the havoc wreaked by the financial industry on the wider economy, and the ability of its executives to continue to reap rewards, many of which are now at the cost of taxpayers. We saw an aspect of this discussion when we used the topic of bonuses to investigate the banker's impression of their entitlement to wealth as a legally valid and, furthermore, ethical stance. The issue of compensation is one that we can use further, to test the claim made earlier in this chapter that politics, via regulation, is encroaching on ground formerly held by the market. What a change that would make indeed. One may even risk Armageddon, we are told.

David Willetts, at the time of writing the UK Minister for Universities and Science, stated (O'Keeffe, 2004: 18) in 2004:

> If you really want to experience a vicious Hobbesian war of all against all, then look to a non-market economy where resources are wasted, where power and influence are all that matters, and where a contract cannot be trusted. What a contrast with the openness, the scope for personal fulfilment, and the sheer diversity of a modern market economy.

What a contrast indeed with a market where banks squandered the wealth of nations for the personal enrichment of their executives, where bonuses were paid to reward massive losses, and where diversity suggested a jungle of financial products designed to deceive customers, mislead regulators and undermine competitors. At the same time, one needs to acknowledge that Willetts was introducing a volume published by the most unashamedly neoliberal think tank in England, the Institute of Economic Affairs (Perry-Kessaris, 2012). If the invective above sounds too extreme, let's adopt the language used by EU regulators who found that excessive and imprudent risk-taking in the banking sector has led to the failure of individual financial institutions and systemic problems in member states and globally. While the causes of such risk-taking are many and complex, there is agreement by supervisors and regulatory bodies, including the G20 and the Committee of European Banking Supervisors (CEBS), that the inappropriate remuneration structures of some financial institutions have been a contributory factor. Remuneration policies which give incentives to take risks that exceed the general level of risk tolerated by the institution can undermine sound and effective risk management and exacerbate excessive risk-taking behaviour (Recital 1, Capital Requirements Directive (CRD) III).

The way English law deals with issues of compensation for company directors owes a lot to the 1995 Greenbury Report. This report (now incorporated into the UK Corporate Governance Code) provided a code of conduct for determining remuneration and recommended the creation of committees consisting solely of non-executive directors which would be tasked with determining issues of pay within firms. The *raison d'être* of the remuneration committee is transparency in rewarding senior executives. Such committees routinely hire consultants to achieve the right mix of incentives to attract executives in what is allegedly a highly mobile international market. The way compensation is structured is meant to enhance the commitment of executives to the long-term performance of the firm. This is, for instance, why share-option packages are used to give the director in question a 'stake' in the firm's performance (to the extent that share price can be taken as a proxy for success).

Like in England, in many jurisdictions there is a requirement that the company's annual report contains a statement of remuneration policy and offers details about the compensation package of its directors (Tricker, 2012: 323). Since 2003, companies quoted on the London Stock Exchange have needed to publish a directors' remuneration report and put it to shareholder vote at the annual general meeting. Since 2002 in fact, shareholders in British companies have had the opportunity to pass non-binding votes on directors' pay. Similarly in the US, SEC rules since 2007 have required the full disclosure of pay packages of top managers. All this, however, did not prevent a link being made as we saw above between excessive compensation and the financial instability that we have experienced since 2008. If the bonus culture is such a dangerous offspring of deregulated capitalism, what has been done about it post crisis? In order to assist us in answering this question, the following section discusses one of the main regulatory initiatives at the EU level aimed at dealing with the issue of incentives in the financial sector, the CEBS Guidelines issued in December 2010.

The CEBS was part of the Lamfalussy (3L3) structures for law-making and supervisory coordination. These included the network-based committees of local supervisors: CESR (securities markets), CEBS (banking), and CEIOPS (insurance and occupational pensions). The latest Capital Requirements Directive (CRD III) required the CEBS to issue guidelines on sound remuneration policies which comply with the remuneration principles included in the amended Annex V of CRD III. This reform of supervisory structures in the EU based on the Lamfalussy recommendations was completed with the creation of four new actors (Regulation (EC) No. 1093/2010): the European Systemic Risk Board, which will be concerned with monitoring macro-prudential, or system-wide, risk and with early warnings; and three new European supervisory authorities, the European Banking Authority (EBA), which takes over the role of the CEBS, the European Securities and Markets Authority (ESMA) and the European Insurance and Occupational Pensions Authority (EIOPA), together called the European Supervisory Authorities (ESAs) (Moloney, 2010: 1332) The ESAs became operational on 1 January 2011.

For details on the CEBS recommendations see Perry-Kessaris (2012: ch. 14), but keep in mind that within all the detail of these and similar measures, it is easy to forget what the objective of intervention was to begin with. Recital 4 CRD III, argues that intervention in compensation structures is justified because excessive and imprudent risk-taking may undermine the financial soundness of credit institutions or investment firms and destabilise the banking system. To avoid all this happening (again) it is important that new obligations concerning remuneration policies and practices should be implemented in a consistent manner and should cover all aspects of remuneration including salaries, discretionary pension benefits and any similar benefits. It is therefore appropriate to specify clear principles on sound compensation to ensure that the structure of remuneration does not encourage excessive risk-taking by individuals or moral hazard and is aligned with the risk appetite, values and long-term interests of the credit institution or investment firm in question. The principles should provide that the design of variable remuneration policies ensures that incentives are aligned with the long-term interests of the credit institution or investment firm and that payment methods strengthen its capital base. Performance-based components of remuneration should also help enhance fairness within the remuneration structures of the credit institution or investment firm. Remuneration, in other words, should be aligned with the role of the financial sector as the mechanism through which financial resources are efficiently allocated in the economy.

In April 2012 the EBA assessed the implementation of the CEBS guidelines, finding the progress of implementation satisfactory in the respective national legal and supervisory frameworks and suggesting that good progress has been reported by the industry with regard to the practices in the governance of remuneration. However, the EBA acknowledged that the scope of the guidelines is one of the areas for concern as considerable variations exist in the extent to which the remuneration requirements are applied beyond the scope of the CRD. Inconsistencies emerged with regard to the identification of risk-takers and there was concern that criteria used to identify staff that have a material impact on the firm's risk profile have not always proved to sufficiently grasp the risk impact aspect of the exercise. Further, the EBA's survey showed that risk alignment practices across the industry remain underdeveloped, namely with regard to the interaction of parameters used for risk management and the structure of bonus pools (EBA, 2012).

We mentioned above the importance of thinking about the effects of remuneration structures on economic efficiency. What, though, is the role of the financial sector in allocating resources efficiently in the economy? Why do European supervisors think that aligning the incentives of executives with their firm's long-term performance is their job? If it is social effects we are concerned about, why is it a good idea to try and influence them by tinkering with internal firm decision-making in issues such as compensation rather than via other means? With the push to complete the European rule book, there is little evidence of any attempt to identify the overarching principles which drive but might also contain the regime. A catalogue of core principles might have made little sense pre-crisis, but the consensus behind a single rule book, coupled with the increasing complexity of the institutional environment, suggests that EU law-making in this area should be subject to some, at least, of the traditional disciplines which apply to financial market law-making, including agreement on the priorities, however vaguely expressed, which a regulatory system should follow (Moloney, 2010: 1376). If the aim of regulating bonuses, for instance, is to punish financiers for their role in the crisis by removing their ability to make obscene amounts of money, why tinker with compensation structures and not simply tax them for earnings that exceed an agreed level of acceptability? If the aim is to make firm performance better, why is this the job of the regulator instead of a responsibility of shareholders? If the purpose is to reduce systemic instability by realigning objectives towards the long term, why leave it to subtle measures such as compensation incentives and not break up financial conglomerates?

For each and every justification of the guidelines, one can present a series of objections, not only along the lines of 'a free market should allow us to do what we want' that we saw uttered by executives in Chapter 1, but along the lines of 'the state can and should run this game'. Why tinker with indirect ways to achieve regulatory goals and not be upfront about the aims of intervention? Perhaps having an open discussion about regulatory aims can enhance the legitimacy of the regulatory product. For instance, where do the new European supervisors draw their legitimacy from? The distinction between input legitimacy and output legitimacy, which distinguishes between legitimacy based on representation and legitimacy based on the achievement of particular goals or outcomes (for example, in the European

Central Bank context, price stability), is a useful one in this context given the challenges posed by traditional representation. Can an output legitimacy model work in this case, given the difficulties in identifying the core objectives of the emerging EU regime (Moloney, 2010: 1378)? All this discussion may remind the reader of debates about the regulation of harmful substances. If we think that smoking, for example, is harmful, why do we regulate the sale, packaging, advertising and availability of tobacco? Why don't we just ban it, like we ban a score of other things that pose a similar or even lesser risk to health? If we think that our societies are being degraded and polluted by the hubris of bankers' excess, why don't we employ more powerful tools to effect change? Would the sky fall, as friends of the IEA claim?

The problem with an output legitimacy model, based on the orthodox premise that economic matters are for technocrats, is that perceptions of failure can destroy reforms for which there initially appears to be political support. Think of the condemnation of excessive bonuses that we have been discussing in this section. Regulatory bodies and politicians seem to agree that something needs to be done about executive compensation. If the rationale for this something is that bonuses were a cause of the crisis, how does one deal with data such as those presented by Fahlenbrach and Stulz (2011) which suggest otherwise? In their paper, the aforementioned researchers suggest that banks with CEOs whose incentives were better aligned with the interests of shareholders performed worse and find allegedly no evidence that they performed better. Banks with higher option compensation and a larger fraction of compensation in cash bonuses for their CEOs did not perform worse during the crisis either, according to this research. Bank CEOs did not reduce their holdings of shares in anticipation of the crisis or during the crisis, we are told, with the consequence that they suffered extremely large wealth losses in the wake of the crisis. If the justification for regulation is based on a 'market fix', correcting a market imperfection on the basis of public interest theories of regulation (like those we presented in the opening chapters of the book), reasons to intervene disappear if the market inefficiency is disproved.

However, if the rationale for intervening in compensation structures was one built on equality and the social effects of runaway capitalism, then a political consensus could deliver change without being held captive by the statisticians. Are we trying too hard to prove things perhaps? Daniel Miller in his excellent book *Consumption and Its Consequences* (2012: vii) says that he found that trying to prove something is usually what prevents us from managing to understand something. Let us ask the question again: why are we so bothered by rewards in the financial industry? The argument in this book is that we can only find out through our democratic processes, and once we have, we can use this knowledge to change our economy and by extension our society. In the concluding chapter of this book (Chapter 6) we will re-examine the ability of the democratic process to determine goals for economic governance, and we will evaluate the potential for causing an economic apocalypse if we were to do so. For the time being, however, we need to proceed with examining illustrative examples of regulatory changes brought about as a result of the crisis. We turn our attention in the following section to the United States and the famous Dodd-Frank Act.

5.5 Regulatory reform in the USA

In July of 2010 the US Congress enacted an extensive financial regulatory reform bill, named the Dodd-Frank Act. This legislation makes wide-ranging and significant changes to a number of aspects of financial services regulation in the United States and represents what many consider a more 'mature' legislative response to the issues raised by the financial crisis. In some respects this Act sets apart the reaction of the United States from that of Europe, where changes have been less wholesale, perhaps understandably considering the disorganising effects of the sovereign debt crisis that has plagued Europe since 2010. Against the harsh background of the financial crisis, the US Congress attempted to ensure that legislation included measures to improve systemic stability, improve policy options for coping with failing financial firms, increase transparency throughout financial markets, and protect consumers and investors. By the time of its final passage, the Dodd-Frank Act included provisions that affected virtually every financial market and amended existing or granted new authority and responsibility to nearly every federal financial regulatory agency in the US (Webel, 2010: 3).

The Dodd-Frank response to the financial crisis can be roughly broken down into three main themes. The first, and arguably the most important of these themes, represents measures taken to avoid future financial crises. The second theme revolves around the provision of improved tools to use in dealing more effectively with the next financial crisis, if and when it occurs. The third theme deals with a significant strengthening of consumer protection in the financial services industry (Cluchey, 2011: 5). The Act created a Financial Stability Oversight Council to oversee the stability of the United States financial system and important aspects of the financial services industry. It also provided substantial regulatory authority to the Board of Governors of the Federal Reserve to ensure the stability and survival of systemically important financial services companies. Banking regulation in the US was to a degree revamped by merging two formerly independent agencies (the Office of Thrift Supervision with the Office of the Comptroller of the Currency). The Act extends the reach of regulators over previously unregulated segments of the market, introducing for instance a new regulatory authority for the regulation of over-the-counter derivatives markets. There are also, for the first time, requirements that advisers to hedge funds register with and submit to regulation by the Securities and Exchange Commission, and that systemically important payment clearing and settlement utilities become subject to detailed regulation. There is expanded authority in the SEC to regulate credit rating agencies. The SEC also benefits from improvements in its management while changes are made to the securitisation process for asset-backed securities The Act further creates a Federal Office of Insurance in the Department of the Treasury to provide limited oversight of the US insurance industry. To a degree mirroring initiatives in Europe, the Act introduces a series of corporate governance reforms, especially relating to executive compensation and board oversight of compensation (Cluchey, 2011: 6).

5.5.1 Supervision

While for Europe it is safe to say that reform does not radically depart from pre-crisis orthodoxy (defined as the desire to maintain the separation between politics and economics), the same cannot be said with the same degree of confidence of the US. One could argue that the new regulatory umbrella group chaired by the Treasury Secretary – the Financial Stability Oversight Council – created by the Dodd-Frank Act with authority to designate certain financial firms as 'systemically significant' and subject them to increased prudential regulation, including limits on leverage, heightened capital standards and restrictions on certain forms of risky trading, allows political as well as technocratic oversight of the operations of the financial industry. The Council is tasked with seeking to identify risks to financial stability, promoting market discipline by eliminating expectations of a federal bailout, and responding to emerging threats to the stability of the financial system. Nevertheless, while the council is authorised to identify and advise regulators on sources of systemic risk and 'regulatory gap' problems, it has no rule-making, examination or enforcement powers of its own.

In order to consider the possible implications of the reform of financial architecture in the US on the American political economy, it is worth explaining in more detail the aims of the Financial Stability Oversight Council. The primary tool available to the Council to protect the financial stability of the United States is to require enhanced prudential supervision of systemically important bank holding companies and non-bank financial institutions by the Board of Governors of the Federal Reserve System (the Fed). In fact, bank holding companies with more than $50 billion in total assets are automatically subject to enhanced supervision by the Board of Governors. Non-bank financial institutions may be subject to the same degree of enhanced supervision upon a vote of two-thirds of the voting members of the Council, including the affirmative vote of the Secretary of the Treasury. The enhanced supervision of these companies can include heightened capital, leverage and liquidity requirements, as well as enhanced public disclosures and overall enhanced risk management. The Council has the responsibility to make recommendations on these heightened prudential standards to the Fed. Additionally, the Fed is given the authority, upon a two-thirds vote of the Council, to impose additional serious restrictions on the activities of those financial companies subject to enhanced supervision.

The Fed has the power to limit acquisitions, restrict products sold, terminate activities of the company, impose conditions on those activities or require a transfer of assets.

The extension of these powers to the Fed is intended to give it the power to mitigate the risk created by these companies to the financial system. In addition to the supervision of systemically important financial companies, the Council will have the general responsibility to monitor threats to the stability of the United States financial system and to respond to those threats. In performing this monitoring function, the Council will be aided by the new Office of Financial Research, established by Dodd-Frank. These powers have the potential to become a significant intrusion on the freedom of financial firms to structure themselves as they choose and to engage in commercial activities which they believe to be appropriate in the marketplace (Cluchey, 2011: 7). Such degree of oversight, coupled with the ability to intervene, arguably sets the US apart from Europe, where the disjoint in the powers of European and national regulators means that the ability to intervene is more compartmentalised and not very likely to be exercised in a consistent and forceful manner. Whether the appetite to intervene exists now or is likely to exist in the future on the part of the Governors is of course another question. Let us not forget that many of the excesses of the sub-prime mortgage market, for instance, went unchecked not due to the lack of legal authority but due to lax enforcement of existing rules by regulators.

Does the empowerment of the Fed, however, represent such a radical departure for US regulatory philosophy as it seems at first instance? It could be argued that the increase in powers for the Fed is exactly aimed at maintaining the appearance of independent regulation and to secure the firewall that separates political decision-making from economic governance. We have to ask ourselves whether enhancing the powers of the Fed (the US central bank), an institution with constitutionally guaranteed independence from the administration, suggests a break with the tradition of de-politicisation. After all, as we discussed in Chapter 2, placing monetary policy and regulatory functions under the control of independent central banks has been the hallmark of the neoliberal revamp of the state–market relationship. It may well be therefore that the creation of the Financial Stability Oversight Council and the new powers handed to the Fed by Dodd-Frank are something quite less than a severe challenge to the US political economy, and not so different in effect from the more technical (agency-based) changes at the EU level.

5.5.2 Crisis management

The second theme of the reforms we mentioned above (enhanced remedial measures for dealing with any new crisis) includes authority for the Fed to impose heightened prudential regulatory standards on systemically important financial institutions. The Act places in the Federal Deposit Insurance Corporation (the FDIC is an independent agency created by Congress to maintain stability and public confidence in the nation's financial system by insuring deposits, examining and supervising financial institutions for safety and soundness and consumer protection, and managing receiverships) new authority, similar to the authority it has over insured depository institutions, to conduct the orderly liquidation of failed financial services companies that pose a threat to the stability of the US financial system. However, the Act does not just add to the powers of existing authorities, but also includes limitations on some of the approaches that were used by regulatory authorities to combat the current financial crisis. These limitations include restrictions on the use of taxpayer funds to bail out troubled financial services institutions. This comes on top of new limits imposed on the Fed relating to emergency lending and emergency financial stabilisation. These limitations have very significant theoretical (and could have serious practical) consequences, as they seem to represent a reversal to contemporary wisdom on the combating of financial calamities. As became evident in 2008, financial safety nets can help protect troubled banks and other financial institutions from default and eventual collapse. In response to bank runs in the Great Depression, the US Congress had enacted section 13(3) of the Federal Reserve Act, empowering the Fed to act as a lender of last resort in 'unusual and exigent circumstances' to banks and other non-bank financial institutions. The Fed used section 13(3) to bail out huge financial institutions, like AIG, at (at least initial) taxpayer expense at the early stages of the financial crisis (Schwarcz, 2011: 10). There is concern therefore whether statutorily defined limits to bailouts are a sensible curb on policy discretion at times of crisis, especially considering the continued fragility of economic recovery in 2013.

The limitations on bailouts contained in the new US legislation bring to mind debates in Europe on the desirability of constitutionally set government debt limits (often known as a 'Schuldenbremse' or balanced budget amendment in the constitution). Germany and France proposed in early 2011 the introduction of debt-limitation rules in national constitutions to deal with the problem of state indebtedness in the Eurozone. If adopted such measures would force countries to amend their constitutions to forbid public deficits exceeding a certain percentage of GDP, similar to Germany's 'debt break', which limits any new borrowing to 0.35 per cent of GDP from 2016. France at the time said that it would introduce its own debt break, which Paris described as a 'golden rule'. Such debt breaks are commonly found in federal states and aim to prevent the indebtedness of regional governments from unbalancing the fiscal position of the whole country. This discussion in 2011 presaged arguments for the deployment of other mechanisms common to federal structures like EU-wide bank deposit insurance and Union banking regulation (ideas very present in policy debates in 2013). One could view these debates as another lurch of the European locomotive towards greater integration (without any of that messy democratic consultation). One wonders, however, whether preventing borrowing is masking the symptoms rather than attempting to cure the disease itself.

The idea of legal limits on policy discretion, be it limits on financial assistance (bailouts) or limits on a sovereign's ability to borrow, is illustrative of the survival of the idea that policy discretion ought to be strictly limited in issues of economic governance. In turn, the perseverance of such attitudes shows that the crisis has not effectively displaced the base-line common sense that operated prior to 2007 built around the de-politicisation of economic decision-making. Economic orthodoxy seeks to constrain the state's ability to intervene in market processes even when the intervention is meant to assist the market (perhaps in order to prevent it from total collapse). We find ourselves therefore in the perverse situation that politically motivated decision-making is so distrusted that even when the intervention is necessary, logical and politically justified, it is still resisted on theoretical grounds. While there is questionable logic in denying bailouts for systemically important institutions at times of acute crisis or for prohibiting state borrowing when the collapse of state services wreaks social havoc, there is a beautiful theoretical symmetry to the unhindered and unassisted market that proves irresistible to market fundamentalists. In testament to the power of market enthusiasts, even in regulatory interventions that aim to change the rules of the game, as in Dodd-Frank, we see more than a few remnants of pre-crisis ideology.

5.5.3 Consumer protection

The third theme of the Dodd-Frank Act is, as we mentioned above, consumer protection. A new Bureau of Consumer Financial Protection is created within the Federal Reserve System with substantial powers to oversee the sale and marketing of covered financial services to consumers. There are provisions designed, for instance, to provide alternatives to abusive pay-day loans. We came across the pay-day loans industry in Chapter 3 when we discussed the evolution of prohibitions on usury from biblical times to the bright new age of the Internet and 4,214 per cent representative APR. The two key provisions of the Act in this area are new rule-making and enforcement powers over pay-day lending (granted to the new Bureau of Consumer Financial Protection) and funding and support for developing low-cost pay-day alternatives as well as providing financial literacy education. The Act also contains provisions improving the protection of investors in securities markets and increasing regulatory enforcement options and remedies for violations of the securities laws. Finally, there is a new set of reforms to the mortgage process intended to make appropriate mortgages more readily available and transparent to consumers.

The educational part of these provisions is of particular interest in allowing us to discover the rationale behind changes to regulatory structures post crisis. Regulators (Hogarth, 2006) believe that data hint at positive relationships between financial education and community involvement and give some hope that financial education programmes really are making a difference in communities. As was aptly put by the *Washington Post* (Singletary, 2012) in the lead-up to the crisis, the bankers did some awful things, but individuals have to ultimately take personal responsibility for their financial decisions. President Obama is quoted in the paper as saying:

> As we recover from the worst economic crisis in generations, it is more important than ever to be knowledgeable about the consequences of our financial decisions... The financial crisis was fueled by a lack of responsibility from Wall Street to Washington. It devastated ordinary Americans, many of whom were caught by hidden fees and penalties or saddled with loans they could not afford. Preventing a recurrence will require both better behavior and oversight on Wall Street and more informed decision-making on Main Street and in homes across our country.

There is increasing concern that calls for improved financial literature and for educating the users of financial services are nothing but a clever distraction from financial reform. In the US there has been significant momentum behind improving financial literature, and Congress even passed the Financial Literacy and Education Improvement Act in 2003, which seems to have had little effect on the 'consumers' of mortgages. One wonders if financial literacy can protect the vulnerable from fraud or whether fraudulent practices ought to be investigated and prosecuted. The Federal Reserve pre-crisis seems to have taken the former view, as evidenced by its persistent lack of interest in curbing the excesses of the mortgage market (Financial Crisis Inquiry Report, 2011: 89). For an illuminating view of the attitudes of regulators in the run up to the crisis, see the Financial Crisis Inquiry Report, published by the US National Commission on the Causes of the Financial and Economic Crisis in the United States. We find ourselves in the peculiar situation therefore of financial firms marketing difficult-to-understand products that are potentially harmful to the interests of their users, while it is the responsibility of the users to educate themselves in order to be able to discern the truth behind advertising and promotional material. All this is reminiscent of the debate as to ownership of guns in the US. Is it more efficient to allow everyone to have guns and to try to convince them/educate them not to use them, or is it simpler not to have guns? Is it more efficient to market wide varieties of financial products that cannot (without significant efforts) be understood by their consumers, or is it easier to mandate that products meet a series of safety/affordability requirements?

Continuing with the theme of having better informed customers and investors, the Dodd-Frank Act deals with the regulation of credit rating agencies. Attention on credit rating agencies has been close in the aftermath of the crisis revealing a score of problems with their operational models. Yet, one cannot help a sense of déjà-vu, as the role of credit rating agencies has been considered time and time again after crises and scandals. For instance, the failure of credit rating agencies to identify and respond to accounting improprieties at Enron and several other large corporations in the late 1990s led to the Sarbanes-Oxley Act mandating the SEC to study the role of the credit rating agencies and to report to Congress with recommendations for additional regulation. Following the report by the SEC, Congress enacted the Credit Rating Agency Reform Act of 2006 which created the system of 'nationally recognized statistical rating organizations' (NRSROs) and required those organisations to register with the SEC (which acquired record-keeping, financial reporting and general oversight responsibility for registered NRSROs). In the Dodd-Frank Act, Congress expanded upon SEC rules introduced between 2007 and 2009 aiming to improve the performance of credit rating agencies. This constituted renewed confirmation that credit rating agencies are of systemic importance to the US financial system, that their performance is a matter of public interest, that as gatekeepers to the securities markets their role justifies public oversight, that they face conflicts of interest requiring monitoring and regulation, and, perhaps most importantly, that their ratings on structured financial products were inaccurate and contributed significantly to the mismanagement of risk by financial institutions and investors, which in turn adversely impacted the health of the economy in the United States and around the world (Cluchey, 2011: 18). Whether reform will help resolve conflicts of interest and deficiencies in the operations of credit rating agencies remains to be seen. If the constant downgrades of sovereign ratings since 2009 are any indication, rating agencies nowadays prefer to be proactive in identifying credit risks.

5.6 Control of compensation in the USA

We saw earlier in this chapter, that the issue of executive remuneration has featured heavily in discussions about regulatory reform in Europe. What has been the response of US policy-makers to the problem of runaway executive pay, especially since the US has been the centre of this race towards extreme compensation packages? Americans certainly share the belief that large financial firm pay structures significantly contributed to excessive risk-taking (Webel, 2010: 19). Between October 2008 and February 2009 the focus was on institutions receiving state support (bailouts) and a series of restrictions on pay by legislation and guidelines were introduced by the US Treasury and Congress aimed at controlling compensation at those corporations. In the fall of 2009 (with guidance issued in June 2010), the Fed, exercising its regulatory role over the banking system, proposed to review bank pay structures to identify any compensation arrangements that provide incentives to take excessive risks (Hill, 2011: 11). Provisions in the American Recovery and Reinvestment Act of 2009 included additional limitations on executive compensation, demanded by Congress, for institutions participating in the Troubled Asset Relief Program (TARP), including a limitation on bonus payments to one-third the value of total annual compensation. In June 2009, the US government took the unprecedented step of appointing a Special

Master for TARP Executive Compensation, with authority to review and approve the pay of senior executives at institutions receiving federal financial assistance. This appointment was described in the financial press as a hard-to-believe turn for the US market economy and evidence of the federal government's increasingly visible hand in corporate affairs (*Wall Street Journal*, 2009). This was proof for market advocates in the US that the Obama administration was tainted with something more than a mere whiff of socialism.

Government actions on the issue of pay, however, have proved to be a very pale shade of socialism, because (as in Europe) the main thrust of initiatives (beyond controlling behaviour in bailed-out firms) has been to empower company insiders to control board performance and pay. This is in stark contrast with what would have been a truly radical turn: controlling corporate pay from outside the firm, on the basis of some socially defined understanding of what constitutes appropriate compensation levels. The policy of empowering corporate insiders to combat unacceptable pay structures underpinned several reform proposals in 2009, such as the Shareholder Bill of Rights, which sought to increase shareholder powers to counteract extreme risk-taking and excessive executive compensation (Schumer, 2009). Some provisions of the Shareholder Bill of Rights related directly to executive remuneration in public companies, such as a mandatory annual non-binding shareholder vote on executive compensation. The problem of risk-taking in financial organisations was also addressed in remuneration guidance, as mentioned above. A concern about the various guidances, however, is that they do not depart from control regimes that we were familiar with pre-crisis. We see therefore in the US a similar situation with what we discovered in Europe when we discussed the CEBS guidelines. We have a series of nice sounding documents that will in all probability succeed in changing the language employed by corporates but not their actual mode of operation. For example, the *Guidance on Sound Incentive Compensation Policies*, issued by the Fed in cooperation with other US banking agencies in June 2010, is principles-based yet accorded with the FSB's *Principles for Sound Compensation Practices* (Hill, 2011: 11). As we have mentioned elsewhere in the book, it is interesting how principles-based regulation has the properties of the Hollywood undead, regularly being written off as inadequate, yet rising to feature in more regulatory guidance.

The way the Dodd-Frank Act deals with the issue of executive compensation is by making amendments to corporate governance regimes. Maybe with the failure of everything else, we should trust in shareholders to put the brakes on corporate excess, even though they have failed to do so again and again in every past bubble and bust? The Dodd-Frank answer is one of structure, or, if you prefer, bureaucracy. The Act imposes new structural requirements on the board of directors of public companies with boards now required to have compensation committees, the members of which must be independent directors, assisted by independent compensation consultants. This mandate builds on earlier requirements imposed by Congress on public companies in the Sarbanes-Oxley Act with regard to audit committees. Also, since 2009 and the US Corporate and Financial Institution Compensation Fairness Act, shareholders in US companies have the responsibility to monitor executive compensation. In addition to the new structural requirements, Dodd-Frank empowers shareholders of public companies by giving them the right to a non-binding vote on the compensation of senior executives of the company (at least once every three years) (Cluchey, 2011: 35). This replicates to a degree the corporate governance regime (mandated by the UK Corporate Governance Code which applies to companies listed on the London Stock Exchange) that existed in the UK prior to the crisis. However, not much substantive change is expected in the US since the non-binding nature of the shareholder votes and the additional provisions of the statute make clear that the votes do not overrule a decision of the directors nor create any new (or alter any existing) fiduciary duty of the issuer or of the directors (Cluchey, 2011: 39). Even if such measures did alter board behaviour in meaningful ways, it is worthy of note that the UK regime (which pre-dated the crisis) did not prevent British financial companies from committing the same mistakes as their US counterparts.

Even if shareholders are given the tools to challenge the board, even if they are supplied with information, it may change little. While compensation disclosure has its uses, it also has significant limitations. Corporate disclosure as mandated by securities laws is difficult (but for the most knowledgeable) to comprehend. Too much information presented in too complex a manner makes it less likely that information will actually be useful to investors and shareholders in making decisions, let alone lead to second-guessing management's decisions on compensation. One wonders if too much information is a way to obscure rather than reveal the truth. In the words of the fictional fire-station captain in Ray Bradbury's *Fahrenheit 451*:

> If you don't want a man unhappy politically, don't give him two sides to a question to worry him; give him one. Better yet give him none … Give the people contests they win by remembering the words to more popular songs or the names of state capitals or how much corn Iowa grew last year. Cram them full of non-combustible data, chock them so damned full of 'facts' they feel stuffed, but absolutely 'brilliant' with information. Then they'll feel they're thinking, they'll get a sense of motion without moving. And they'll be happy, because facts of that sort don't change.

Could it be that giving shareholders all the information they could possibly want on executive remuneration will cause them to do absolutely nothing, yet feel empowered?

5.7 Conclusion

This chapter has offered a glimpse into regulatory responses to the financial crisis. Due to the limitations in the scope of this work, we cannot in fact offer a comprehensive comparative analysis of policy responses to the credit crunch and to the European economic and debt crises; one could fill a few books just with descriptions of the new market-supervisory structures in the US and Europe. Offering such an analysis is not necessary anyway for our purposes, as the key issue in this part of the book is not to describe what is being done in detail, but what is being revealed as to the thinking behind policies. Do we see in fact a change of tone, of flavour, of ideological direction in these reforms that suggests a boundary is being revealed, separating pre- and post-crisis thinking? Or do we discover a continuum that seems to treat the Great Recession like a hiccup, a normal incidence of market disequilibrium that does not require anything radical as a response? In answering this question we have looked at the new market regulatory structures in the EU and the Dodd-Frank Act across the Atlantic. We have also used the example of controls over executive compensation, in both Europe and the US, as a proxy for wider views on the role of the state and the scope of markets.

The conclusion of the analysis offered in this chapter is that the Great Recession is not achieving what the Great Depression inflicted in terms of general thinking about the place of state regulation in markets. We see again and again that even when significant changes are being made to regulatory frameworks, the underlying orthodoxy is not being challenged. While we agree now that more sections of the market ought to be regulated, and that regulators ought to have more powers to act more quickly and to spot systemic effects sooner, we are not faced with a challenge to the pillars of neoclassical thinking. Markets are still seen as the most efficient way to achieve beneficial social outcomes (whatever they may be). Market regulation is still seen as a technical exercise that ought to be carried out by experts, and not to be put to the democratic test of election platforms. While we are faced with a major failure of market discipline, we still regard the state as suspect, as incapable, as corrupt or corruptible. Even though we just saw soft law and self-regulation fail, we think that we ought to give it another chance. Is this the right time, we wonder, to impose compliance costs on a market struggling to find its feet? Maybe if we pretend that everything is going to be OK, the market will regain its stature, profits will rise again and we will ride an ascending growth curve long enough to make the next crash not matter. Who knows, maybe Minsky was wrong and this time the slightly improved regulatory mechanisms will negate capitalism's tendency to unravel. Maybe we have learned the lessons we failed to remember long enough after every single previous crash. Maybe this time it's different. Or maybe it is not.

What is clear is that as democratic societies we still have not found the strength to identify the underlying reasons that guide our policy impulses. As this book has asked in a number of places, why are we bothered about large bonuses and executive remuneration structures? So long as we do not find the confidence to say we do not like bonuses because they are incompatible with a shared vision of a healthy society and we hide behind technical language and rationalisations along the lines of incentives to risk-taking, we will never manage to change the way markets see themselves and the way market players behave. Yet, in order to make an argument based on visions of an appropriate and good society, we need to find a way to define what is good. Accepting the de-politicised nature of markets means we cannot use our democratic structures to define social goods. We are doomed therefore to repeat the past, to lose sight of what is important and to remain vulnerable to arguments based on the most 'efficient' ways to achieve ill-defined outcomes. I do not see in what this chapter has examined (and much more besides) reason to be very optimistic that we are leaving financialised capitalism and its excesses behind. So long as we do not break out of the neoliberal straightjacket that has contained thinking about the state–market relationship for the last three decades we will not be able to chart a route to a different future. What may a different future look like, you may ask? That is the topic of the next and final chapter of this book, where we will address directly the question: what is our future likely to look like if we keep on the present path, and what could we do to carve a different path?

6 The market–state balance revisited

We have become slaves to economic efficiency trying to hide from the fact that acknowledging inequalities of wealth leads efficiency to become a mechanism to perpetuate unfairness.

6.1 Introduction

In the previous chapters, this book laid out a thesis that can serve as the basis for a new political economy in western democracies. It was noted early on that capitalism should not be taken as a given, natural state of affairs. It should be seen rather as a fragile system whose survival depends on the existence and maintenance of a social contract. This social contract represents a class compromise, the agreement of those who have little to tolerate the lifestyles of those who have plenty. This social compromise rests on a foundation of law. The law can be seen therefore as a conduit of legitimacy from the wishes of the many to the choices of the few. The preceding chapters also put forward the argument that mandatory rules backed by the force of law often remain the best way to control and contain market behaviour in a way that the common good is guaranteed and the social contract is not threatened. Faced with a great crisis of finance, a recession, rising unemployment and poverty we can no longer be complacent and rely on the security services to keep the inhabitants of the estates away from the streets of Kensington (to take London as an example). In fact, why is it that, in an environment of hardship and austerity, those who have little should defer to the expertise of the rich, fortified behind their gated communities, policed streets and Porsche Cayennes? When does the hubris of supposedly disgraced banking executives floating away with their golden parachutes become unbearable for the teenager who is not in education, employment or training (the government-christened NEET)? When will we begin to see the pattern linking the London riots of 2011, the rise of the far right in Greece and other European countries and the inability of 'orthodox' thinking to reinvigorate a dying democracy? In Charlie Brooker's dark comedy series *Black Mirror*, aired in the UK early in 2013, one of the episodes featured a cartoon character (something like the infamous Gummy Bear) who runs as a candidate in an election and then becomes the face of a global tyranny. The reason for this fictional bear's success was the disdain it represented against a political class that seemed to stand for nothing other than its own survival. Is this a silly comic sketch or a herald of things to come? When politics seems unable to decide anything that matters, is it anything more than a career path for certain people? If democratic decision-making is only about peripheral unimportant issues, what is the purpose of the political establishment rather than self-perpetuation?

This book argues that a larger role for politics in economic decision-making and a greater role for law is necessary to offer a way out of the crisis. Such an enhanced role for law can help reconnect the popular will with economic decision-making, to stop the slide towards a dictatorship of finance, rule by experts and increasing social discord. A return to law and to democratic legitimation of policy may well involve the reversal of deregulation and a change in the market–state relationship away from market freedoms and towards greater state involvement in economic decision-making. The preceding discussion has stressed that resistance to state intrusion often negates democratic choice because it entails a rejection of democratic politics. Hayekian notions of the rule of law reduce law to a base for market transactions, as opposed to a tool aimed at achieving social justice. Market worshippers rely on a limited understanding of the function of law, as the protector of property rights, yet the law is something more. We have become slaves to economic efficiency trying to hide from the fact that acknowledging inequalities of wealth leads efficiency to become a mechanism to perpetuate unfairness. We forget that more choice for consumers can mean less choice for citizens.

The reader may wonder why should we even attempt to maintain capitalism, why should we reduce our expectations of justice to the confines of a capitalist society? The answer is that maybe we should not, but we need to be having this discussion. This book is meant to raise consciousness that we can no longer continue with business as usual. The Financial Crisis, the Great Recession, the European Debt Crisis have been game changers that prevent us and our elites from falling back on known, short-term fixes for long-term problems. Now is the time to discuss whether we want capitalism to survive, whom it should serve and how best to contain it so that it does not breach the promises democracy makes of shared prosperity, equality, justice. It may be that if we have a truly open discussion via our democratic institutions, we may decide to try something other than capitalism. It is the author's belief that at this point in human history, ownership of the outcome of the debate is more important that the type of balance to be struck between markets and states. We are at a crossroads when governments will either regain the popular mandate to structure economic institutions, or we will have to choose between democracy and economic 'logic'. No one thinks we could have a repeat of the political conditions of the 1930s in Europe. But why not? How many years of massive unemployment does it take for social cohesion to break down? How many conflicts do we wish to see before we realise that we had an opportunity to change things before someone changed them for us? Are we confident enough that it will all be fine in the end to afford to be so complacent?

This final chapter of this work concludes our investigation by reflecting on possible futures for the state–market relationship and the role of democratic politics and the law in our societies. The chapter begins by considering the evolution of norms in regulating markets through adjudication processes. A significant part of the way market freedoms evolve is dependent on court and tribunal interpretations of rights. It is often observed that the creation of an initial framework for investor protection can be modified in unintended ways through the adjudication process. This is something that has come to be a concern to policy-makers, not only in jurisdictions sceptical of market supremacy, but also in the US as the experience of NAFTA arbitrations and the curbs they place on national policy discretion shows (Sornarajah, 2010). Chapter 6 selects the example of investor–treaty arbitrations to investigate two areas. The first is the capacity of investor protection provisions to undermine state efforts to deal with the problem of sovereign debt (with Greece as the central example); the second is the effect adjudication has on regulators, which is often to cause them to shy away from regulating in controversial areas (as investor claims against Canada under NAFTA suggest). The chapter then proceeds to consider options for controlling market cultures beyond the law, by offering an investigation of self-regulation and voluntary initiatives. The argument made here is that while there is a place for voluntarism, self-regulation is not an adequate tool to change deficient corporate cultures like that of the financial industry so centrally implicated in the financial crisis. The chapter concludes by speculating as to the future role of politics, its impact on market regulation and the evolution of legal regimes; it warns against assuming that the consequences of the current disconnect between democracy and economic decision-making will be benign. The concluding part also addresses two key reservations that the reader is likely to have had throughout this work: how realistic is to expect politicians to do a better job, and why stick with capitalism? The reflection below seeks to offer convincing answers to both these questions, without prejudging the result of the popular democratic debate that is being advocated throughout the book.

6.2 The market–state balance in courts and tribunals

In earlier parts of this book, when we presented the history of regulation, we noted that in a number of jurisdictions, especially in the US, litigation preceded state-mandated regulation as a mechanism for controlling market behaviour and for ensuring the correspondence of business interests with the public's perception of common goals and goods. The expansion of regulation (and its fluctuating reach) since the early twentieth century has gone hand in hand with other efforts to channel market activity, including private ordering via litigation and various voluntary initiatives. Determining how a state defines its ability to control market activity, as we have seen, includes the extent to which litigation processes are allowed to restrict state discretion. This is a fairly complex way of saying that if we want to empower states over markets and in the process return some of the power to determine a political economy to the democratic process, we need to consider how regulation can influence market behaviour more effectively, and how litigation processes can be contained so that they do not undermine state policy initiatives. Especially when considering the latter, we need to think how changes introduced in the law by courts and tribunals can affect the rights of private parties to block state initiatives in the future. Policy-makers, in other words, need to access how a measure that seems to guarantee market freedoms now may negatively affect the choices of their peers 40–50 years later.

In *Neoliberalism and the Law* (Glinavos, 2010a) we came across the notion (central to economic orthodoxy) that the state ought to leave private persons to direct changes in the law primarily through litigation or self-regulation. Indeed, a correlation between judicial rule-making and market principles has a long pedigree in Anglo-American legal thought. The belief that the common law generates more market-friendly, efficient legal rules is, of course, one of the main claims of Richard Posner (1972) as we saw earlier in the book. Posner expressed a strong preference for the common law over statute on efficiency grounds. Rules created through the processes of the common law, Posner argued, tend to promote economic efficiency while those created through statute do not. Courts have the capacity, according to this argument, to establish through case law sets of rules consistent with the effective functioning of a free market (Manne, 1997–8: 31). It is observed in fact that common law judges have a strong preference for protecting private property and contractual rights. Posner arrived at this conclusion by examining common law doctrines and rules found to be consistent with economic efficiency, concluding that the common law could best be understood as a mechanism for achieving market-efficient outcomes.

Can reliance on litigation, however, disengage the state from the field of regulation and render democracy irrelevant? This final chapter of the book attempts to answer this question by examining market-led dispute resolution processes in the field of investor–state disputes. Can market-friendly law changes today herald a future where policy is made in the courts and tribunals instead of being chosen by citizens? The following discussion uses the example of a Treaty concluded in 1961 which can still alter (fifty years later) state options in dealing with the sovereign debt crisis.

6.2.1 Treaty rights and investor disputes

One of the key messages in this book is a warning about the wide-ranging set of consequences market-friendly legal provisions have for the operation of the economy. Legal changes can set in motion events far removed from the intentions of policy-makers at the time, something that is well demonstrated in the various facets of the crisis. While everyone is aware of the way financial innovations led to unintended consequences, for example how efforts to manage and disperse risk led to the amplification of systemic risks, it is not fully appreciated how market-friendly law reforms have a trajectory that leads to ever decreasing policy discretion in the medium and long term. To reiterate a point often made in this book: locking up market-friendly policies with legal means is not always desirable. A democratic polity is based on the ability to change course, and the fundamental *raison d'être* of a democracy is to allow the people to determine what are public goods and how they ought to be obtained and distributed. Elevating issues of economic decision-making beyond the reach of the democratic processes may be positive for the 'investment climate' in the short run, but can lead to instability and threaten the very existence of a market in the long run. It is not therefore anti-market to suggest that market democracy needs to retain policy discretion on issues of economic governance. Policy discretion is a shock absorber, without which advocates of increasing liberalisation (and the further use of law to cement pro-market reforms) may find themselves faced with a revolution. To illustrate the potential of market-facilitative law reform to undermine policy discretion in the long run, this section presents a case study on the operation of bilateral investment treaties that goes to the core of the crisis: the ability of governments to choose between a series of options, including default, in dealing with unsustainable public debt.

Bilateral investment treaties (BITs) are the most common vehicle for the facilitation and protection of foreign direct investment. A BIT for the protection and promotion of foreign investments can de defined as a legally binding international agreement between two states where they each promise reciprocally to observe the standards laid down by the treaty in their dealings with investors from the other state (Muchlinski, 1999: 617). BITs aim to create a stable investment environment in the interests of development and to protect the foreign investor from arbitrary treatment by the host government that can detrimentally affect the profitability of the investment. BITs may provide for specific standards both in the pre- and post-investment stage (with post-investment treatment being more commonly regulated). The OECD characterises BITs as an increasingly important vehicle for protecting and promoting investment flows by providing legal security to investors and their investments (OECD, 2001). They presently represent the principal instrument for agreeing on specific rules for the legal protection of foreign investment (Cremades, 2000). Expropriation under BITs can occur only in accordance with international law standards, be non-discriminatory and followed by the payment of prompt, adequate and effective compensation. Modern BIT and multilateral practice provides enhanced protection against expropriation through expanding the definition of investment in order to protect contractual aspects of investments. Recent BITs place emphasis on safeguarding the sanctity of contract by guarding against regulatory takings and other governmental action that thwarts legitimate expectations of the investor (Waelde, 1996). Furthermore, investors are guaranteed unrestricted transfer of funds in freely convertible currencies. Disputes between the foreign party and the host government are commonly referred to international arbitration, subjected to procedures already agreed in the context of investment agreements away from the jurisdiction of the local courts or the administrative tribunals of the host country. The exhaustion of local remedies is normally not required for the submission of a dispute to arbitration.

Investment treaties become relevant to the sovereign debt crisis through the consequences of debt restructuring (known as workouts). Debt restructuring, by definition, reduces the value of a sovereign bond and could be seen as a violation of not only the capital transfer provisions of a BIT, but also of 'fair and equitable treatment' (if, for example, domestic creditors are treated differently to foreign ones) and could also potentially constitute an 'expropriation'. By filing investor–state claims under a BIT, bond holders can attempt to circumvent official restructuring processes, as the Italian bond holders attempted to do in *Abaclat* v. *Argentina* (ICSID Case No. ARB/07/5, 04.08.11), by suing the defaulting state in order to recoup the face value of their bonds. Even when debt-related claims during a restructuring are not permitted, prohibitions may not apply where the measures violate national treatment or most favoured nation provisions, even though a nation in crisis may be justified in giving domestic bond holders priority under a sovereign debt restructuring in order to protect the banking system or ensure fulfilment of wage and pension commitments (Kelsey, 2011: 9). Think, for example, of the losses investors suffered on the swap of Greek bonds agreed in March 2012 discussed in Chapter 4. Even those investors who agreed to the swap could potentially complain of discriminatory treatment considering that other lenders like the ECB, the IMF and EU member state central banks had not taken commensurate haircuts on their holdings of Greek debt.

If investors consenting to the swap may feel aggrieved when considering possible violations of their rights under treaties, those who have not consented (known as holdouts) are likely to have a wider range of grievances to bring to investment arbitration (principally complaints about expropriation). International law generally addresses the issue of expropriation by defining it as a compulsory transfer of property rights and refers to regulatory takings variably as indirect expropriation, disguised expropriation or creeping expropriation. While it is generally required that governments will need to offer compensation for actions amounting to expropriation, it is accepted that states are not liable for economic losses arising from bona fide regulation within the accepted scope of 'police powers' including the operation of competition law, consumer protection, securities regulation, environmental protection, land planning and other similar legislation (Wagner, 1999: 518). In reviewing the decisions of the Iran–US Claims Tribunal, for example, one of its members concluded that under international law, liability does not arise from actions that are non-discriminatory and are within the commonly accepted taxation and police powers of states (Aldrich, 1994: 609).

The key issue is, therefore, whether a reduction in the face value of a sovereign bond is an exercise of legitimate state powers or a form of expropriation that gives rise to a claim for compensation under international law. This question brings us back to our consideration of Greece and its recent debt restructuring.

Greece's troubles are roughly similar to Argentina's as we saw in Chapter 4. After Argentina went ahead with its debt settlement offer, holdouts and some observers of the restructuring were furious, going so far as to call Argentina a 'rogue creditor' (Porzecanski, 2005). Some holdouts, among them numerous vulture funds (see below), took the litigation route in the United States, where at least 158 suits have been filed (Hornbeck, 2010). For the first time ever, a number of those holdouts filed claims under BITs to the International Center for the Settlement of Investment Disputes (ICSID). In September 2006, about 180,000 Argentine bond holders filed a claim under the Italy–Argentina BIT for approximately $4.3 billion. The creditors claimed that the Argentine restructuring was tantamount to expropriation and violated fair and equitable treatment standards under the treaty (Waibel, 2011). Argentina was still left with a significant debt load and was short of the 90 per cent threshold for the restructuring to be seen as successful (so that the rest of the holdouts could essentially be ignored). Argentina launched another take-it-or-leave-it exchange from May to June of 2010 for $18 billion of its debt, offering a 75 per cent haircut under the same rationale as in 2005. As was the case with the 2005 swap, the bonds were exchanged for bonds with collective action clauses (CACs) and were linked to GDP, meaning that the bonds pay out more when the economy is growing fast and less during slowdowns. Sixty-six per cent of the bond holders ($12.1 billion) tendered, while $6.2 billion worth of bond holders continued to litigate either through domestic courts or through ICSID (Hornbeck, 2010).

The Argentine precedent demonstrates that there are always some 'holdouts' during a restructuring, disgruntled investors who refuse to negotiate and demand the full value of their investment, even in desperate situations for the countries involved. There are also so-called 'vulture funds', which purchase debt when it is of very low value before or after a restructuring and then file suits to increase the value of their investment (Thomson and Runciman, 2006). The tribunal's decision on jurisdiction in *Abaclat* offers hope to investors seeking to bring claims under BIT provisions against sovereigns for debt restructurings. The fact that the tribunal in *Abaclat* did not rule on whether compensation was indeed payable does not detract from its immense value in characterising financial investments (in the form of purchases of sovereign bonds) as worthy of protection under BITs. Indeed, many BITs treat 'any kind of asset' as a covered investment and therefore include sovereign bonds. More recent treaties explicitly list sovereign bonds as covered by the treaty. As *Abaclat* demonstrates, in terms of general jurisdiction and coverage, an arbitration claim against sovereign debt restructuring depends on several issues, including whether the tribunal finds that it has jurisdiction (which requires an investment to have been made), consent by the sovereign party to arbitration or a claim based on the investment agreement itself. In terms of jurisdiction, the consent of the sovereign party will be governed by the investment agreement in the treaty. This is where the 'definitions' provisions of BITs come in. If an agreement clearly includes bonds and other debt instruments as covered investments, then the country has consented to jurisdiction for those claims. By extension, then, any limitation within the BIT to those claims is a limitation on consent (Cross, 2006). We are entitled to wonder therefore if the Argentine débacle is a forerunner of what can happen to Greece.

According to UNCTAD Greece has signed 38 BITs with other countries within and outside the European Union. A study of the provisions of all these is beyond the scope of this discussion; however, the Greece–Germany BIT of 1961 is an indicative case. The Germany–Greece BIT was concluded between the Federal Republic of Germany and the Kingdom of Greece on 27 March 1961 with the aim of enhancing economic cooperation between the two countries and to create fertile conditions for capital investments. Article 1(2) offers investors Most Favoured Nation (MFN) treatment on capital investments, while Article 2 extends MFN status to professional and economic activity more generally. Article 3(2) offers full protection and security to investments and specifies that expropriations are only possible in the public interest on the payment of compensation. Such compensation must correspond to the value of the expropriated funds and must be paid without delay. Compensation payments and their legality are subject to judicial review in the normal courts of law. Losses due to war, insurrection or civil unrest are compensable on the National Treatment standard, while fund transfers abroad benefit from MFN treatment (Article 3.3). Article 7 offers a clause that guarantees that protected investors will benefit from possible future agreements between Germany and Greece offering improved protection standards.

Article 8 contains definitions of protected investments. It contains property rights over chattels and real property, land-based rights such as mortgages, loans, leaseholds, etc., equity and other rights over companies, promissory notes and receivables, intellectual property rights, design rights, technical know-how, business names and good will as well as rights derivative from the foregoing. The article further specifies that changes in the form of the above, in accordance with the law, does not alter their nature as protected investments. Receivables are defined as amounts accruing from investments during specified time periods in the form of participation rights in profits or interest. The Protocol to the Treaty specifies in paragraph 2(a) that the provisions of Article 3(2) – compensation for expropriation – apply to the transfer of investment capital to public ownership. However, state actions taken on behalf of creditors or investors in case of insolvency or administration are not considered expropriations (para. 2.b). Only the removal or reduction in the exercise of property rights is considered expropriation. Article 11 provides for dispute resolution processes, requiring that disagreements not resolved via mediation are referred to binding arbitration. The wording of the article limits the rights to commence arbitration to the state signatories (as opposed to giving unilateral rights to commence actions to private investors) with the process of appointing the tribunal specified in the Treaty. However, as both Greece and Germany signed onto the ICSID in 1966, there is a strong argument in favour of the position that the relevant tribunal would now be the ICSID centre. It is far from clear, however, whether the ICSID Convention helps overcome the inability of individual investors to commence arbitration written in the BIT. In April 2012 the German government in letters to investors refused to lend assistance in commencing arbitration against Greece on the basis of rights in the Treaty. Perhaps, signing onto ICSID could be considered as offering improved standards to investors, which under Article 7 (discussed above) helps open the arbitration provision to private as well as state actors.

This treaty could arguably offer holdouts on the Greek restructuring an opportunity to obtain a result superior or alternative to payments on credit default swap (CDS) contracts, and in any case it gives enough ammunition to investors to continue with actions intended to harass the Greek government into a settlement with holdouts as it tries to put the debt troubles behind it. On 9 March 2012 the Greek government exercised the powers it granted itself with Law 4050/2012 and activated collective action clauses on Greek bonds forcing holdouts to participate in the debt swap offer it launched in February 2012. On 14 March the International Swaps and Derivatives Association (ISDA) declared a credit event which allows the payment of credit default swap contracts on Greek debt. The analysis in this section indicates that, considering the precedent of Argentina and the reasoning of the Tribunal in *Abaclat* in 2011, there is an opportunity for investors to pursue the Greek government for compensation under the terms of bilateral investment treaties Greece has signed. In particular the Germany–Greece BIT of 1961 could offer fertile ground for arbitration under the International Center for the Settlement of Investment Disputes. While there is no guarantee of success, there is enough legal justification for commencing action, and no doubt many holdouts will take that route.

Greece has set a remarkable precedent in being the first developed country to default on its debt in living memory. While a number of European nations are continuing to live in circumstances of questionable solvency (with Cyprus being a prominent example in the spring of 2013), Greece has been the focal point of the debt crisis that has been a consequence of the financial turmoil that began in 2008 with the collapse of Lehman Brothers in the US. The events in Greece since 2010 will occupy policy-makers and market participants for the foreseeable future. They will also occupy courts and arbitral tribunals in multiple jurisdictions. The purpose of this section has been to offer a first glimpse in what will become a major issue for discussion for legal scholars for years to come. In the same way that Argentina's default led to legal actions that are still to reach a conclusion, legal advisers will be grappling with the issues raised by Greece's workout well into the 2020s. This of course assumes that the European debt crisis stops here and does not lead to more workouts and defaults in other member states. This study is not an authoritative one, and draws heavily on the existing literature on the subject. Such a study is useful nevertheless, it is hoped, as it collates impressions as to the state of relevant law and can serve as a starting point for further research. The message for investors seeking to sue Greece for their losses is that they have a long and hard road ahead of them, but the very fact that a road exists is reason for optimism that a possibility of recouping some of their losses survives. This possibility is heightened for investors protected under BITs that Greece has signed and for those seeking to challenge the constitutionality of the workout in national courts.

Whether investors should pursue this lengthy legal battle is another question. When there is money to be made, someone somewhere will always consider litigation options, regardless of the damage such action may cause to the country concerned and its prospects for recovery. In a way, the possibility of legal actions on this topic is a consequence of decades of foreign direct investment liberalisation coming back to haunt us. Who would have thought in 1961 that a BIT signed to encourage investment funds into the country would allow vulture funds to pick at Greece's fiscal corpse in 2013? If there is a wider message to draw from this discussion, it could be that policy-makers need to think harder when balancing the need for investment with policy freedom in the long run.

6.2.2 Freezing policy discretion: the fear of losing

The discussion above presented the challenges to policy space represented by elevating market freedoms to the higher regions of the legal space, beyond the reach of normal law-making institutions. It is possible, however, as I discussed in a paper published in the *European Journal of Law Reform* (Glinavos, 2011), that the danger of constitutionalising market freedoms is becoming detached from the decisions of actual courts and tribunals. As the discussion below demonstrates, it is entirely possible that a combination of market pressures and the fear of potentially losing in litigation arenas serves to disarm the state, before any changes are apparent in the law itself. There is indeed evidence that the contemporary international legal framework offers opportunities to investors to challenge and control state action via what has been described as a 'regulatory freeze'. This means that changes to the way states behave are not being made because courts and tribunals have significantly expanded definitions of expropriation in order to massively restrict state regulatory discretion. On the contrary, a regulatory freeze is the consequence of states' own reluctance to legislate/regulate in areas where challenges might be brought. The costs of litigation and the potential of decisions adverse to the state (mandating compensation for investors), even if they are largely remote in areas still considered an exercise of legitimate state 'police powers', make legislators doubly careful before upsetting market expectations via expanding regulation (for example in pursuit of environmental objectives). We find therefore a frightening symmetry between the fear of markets in the way Krugman described it (in Chapter 4) and the voluntary withdrawal of regulators from areas where challenges are brought under BITs or the investment chapters of free trade agreements, such as Chapter 11 in NAFTA.

As we saw earlier in this chapter, It is not a new idea in international law that foreign owned property should be protected from expropriation. Protection is commonly achieved by giving property owners a right to compensation for the value of the lost or expropriated property. Also, national constitutions contain to varying degrees mechanisms to protect economic rights, most specifically private property rights. One of the core functions of constitutional drafting, in fact, is to achieve a balance between the protection of the rights of citizens to enjoy their property and the ability of governments to control private actors' behaviour within the national economy. A balance is usually found on an intermediate point between absolute protection of private property rights and limitless government power. This balance in national constitutional provisions translates as limits on expropriation and provisions for compensation in the event of government takings. This discussion is of contemporary significance because in the last two decades (primarily) investors have made claims for compensation based on government regulations seeking to place restrictions on the legal use of property (such restrictions affecting its value, but without actually removing the owner's title to the property). This development has led to the creation of a doctrine of 'indirect expropriation' that is of concern because of its capacity to conflict with the till recently dominant notion that states can regulate without having to pay compensation when such regulation constitutes an exercise of their legitimate 'police powers' such as taxation, the protection of public health and welfare. Concern stems from the argument that allowing a doctrine of indirect expropriation to eat away at the sphere of government discretion under the umbrella of police powers will severely limit the capacity of governments to legislate in order to promote general welfare (Wagner, 1999: 466). Obvious victims of these trends can be regulations to address environmentally damaging behaviour contributing to climate change, to use a single prominent example.

The core idea underpinning the framework of investor protection therefore is the payment of compensation for expropriation. For there to be a recovery for expropriation, however, in almost all jurisdictions, there is a requirement that there must be a taking of property. Defining what constitutes expropriation or taking has been a matter of significant controversy both in dispute resolution fora and in national courts. The argument being made here is that expanded definitions of expropriation, that include regulatory measures that affect profitability, harm states' capacity to govern their sovereign territories and constitute part of an emerging global constitutional order that rates market freedoms as more important than other social and political objectives (Glinavos, 2011). It is worth repeating here the reason for concern arising from the requirement for compensation for indirect expropriation. If states are threatened with the need to compensate in increasing regulatory spheres when regulation affects the profitability of investments, states will be less likely to legislate in the common good, especially on environmental protection issues, when doing so incurs costs of preventing or defending litigations. In principle, NAFTA (Article 1110) does not prevent a state from introducing an expropriatory measure to ensure that investment activity in its territory, for example, is undertaken in a manner sensitive to environmental concerns. References to 'public purpose' clearly allow this, provided that compensation is paid to the investor (Baughen, 2006: 222). But it is the payment of compensation in itself that is exactly the problem here. Why should a state be forced to compensate polluters when exercising its legitimate power to control their damaging behaviour?

There are already cases illustrating the existence and evolution of the trends described above within NAFTA. The case of *Ethyl Corporation* v. *Canada* (NAFTA Chapter 11 Tribunal, 24.6.1998) which was settled before the tribunal had the chance to make an award, involved Canadian environmental regulations that prohibited the import and trade in certain chemical components of gasoline due to their potentially harmful effects on health and the environment. Immediately upon the bill becoming law the US corporation Ethyl and its wholly owned Canadian subsidiary filed a notice of arbitration pursuant to NAFTA's investment chapter. Ethyl claimed among other things that the Canadian law constituted an expropriation of its business in Canada and was as such subject to compensation under Article 1110. The reason for the damage to Ethyl's business was that its Canadian subsidiary was the sole Canadian importer, processor and distributor of the substance in question (Wagner, 1999: 491–2). Ethyl's argument was that BITs containing similar provisions to NAFTA's investment protection provisions required compensation for 'indirect expropriation' where the effect of regulatory measures is tantamount to direct expropriation. Ethyl claimed that the purpose of Article 1110 was to protect investors' property rights from government infringement by requiring compensation. This supposedly did not negate the government's sovereign rights to legislate over its territory, while at the same time protecting the expectations of investors. Ethyl also drew arguments from the jurisprudence of the GATT dispute resolution panel on Article XX(b) which permits trade restrictions where necessary to protect human, plant or animal life or health. They suggested that Article XX(b) requires governments to choose the least trade restrictive measures, and Canada's action in banning trade in these substances was not necessary to achieve the stated objectives or environmental protection. The Ethyl case did not get the chance to lead to an award as the Canadian government repealed the law after losing before a domestic trade panel on a separate action. Similar arguments were employed in the S. D. Myers case (*S. D. Myers, Inc.* v. *Canada*, Ad Hoc Tribunal, 30.12.2002) which involved a claim for compensation against Canada for losses arising out of a ban on the export of chemicals which the

US company claimed to amount to expropriation of its contracts to treat such chemicals (Wagner, 1999: 496). The result of the case was similar to the one in *Ethyl*, as Canada repealed the law instead of defending the action.

It is widely accepted that the international investment arbitration regime embodied in NAFTA and BITs was intended to limit governments' exercise of public power by giving international capital enforceable protection against certain forms of state intervention in the economy, including protection against expropriation. The belief that foreign direct investment will come after an investment treaty is concluded leads states to surrender sovereignty. This happens because the state on the receiving end subjects itself to external protection of investors through outside dispute resolution mechanisms, insulated from the reach of local laws. As a result, market actors have invoked treaty rights aggressively to inhibit public welfare regulation, with at least some success. Even though governments have won most Chapter 11 cases, arbitral panels have taken a broad view of what can count as measures 'tantamount to expropriation', effectively restricting governments' ability to regulate corporate activities in what they see as the public interest (Wood and Clarkson, 2009: 5). Wood and Clarkson (2009) argue that, despite the fact that investors have actually lost in most cases challenging regulations that reached their conclusion, there is still room for concern in the wake of *Methanex* v. *USA* (NAFTA Chapter 11 Tribunal, 3.8.2005). While *Methanex* ruled that non-discriminatory regulation of general application does not amount to expropriation unless the regulating government gave the investor a commitment not to regulate, other Chapter 11 tribunals have held that Article 1110 does cover non-discriminatory regulation that might be said to fall within an exercise of a state's so-called police powers (*Pope & Talbot Inc.* v. *Canada*, Ad Hoc Tribunal, Interim Award, 26.6.2000).

The Canadian cases discussed above seem to confirm the concerns of commentators. One result of NAFTA's provisions is not so much that governments actually lose cases brought against them by investors, but that governments choose to shy away from regulation when faced with a risk of losing. When the effect of this 'regulatory freeze' is to prevent regulation from coming into place, then the outcome is the same as outlawing the legislation on the basis of a hardcore, pro-market interpretation of treaty provisions. It is a win for business and investor interests, but is it a win for society, and is it a win for democratically expressed popular choices?

6.3 Leaving the law behind: voluntarism

If changing the law is impossible due to resistance from markets, regulation is risky due to the danger of overkill and we cannot trust adjudicators to strike an appropriate balance in the market–state relationship, what are we left with? Neoliberalism's favourite regulatory tool, self-regulation, has a long history, rooted in the perceived failure of mandatory mechanisms to achieve regulatory aims. We have often mentioned in this book areas where self-regulation was mistakenly thought to be most suited to the regulatory task, as we have also seen plenty consequences of its failure. Despite our earlier brushes with these concepts, however, it is worth devoting some space in this final chapter to a more systematic treatment of the theory behind the supposed virtues of voluntarism.

The concept of self-discipline and voluntary self-regulation is one that has become quite prominent in the literature, even outside the market advocates that consider any form of state intrusion as a violation of the rule of law. A good example to consider here is how voluntarism has been presented as a solution to the problem of corporate misbehaviour as it relates to the human rights impacts of international business activity. Voiculescu, for instance, has considered how legal, regulatory and ethical, voluntary normativity strive for balance (Voiculescu and Yanacopulos, 2011: 10), suggesting that the proliferation of voluntary compliance initiatives in the field of multinational business legitimise self-regulation. Are voluntary codes of conduct a digression used by corporate actors to avoid domestic and international regulatory intervention, or are they pragmatic ways to influence corporate culture through dialogue, cooperation and constructive compromise?

There is a view that initiatives such as the Global Compact, the OECD Guidelines for Multinational Enterprises and the UN Guiding Principles on Business and Human Rights along with the standardisation of corporate social responsibility (CSR) principles have made the voluntary approach attain more predictable and measurable outcomes. On the topic of measuring outcomes, there is an evolution of systems in operation or development such as SAI, ISO, AA 1000 Assurance Standards which use key performance indicators, alongside the developing practice of independent verification of CSR reporting. The above can combine therefore in offering support to the argument that voluntary initiatives can be something beyond pretty dressing for corporate branding exercises. There has been some recognition of the above by legislators as evidenced by the introduction of CSR concepts in legislation (for example, s. 172 of the Companies Act 2006) or in listing rules for stock exchanges (and in the UK Corporate Governance Code). This is despite the impression that the work of UN Special Representative John Ruggie (the Protect, Respect and Remedy framework) concluded in 2008 (Ruggie, 2008) constitutes a move towards a more interventionist approach.

There is a difference, however, between enforcement problems for norms in fields that exist primarily in the international law domain, like human rights, and those that have their bases in national law, like financial regulation. While it is fair to suggest that disciplining multinational corporations in a multi-jurisdictional environment (to prevent them, for example, from taking advantage of lax labour laws in developing states) may require less mandatory and more voluntary commitments, it is not accurate to extrapolate from this lessons for all areas of the regulatory effort. Voluntarism in the financial business domain has more to do with legitimising laissez-faire and less to do with effective enforcement of norms. The literature on principles-based regulation, for instance, is one of the best examples of a deregulatory philosophy that envisages a marketplace operating on the basis of self-control rather than on statutory imposition of norms determined by political forces. According to Black (2008: 8) the rhetoric of principles-based regulation invokes a reframing of the regulatory relationship from one of directing and controlling to one based on responsibility, mutuality and trust. Regulators are seen as moving from a directing relationship of telling and doing to a relationship in which they communicate their goals and expectations clearly in principles and apply those principles predictably, adopting a self-reflective approach to the development of processes and practices to ensure that these goals are substantively met. Critically, according to Black, both regulators and firms trust each other to fulfil their side of this new regulatory bargain.

The UK's Financial Services Authority (FSA), shortly before the shock of the credit crunch in 2008, had fully underwritten this type of regulation as the 'optimum' method of influencing the market. The FSA even noted (2007: 3) that it aspired to push a regulatory agenda without rules and traditional compliance techniques, despite the EU Commission's reservations. It is fairly shocking therefore how fast the FSA performed a volte-face subsequent to the events of 2008, and how it began to deconstruct its own rhetoric of self-regulation. Even though examples abound, one can highlight the abandonment by the FSA of its Banking Codes (the voluntary codes of conduct of the banking industry vis-à-vis business and consumer clients) from November 2009 in favour of a traditional, continental, involuntary control system of clearly determined rules (Glinavos, 2010b: 541–2). Yet, even more surprisingly, the FSA returned to a promotion of self-discipline shortly after and up to the point of its dissolution in 2013. In February 2010, forgetting perhaps the little interlude of dissatisfaction with principles-based regulation, the FSA, responding to proposals for a European Union directive on the regulation of hedge funds and private equity firms, highlighted concerns that a tight legal framework governing all types of alternative investment businesses will be open to challenge and proceeded to put forward proposals for a principles-based approach to regulation, mimicking the model used by the FSA prior to the crisis (Inman, 2010). This little episode on the magnetic pull of self-regulation on thinking at the FSA demonstrates that the choice of voluntarism over mandatory rule-making has more to do with the ideological climate that serves as a background to policy choices than media-projected excuses based on 'efficiency'.

The aim here is not to argue against voluntarism per se, but rather to show the limitations of self-ordering. Corporate social responsibility may have a role to play in curtailing corporate excess in manufacturing practices across the seas, but we cannot use CSR as a tool to restrict corporate excess in the financial markets. Some things are still the domain of law emanating from the democratic political process, and no amount of economic orthodoxy doublespeak can change that. Parker (McBarnet et al., 2007) in fact asserts that CSR has a different purpose and objective to regulation by way of law, as law is centrally concerned with accountability rather than responsibility more generally. The law is about holding people to threshold criteria of good conduct and performance. Responsibility goes beyond accountability to ask how much people care about their duties, ideals as well as obligations, values as well as rules. Traditional legal regulation of business is primarily concerned with accountability (McBarnet et al., 2007) and this is certainly true of those industries most implicated in the current crisis. While the concept of CSR is increasingly being developed by individuals or groups who invoke the law, a distinction is maintained between what should be the domain of law, and what is the domain of softer types of rule-making. While law and regulatory enforcement action are being used by consumers, employees and NGOs as well as governments to encourage and enforce corporate economic, social and environmental responsibility, the law has a link to legitimacy (via the democratic structures that produce it) distinct from any 'ownership' of rules that come from the voluntary involvement of stakeholders. While we can concede that discussions of 'meta-regulation' involving sophisticated frameworks combining mandatory and softer forms of compulsion are relevant, we cannot avoid the fact that cultural changes that express a society-wide political consensus need to be expressed through 'traditional' forms of mandatory regulation backed by law.

We can conclude therefore that while there may be a place for voluntarism and self-regulation, and good reasons for separating legal accountability from wider moral responsibility, this is not where the debate is premised at the moment. The use of voluntary initiatives as an alternative to mandatory, rules-based regulation is not explained by a search for efficiency, but dictated by the neoliberal logic of de-politicisation and distancing of the state from economic management. This realisation brings us back to a central point made by this book. Law can be used as a reflection of society's view of what the goals of policy should be. Types of influencing market behaviour, including voluntarism, are means of achieving those goals. So long as the goals are set, it is of lesser consequence what the means employed are, as they can seek efficiency within a larger legitimate universe. What we have at the moment, the promotion of self-ordering in a purposeless system (or, to a degree, a system without democratically determined aims), is a travesty of legitimate governance.

6.4 The future: politics and extremes

The main message of this book has been a call for more politics or, if you prefer, more political input into economic decision-making. The reason offered for this has been an assumption that a closer connection between the democratic political process and economic decision-making will help both alleviate some of the harsher aspects of capitalism and reaffirm a social contract in favour of capitalism that guarantees peace and prosperity. There are two central objections to this thesis that the reader possibly had at the very beginning, but can only be addressed directly now, at the end of the work, after the entire argument has been laid out. First, even if it sounds plausible in theory, can this call for 'more politics' work in practice? Second, why insist on capitalism? Shouldn't an empowerment of the imagination towards a better capitalism also allow a non-capitalist alternative? We will begin by considering the first objection, the nature of politics and the practicality of proposals for more engagement between politics and economics.

I recently wrote a review of Habermas' last book (2012), online, arguing that his view that the economic calamities engulfing Europe are an opportunity for democratisation in a cosmopolitan federal state is unrealistic and therefore irrelevant. Why should my call for an end to the de-politicisation of economic decision-making be more realistic, and even if it were, would it have the outcomes I wish it had? In order to answer this question we need to have a closer look at the 'technocrats', those undemocratic rulers that I have been complaining about in this book. Let us take, for example, the government of Papademos in Greece. Lucas Papademos is a banker (formerly of the European Central Bank) who served as Greek prime minister from November 2011 to June 2012. His short-lived government suffered from being constantly undermined by its supposed political backers and was dealing with an extraordinarily difficult situation constantly facing bankruptcy while having to negotiate the terms of the 'haircut' and to comply with the conditions of the Greek bailout. How should we view Papademos on the basis of the analysis offered in this book? Should we treat him like a technically competent messiah, coming after politicians, especially George Papandreou who, due to a mix of petty calculation and incompetence, turned a great economic problem into a national catastrophe? Or should we treat him like a usurper, an embodiment of economic orthodoxy, a banker representing bankers' interests, a collaborator of the Troika, placed in a position of authority in order to implement a reform package that lacked popular legitimacy?

To borrow an example from Greece's neighbouring jurisdiction, how should we judge the tenure of Mario Monti in Italy? Prime Minister Monti announced in December 2012 that he would resign once the 2013 budget was approved, bringing forward an election due in 2013. This announcement came two days after Silvio Berlusconi's party withdrew parliamentary support for the technocrat government and hours after Berlusconi said he would run to become premier for a fifth time on a platform that attacks Monti's economic record. Monti is an economist who served as a European Commissioner for almost a decade and took over as prime minister (like his colleague Papademos) after Berlusconi's resignation in November 2011. Monti has been hailed almost universally as Italy's saviour after the catastrophic last stages of Berlusconi's government, with success for Italy being measured on the size of the spreads of its borrowing costs over those of Germany's. Monti is deemed to have ushered in a turning point in Italian politics, helping change Italy into a serious country again in the eyes of foreign investors and also for many of its own citizens (Donadio, 2012). Monti's premiership, however, as the *New York Times* aptly observed, underscored the clash between the economically sound and the politically sustainable. While he has reassured investors and helped keep Italian borrowing rates down, the tax increases and spending cuts passed by his Parliament have eroded law-makers' standing with voters, in a similar (but not as definitive) manner as Papademos' efforts exhausted the Greeks, who expressed themselves in two successive elections by throwing themselves to the extremes of the political spectrum. Monti is also an example of what happens when 'technocrats' half-engage with the political process. After initially declaring that he did not wish to run in the election yet would be happy to be anointed premier again by any subsequent winner, he relented and headed a centrist coalition. In the election of February 2013, Monti's party gained only 10.6 per cent of the vote.

It is difficult to resist the conclusion that voters reject austerity in the South of Europe. This book argues, however, that the rejection is not simply of austerity, but of something greater. The rejection is of the lack of ownership of policy, of powerlessness and of disenfranchisement. When the predominant response to financial crisis has been to hand the keys to supposed experts, then what is the reason for the public to accept the expert medicine, especially when it does not seem to be working? If the prescription is correct, why not argue its merits in the political arena and convince the public as to its adoption? Isn't that what a democratic polity is supposed to be about, choice? Why are we all so keen on choice as consumers? Why indeed does the British government assume we need to choose schools and health providers, to rate our GPs and get rid of our schoolteachers, yet it considers us unable to debate and vote on the content of economic policies? Why are we meant to be intelligent enough to pick insurance and financial products that would baffle a maths professor, yet we are considered inadequate to follow a debate on the best way to climb our way out of the hole the financial collapse has left us in? Is this all a little convenient? Are we, to borrow again from Bradbury, being flooded with information about things that do not matter so that we acquiesce about the things that do? Are we being told to fear the markets to keep us quiet so that we do not challenge the legal bases that allow sentiment and market whim to govern our fates? It is paradoxical that the Conservatives in the UK wish to distance the country from the allegedly unelected bureaucrats of Brussels, yet at the same time tell us that austerity and debt reduction are inevitable, as they are dictated by the markets? What difference does it make, one wonders, whether your ruler is an unelected 'Eurocrat' or an elected Tory if there is no choice anyway? Is the universe of technocracy that has so quickly descended upon Europe as a response to the European Debt Crisis a blessing or is it a cloak for a dictatorship of finance? Are our new, unelected rulers benign or are they disinterested in the fate of those who have less, who are unemployed or studying at the wrong school? Is the system we have one that can persist, or one that will crumble? At which point does the reaction to capitalist excess turn into a revolution or, in the absence of a motivating ideology that can channel reaction to creativity, just anarchy?

How realistic is it to expect politicians to do a better job than technocrats and to use the law to channel the popular will, as opposed to using it for their own interests as the capture theory of regulation would have us believe? The answer to this is that we get the politicians the system allows us to have. In an environment where large swathes of policy are beyond the reach of the democratic process, politics attracts people who view it as a career rather than people who have a vision. We see the rejection of our current political class in people's unwillingness to participate in traditional party politics. What is presented as apathy and disinterest in politics (low turnouts in elections, low membership in political parties) is not disinterest but a very clear political stance. There is further evidence for this in the fact that parties at the extremes of the political spectrum recruit followers at rates not even dreamed of by the standard political parties. The people in the extremes may be populists, misguided or plainly wrong about many things, but they share one thing: drive. For political agitators, politics is not a career path, it is a calling. This appeals to a public disengaged from those politicians who are used to telling us how things are and why nothing can be done about it. Political disaffection that can be defined as the subjective feelings of powerlessness, cynicism and lack of confidence in the political process, politicians and democratic institutions, but with no questioning of the political regime, turns in time to wholesale rejection of the system. That can take the form of the 'let it all burn' nihilism exhibited in many a Greek protest, or it can lead to support for anti-systemic, anti-democratic political formations, like Golden Dawn in Greece or España2000 in Spain (Mason, 2012). It is outside the scope of this work to present the literature on political disaffection and its consequences on European democracy, but one can consult the recent title by Torcal and Montero (2006) for a summary of the research in this area. What is within the scope of this work is the link the political process has with the production of law, and the link law has with the legitimacy of economic decision-making. The next and final section of this chapter will reflect on how the future could be different if we were to use law to make these connections. It will complete the discussion of how politics could be better, different, and then it will address the second of the questions posed above, why persist with capitalism?

6.5 An alternate future: law as peacemaker

This work, like *Neoliberalism and the Law* (Glinavos, 2010a), is hopeful as it imagines a different future where a better political class becomes an instrument of channelling popular desires, rather than a professional elite that manipulates and preys upon its people. The key argument made here is not that we get the politicians we deserve, but rather we get the politicians that the system allows for. If we were to change the system, if we were to re-establish a foundation of law as a representation of a novel social contract, what would capitalism look like? An open debate about what capitalism is for, what financial markets are for, what should be the rewards for those that run the commanding heights of the economy and to what degree wealth should be redistributed, forms the basis upon which a better system can be built. In order to have this debate we need political platforms that propose different visions of social and economic organisation. For this to happen, we need to break through the fear of reprisals from the markets. We need to reassert our status as *homo sapiens*, rather than *homo economicus*, to allow ourselves to think without being boxed in by neoclassical assumptions. We should be free to be economically irrational if we are to remain socially engaged.

It is important at this point to reiterate that the contribution of this idea is one of method rather than a proposal of substantive content. I cannot and do not want to prejudge what the outcome of the debate should be. One could even argue that it does not matter what the outcome of the debate is because it will be a chosen outcome. If the system is built in a way that the goals of economic policy reflect a new social contract, then no matter what the decision is, the public will have a stake in the process. Establishing a foundation of law that sets new outer frameworks to market activity and inaugurates a new balance point in the market–state relationship will ensure the maintenance of peace only if it is the product of choice. If the people own the process, choose what matters, then social conflict will recede. Will this be terrible for markets, if the choice significantly diverges from the norms of today? Does it matter? Should we aim to endlessly appease the markets, to preserve expectations, reduce uncertainty and end up risking social collapse? Should we sit by till the Greeks elect Golden Dawn to run a fascist dictatorship before we realise that the investment climate was not that predictable anyway?

Opening up the debate, allowing ourselves to challenge the sacred tenets of neoclassical economics, risking the abandonment of neoliberal ideology, will empower a new generation of politicians that will channel and enhance this social consultation. Imagine what the political debate would be like if a political party could argue for redistribution of wealth and taxation without being shouted down by market advocates as being unscientific and irrational. The answer can be offered therefore. It is not unrealistic to extend politics to help us determine the goals of our economic system. It is not unrealistic to expect politics to help us break out of the confines of 'orthodoxy'.

If a break with orthodoxy is the aim, however, why resist the next step: to reject capitalism? Is it cowardly to suggest that a debate is to be had without signifying a potential conclusion? Is it limiting to state, as we have at the beginning of the book, that the aim of these proposals is not to dethrone capitalism? Wouldn't a new balance be more securely achieved by trying to abandon the idea of market liberalism altogether? The reason why this book has argued for ways to use law to improve the legitimacy of market structures, to strengthen as well as to humanise capitalism, is that the continuation of market democracy is the only guarantee that the system will remain democratic. This is not to say that the outcome of the debate, the birth of a new social contract, can only take place against a capitalist background. It is rather a warning that politics of a nature radical enough to be extreme and undemocratic represents a negation of the value of the whole process aimed at reconnecting politics with economic decision-making. History does not bode well for non-capitalist alternatives, be they the Stalinist communism of the likes of the Greek Communist Party or the Fascist ramblings of Golden Dawn.

A reconnection between economics and politics, the use of law as a tool to channel the popular will to governance outcomes, is pointless if it is to result in the dissolution of the very notion of legality. We will not benefit as a democratic society from the politicisation of law and from a return to law as a sub-branch of party ideology. While this book has been critical of the way the notion of the rule of law is abused by a pro-market establishment, it is not suggested that the politicisation of the judiciary and a submersion of law to political interests is the way forward. There is in other words a way to reverse de-politicisation and to regain legitimacy for the capitalist project without recreating Socialist law and Stalinist lawlessness. How does the delicate theorising offered here deal with potential side effects if the book's proposals were to be applied in practice? Will a win of (for example) Syriza in the next Greek election and an attempted change of course via rejection of economic orthodoxy be a practical example of the lessons of the book? Even though the author's view of Syriza is not positive, a debate about the nature of the economy, of the trajectory of a country and of what counts as a public good is entirely consistent with what has been argued here. To continue with this particular example, will an election of such a group herald disaster? If the choice of the platform proposed by a political party signifies the acceptance of their vision of society, then the outcome (even if disastrous in economic terms) is likely to be less conducive to social conflict than a disaster that comes after the imposition of policies that lack legitimacy and popular support. It is my belief that if one were to choose between two evils, two scenarios of economic collapse, the one that comes after democratic choice is always to be preferred to the one that comes after the imposition of 'the rational thing to do'. A wrong choice can be dealt with in the next election; when the 'rational' turns out to be wrong, however, the outcome is likely to be much more dangerous.

6.6 Conclusion

This chapter has considered how the state–market relationship is seen through the process of dispute resolution and has reflected on the effects of embedding pro-market policies in legal structures beyond the reach of the normal legislative process. In fact, investor–state disputes and the way they are resolved is significant in revealing the often unintended consequences of market-friendly measures. The point made here is that even well-intentioned mechanisms can end up limiting policy discretion in unanticipated ways, both due to the findings of tribunals and because of the fear they generate of the consequences of losing in an arbitral forum. The chapter then proceeded to question the very use of mandatory legal provisions as the background to regulation, examining the role of voluntarism and self-regulation. The conclusion has been that while there may be a place for voluntarism in the design of regulatory frameworks, self-regulation fails to adequately reflect political demands and risks further segregating the political process from economic decision-making, something that we have identified throughout as a very dangerous route to follow for the survival of democracy itself. The solution is not therefore to withdraw from law, in its traditional incarnations, but to embrace it. In order to avoid having the corrosive effects of de-politicisation combining with the crisis to threaten the stability of the political system through a lurch towards extremism, we need to recapture the role of law as a tool to achieve social peace, as a conduit to equity and the defender of justice. If this entails a shrinking of market freedom, then so be it.

Do we see any evidence that would lead us believe that such a return of law as a conduit for political demands (as opposed to a protector of economic orthodoxy) is upon us? As this book goes to print, there are indeed some indications that may make us optimistic, despite the overall cautious tone Chapter 5 adopted when discussing regulatory changes as a response to the crisis. Let us just mention three measures being discussed in the spring of 2013. The book has spent some time discussing the issue of executive remuneration and bonuses as a proxy for attitudes to market freedoms and as a gauge of the forcefulness of regulatory responses to the crisis. We have also discussed in places the example of the payday loans industry as an illustration of the excess of laissez-faire attitudes and its consequences on consumer welfare. These are fields that can also help us assess how policy impulses are being revealed currently. In February 2013 in a meeting of officials from the 27 countries of the EU with MEPs and the European Commission, it was agreed to cap bankers' bonuses broadly at a year's salary, with the proviso that the bonus could be doubled subject to majority shareholder approval. This of course caused significant consternation to the British delegation which (habitually) was in Brussels aiming to safeguard the interests of the City. This agreement was then approved by the EU finance ministers' meeting on 5 March 2013. Only a few days earlier Swiss voters had overwhelmingly backed proposals to impose some of the world's strictest controls on executive pay, supporting plans to give shareholders a veto on compensation and ban big payouts for new and departing executives. That very same week the Office of Fair Trading in the UK (OFT, 2013) published the final report on the OFT's compliance review of the £2 billion payday lending sector. The review found evidence of problems throughout the lifespan of payday loans, from advertising to debt collection, and across the sector, arising from pervasive irresponsible lending. The review suggested fundamental problems with the operation of the payday market that go beyond non-compliance with the law and regulations, leading to the recommendation that a full investigation by the Competition Commission is needed to identify and, if appropriate, impose lasting solutions to make this market serve its customers better. Can we take these indications as evidence that the mood is changing towards a retreat from treating market solutions as primary in the organisation of our political economy? Perhaps, considering what we have reviewed in this book, we cannot quite yet say that, but one can still detect a change of tone in the spring of 2013. We can perhaps be optimistic that a debate is beginning to take place in order to challenge perceived wisdom and the sacred tenets of 'orthodoxy'. With some luck, we may even be allowed to test such emerging iconoclasm in elections.

Epilogue

Often in the pages of this book the reader has been directed to sources of interest and further reading that serve as an entry point to a wide literature having similar objectives to this work. There is indeed a wealth of heterodox literature that tries to challenge current orthodoxy. There are two questions that arise from this realisation. First, what is the point of yet another book offering a heterodox view, trying to challenge neoclassical assumptions? Second, if heterodoxy is so well documented and its thesis so well put, why is it not successful in dislodging the status quo? To answer the first question we have to return to the book's main claim to novelty, the interdisciplinary treatment of the issues which includes a legal perspective. While there are many wonderful works that raise similar concerns about the undemocratic effects of financialisation and explain the corrosive effects of inequality on the body politic, there are fewer works that try to examine what these insights mean for the role of law and the place of law reform in influencing economic organisation. It is hoped therefore that by reading this book the audience has gained an appreciation of how the heterodox message can be translated into legal practice. One of the key themes of the book, the disengagement of the political process from norm creation and the surrender to technocracy, offers a way to bring together debates about democratic re-engagement and economic policy-making. The conduit for legitimacy, as this book claims, is the law. We can – and should – use our powers as citizens to influence law creation in order to sculpt the society we seek.

In order to answer the second question – the failure of heterodoxy to translate a win over theory to a win over practice – we can explore the notion of epistemic communities we utilised in Part 1 of the book when explaining the role of ideas and how they can be transmitted from academic discourses into practice. The reason why the heterodox message fails to translate into policy, despite the ever obvious weaknesses of neoclassical orthodoxy, is because critical academia has failed to project a message consistent enough to offer a platform for change politicians can adopt. There are multiple reasons for this that are explained well in the literature emanating from political science and that are beyond the scope of this discussion. One thing is certain, however. The crisis offers an opportunity (as has often been mentioned) to seize the day and channel the heterodox message to politicians and citizens in a usable and practical format. The failure of orthodoxy, as represented by austerity, for example, to resolve the European debt crisis leaves a political opening for different solutions. It is exactly for these reasons that this book has argued that now is the time to begin a discussion about the purpose of markets, the nature of finance, the role of law and the place of regulation. It is only via this discussion, now in the midst of the crisis, that a concrete challenge can be brought against orthodoxy. Can such an effort be successful? Can we trust the European left (for example) to deliver a re-evaluation of the state–market balance in practice? This work suggests that maybe this is the wrong question to ask. The right question could be: what will happen if the left fails to articulate a message that challenges failed orthodoxy? Where will the public turn when the right fails to deliver the fruits of austerity to the many (because there will always be rewards for the few), while the left promises the same orthodox policies but with a friendlier face? Is it inconceivable to think that if we do not use democracy to re-establish a social contract to support liberalism, we may end up with powerful extremes? Is it impossible that the discredit attached to politics will deliver us into the hands of deluded 'socialists' and fascist demagogues? Is it the place of a book about the law to pose these questions, you may ask? If not in a book about the law, about the source of the power to effect change, then where should these concerns be raised? Now is the time to stop arguing about the means to achieve ill-defined outcomes and to have a discussion about the goals of a market economy. Now may be the last opportunity we have to offer an opinion, as a democratic society, about what economics, finance, the law, are for and how they are used. If we choose not to ask these questions we may have in front of us a future of scientific technocracy that may or may not be benign, or worse, a future where the pretence of democracy is abandoned and with it our freedom is lost. Now is the time to stop asking for choices for consumers and start demanding choices for citizens.

Bibliography

Aldrich, G. (1994) 'What constitutes a compensable taking of property? The decisions of the Iran–US Claims Tribunal', *American Journal of International Law*, 88: 585.

Aman, A. (2004) *The Democracy Deficit: Taming Globalization Through Law Reform*. New York University Press.

Amato, M. and Fantacci, L. (2011) *The End of Finance*. Polity Press.

Andersen, K. (2009) 'The avenging amateur', *Time Magazine*, 10 August. Available on http://www.time.com/time/magazine/article/0,9171,1913776,00.html (last accessed 13 March 2013).

Arner, D. (2009) 'The global credit crisis of 2008: causes and consequences', *International Lawyer*, 43: 91–136.

Athanassiou, P. (2009) *Withdrawal and Expulsion from the EU and EMU: Some Reflections*, Legal Working Paper Series, No. 10. ECB.

Avineri, S. and de Shalit, A. (eds) (1992) *Communitarianism and Individualism*. Oxford University Press.

Baker, E. (1975) 'The ideology of the economic analysis of law', *Philosophy and Public Affairs*, 5 (1): 3–48.

Bank for International Settlements (2008) 'OTC derivatives market activity in the first half of 2008', 13 November. Available on http://www.bis.org/press/p081113.htm (last accessed 17 March 2013).

Bank of Greece (2012) *The Bank of Greece Interim Report on Monetary Policy 2012*, 3 December. Available on http://www.bankofgreece.gr/Pages/en/Bank/News/PressReleases/DispItem.aspx?Item_ID=4107&List_ID=1af869f3-57fb-4de6-b9ae-bdfd83c66c95&Filter_by=DT (last accessed 17 March 2013).

Banque de France (2008) *FSR Financial Stability Review*, February. Available on http://www.banque-france.fr/fileadmin/user_upload/banque_de_france/publications/Revue_de_la_stabilite_financiere/rsf_0208.pdf (last accessed 16 March 2013).

Barton, T. (1989) 'Prospects for a general theory of economic regulation', *Washington and Lee Law Review*, 46 (1): 41–62.

Baughen, S. (2006) 'Expropriation and environmental regulation: the lessons of NAFTA Chapter 11', *Journal of Environmental Law*, 18 (2): 207–28.

BBA (British Banker's Association) (2010) Response to CEBS CP42, 8 November. Available on http://www.bankfacts.org.uk/download/6241 (last accessed 13 March 2013).

Benmelech, E. and Moskowitz, T. (2007) *The Political Economy of Financial Regulation: Evidence from U.S. State Usury Laws in the 18th and 19th Century*, Working Paper 12851. NBER.

Berglund, S. (2006) 'Prison or voluntary cooperation? The possibility of withdrawal from the European Union', *Scandinavian Political Studies*, 29 (2): 147–67.
Berle, A. and Pederson, V. (1934) *Liquid Claims and National Wealth*. Macmillan.
Bernanke, B. and Mishkin, F. (1997) 'Inflation targeting: a new framework for monetary policy?', *Journal of Economic Perspectives*, 11 (2): 97–116.
Bernhard, W. (1998) 'A political explanation of variations in central bank independence', *American Political Science Review*, 92 (2): 311–27.
Black, J. (2008) *Forms and Paradoxes of Principles Based Regulation*, LSE Legal Studies Working Paper No. 13/2008.
Blinder, A. (1999) *Central Banking in Theory and Practice*. MIT Press.
Blundell, J. (2007) *Waging the War of Ideas*, 3rd edn. Institute of Economic Affairs.
Blyth, M. (2001) 'The transformation of the Swedish model – economic ideas, distributional conflict, and institutional change', *World Politics*, 54 (1): 1–26.
Bradbury, R. (2008) *Fahrenheit 451*. Harper Voyager
Brittan, S. (1982) *How to End the Monetarist Controversy*. Institute of Economic Affairs.
Bruchey, S. (1988) *The Wealth of a Nation: An Economic History of the US*. Harper & Row.
Bruno, M. and Easterly, W. (1996) 'Inflation and growth: in search of a stable relationship', *Federal Reserve Bank of St Louis Review*, 78: 139–46.
Callinicos, A. (2010) *Bonfire of Illusions: The Twin Crises of the Liberal World*. Polity.
Campbell, T. (2001) *Justice*. Macmillan.
Carnegy, H. (2012) 'French court says tax is unconstitutional', *Financial Times*, 29 December. Available on http://www.ft.com/cms/s/0/d5846b16-51b2-11e2-abb6-00144feab49a.html#axzz2Nk1UfQ2q (last accessed 16 March 2013).
Carruthers, B. and Stinchcombe, A. (1999) 'The social structure of liquidity: flexibility in markets and states', *Theory and Society*, 28: 353–82.
Chang, H.-J. (2002) *Kicking Away the Ladder: Development Strategy in Historical Perspective*. Anthem Press
Chapman, M. (2009) *Don't be Fooled Again: Lessons in the Good, Bad and Unpredictable Behaviour of Global Finance*. Financial Times/Prentice Hall.
Chernow, R. (1994) *The Warburgs: The Twentieth-Century Odyssey of a Remarkable Jewish Family*. Vintage.
Clark, A. (2011) 'GSK chief executive Andrew Witty warns that drive for profits is undermining public trust in big companies', *The Observer*, 20 March. Available on http://www.guardian.co.uk/environment/2011/mar/20/firms-quit-britain-tax-reasons (last accessed 14 March 2013).
Cluchey, D. (2011) 'The financial crisis and the response of the United States: will Dodd Frank protect us from the next crisis?', in *The Financial Crisis of 2008: French and American Responses*, Proceedings of the 2010 Franco-American Legal Seminar. Available on http://papers.ssrn.com/sol3/papers.cfm?abstract_id=1831661 (last accessed 17 March 2013).
Coase, R. (1960) 'The problem of social cost', *Journal of Law and Economics*, 3: 1–44.
Coggan, P. (2011) *Paper Promises: Money, Debt and the New World Order*. Allen Lane.
Cohen, G. A. (1991) *Incentives, Inequality, and Community*, The Tanner Lectures on Human Values, 21 May. Available on http://www.tannerlectures.utah.edu/lectures/documents/cohen92.pdf (last accessed 14 March 2013).
Cohen, G. A. (1994) 'Back to socialist basics', *New Left Review*, 207: 3–16.
Cohen, M. (2011) *Argentina's Economic Growth and Recovery: The Economy in a Time of Default*. Routledge.

Craig, D. and Porter, D. (2006) *Development Beyond Neoliberalism?* Routledge.

Craig, P. and De Búrca, G. (2003) *EU Law: Text, Cases and Materials*. Oxford University Press.

Cremades, B. (2000) 'Promoting and protecting international investments', *International Arbitration Law Review*, 3 (3): 53.

Cross, K. (2006) 'Arbitration as a means of resolving sovereign debt disputes', *American Review of International Arbitration*, 17: 335–89.

Cukierman, A. (1994) 'Central bank independence and monetary control', *Economic Journal*, 104: 1437–48.

Damaska, M. (1982–3) 'Activism in perspective', *Yale Law Journal*, 92: 1189.

Das, S. (2011) *Extreme Money: The Masters of the Universe and the Cult of Risk*. Financial Times/Prentice Hall.

Davies, H. (2010) *The Financial Crisis*. Polity.

De Larosiere, J. (2009) *The High-Level Group on Financial Supervision Report* (The DLG Report). Available on http://ec.europa.eu/internal_market/finances/docs/de_larosiere_report_en.pdf (last accessed 17 March 2013).

Debelle, G. and Fischer, S. (1994) *How Independent Should a Central Bank Be?*, Federal Reserve Bank of San Francisco, Working Papers in Applied Economic Theory, Paper 94–05.

Desmet, P., Cremer, D. and Dijk, E. (2011) 'In money we trust? The use of financial compensations to repair trust in the aftermath of distributive harm', *Organizational Behaviour and Human Decision Processes*, 114 (2): 75–86.

Dickson, P. (1967) *The Financial Revolution in England: A Study in the Development of Public Credit 1688–1756*. Macmillan.

Donadio, R. (2012) 'Next act in Italian drama: exit Monti the technocrat, enter Monti the politician?', *New York Times*, 9 December. Available on http://www.nytimes.com/2012/12/10/world/europe/stage-is-set-for-turmoil-in-italy.html?hp&_r=1& (last accessed 18 March 2013).

Dor, E. (2011) *Leaving the Euro Zone: A User's Guide*, 2011-ECO-06 Working Paper Series, IESEG School of Management. Available on http://my.ieseg.fr/bienvenue/DownloadDoc.asp?Fich=1046781054_2011-ECO-06_Dor.pdf (last accessed 17 March 2013).

Dyson, K. and Marcussen, M. (2009) *Central Banks in the Age of the Euro Europeanization, Convergence, and Power*. Oxford University Press.

EBA (2012) 'Survey on the implementation of the Guidelines on remuneration policies and practices', 12 April. Available on http://www.eba.europa.eu/News-Communications/Year/2012/Survey-on-the-implementation-of-the-Guidelines-on-.aspx (last accessed 17 March 2013).

Economist, The (2008) 'Diagnosing depression: what is the difference between a recession and a depression?', Economic Focus, 30 December. Available on http://www.economist.com/node/12852043?story_id=12852043 (last accessed 17 March 2013).

EFAMA (European Fund and Asset Management Association) (2010) Response to CEBS Consultation Paper on Guidelines on Remuneration Policies and Practices (CP42), 12 November. Available on http://www.efama.org/Publications/Public/Corporate_Governance/10-4098_EFAMA%20Reply%20to%20_CRD_3_Guidelines_Remuneration_%28CP42%29.pdf (last accessed 13 March 2013).

Eggertsson, G. (2005) *Great Expectations and the End of the Depression*, Federal Reserve Bank of New York Staff Report No. 234. December.

Eliot, G. (1860) *The Mill on the Floss*. William Blackwood.

Emmanouilidis, J. (2007) *Withdrawal or Creation of a New Union – A Way Out of the EU's Constitutional Dilemma?* Bertelsmann-Stiftung.

European Commission (2011) 'Internal market: awareness, perceptions and impacts', *Eurobarometer Qualitative Studies*, November. http://ec.europa.eu/public_opinion/archives/quali/5983_awareness_en.pdf (last accessed 13 March 2013).

EVCA (European Private Equity and Venture Capital Association) (2010) Industry Response to the CEBS Consultation on the Guidelines on Remuneration Policies and Practices, 8 November. Available on www.evca.eu/WorkArea/linkit.aspx?LinkIdentifier=id&ItemID=6030 (last accessed 13 March 13).

Fahlenbrach, R. and Stulz, R. (2011) 'Bank CEO incentives and the credit crisis', *Journal of Financial Economics*, 99: 11–26

Fama, E. F. (1970) 'Efficient capital markets: a review of theory and empirical work', *Journal of Finance*, 25: 383–41.

Featherstone, K. 2005) '"Soft" co-ordination meets "hard" politics: the European Union and pension reform in Greece', *Journal of European Public Policy*, 12 (4): 733–50.

Financial Crisis Inquiry Report (2011) *Final Report of the National Commission on the Causes of the Financial and Economic Crisis in the United States*. Available on http://www.gpo.gov/fdsys/pkg/GPO-FCIC/pdf/GPO-FCIC.pdf (last accessed 17 March 2013).

Financial Services Authority (2007) *Principles Based Regulation: Focusing on the Outcomes that Matter*. FSA. Available on http://www.fsa.gov.uk/pubs/other/principles.pdf (last accessed 18 March 2013).

Financial Stability Board (2009) *FSB Principles for Sound Compensation Practices*. Available on http://www.financialstabilityboard.org/publications/r_090925c.pdf (last accessed 16 May 2013).

Fishback, P. and Kantor, E. (2000) *A Prelude to the Welfare State: The Origins of Workers' Compensation*. University of Chicago Press.

Frank, T. (2012) *Pity the Billionaire: The Hard-Times Swindle and the Unlikely Comeback of the Right*. Harvill Secker.

Friedman, M. and Schwartz, A. (1963) *A Monetary History of the United States, 1867–1960*. NBER.

FSA (Financial Services Authority) (2010) Policy Statement 10/20: Feedback on CP10/19. Available on http://www.fsa.gov.uk/pubs/policy/ps10_20.pdf (last accessed 13 March 2013).

Fukuyama, F. (1992) *The End of History*. Penguin Books.

Fung, K. and Lau, L. (2003) 'Adjusted estimates of United States–China bilateral trade balances: 1995–2002', *Journal of Asian Economics*, 14 (3): 489–96.

Furceri, D. and Mourougane, A. (2009) *Financial Crises: Past Lessons and Policy Implications*, Economics Department Working Papers No. 668. OECD.

Galbraith, J. K. (1992) *The Great Crash 1929*. Penguin.

Geary, A., Morrison, W. and Jago, R. (2009)) *The Politics of the Common Law: Perspectives, Rights, Processes, Institutions*. Routledge.

Geoghegan, T. (2012) 'Is Greece's the longest recession in history?', *BBC News Magazine*, 28 February. Available on http://www.bbc.co.uk/news/magazine-17102525 (last accessed 17 March 2013).

Germain, R. (2010) *Global Politics and Financial Governance*. Palgrave Macmillan.

Glaeser, E. and Shleifer, A. (2003) 'The rise of the regulatory state', *Journal of Economic Literature*, 41: 401–25.

Glinavos, I. (2008) 'Neoliberal law: unintended consequences of market-friendly law reforms', *Third World Quarterly*, 29 (6): 1087.

Glinavos, I. (2010a) *Neoliberalism and the Law in Post Communist Transition*. Routledge.

Glinavos, I. (2010b) 'Regulation and the role of law in economic crisis', *European Business Law Review*, 21 (4): 539–57.

Glinavos, I. (2011) 'Investor protection v. State regulatory discretion', *European Journal of Law Reform*, 13 (1): 70–87.

Glucksmann, A. (2009) 'The postmodern financial crisis', *City Journal*, 19 (1). Available on http://www.city-journal.org/2009/19_1_snd-postmodern-financial-crisis.html (last accessed 16 March 2013).

Goldstein, J. (1993) *Ideas, Interests, and American Trade Policy*. Cornell University Press.

Greek Ministry of Finance (2012a) Press Release, 24 February. Available on http://blogs.reuters.com/felix-salmon/files/2012/03/Greek.Min-Fin-Press_Release_Feb.24-2012.pdf (last accessed 17 March 2013).

Greek Ministry of Finance (2012b) Press Release, 9 March. Available on http://av.r.ftdata.co.uk/files/2012/03/9-MARCH-2012.pdf (last accessed 17 March 2013).

Griffiths, B., Sirico, R. A., Barry, N. and Field, F. (2001) *Capitalism, Morality and Markets*. Institute of Economic Affairs.

Groenewegen, J., Spithoven, A. and Van den Berg, A. (2010) *Institutional Economics: An Introduction*. Palgrave Macmillan.

Gup, B. E. (ed.) (2003) *Too Big to Fail: Policies and Practices in Government Bailouts*. Quorum Books.

Haas, P. (1990) *Saving the Mediterranean: The Politics of International Environmental Cooperation*. Columbia University Press.

Haas, P. (1997) *Knowledge, Power, and International Policy Coordination*. University of South Carolina Press.

Habermas, J. (2012) *The Crisis of the European Union: A Response*. Polity Press.

Hale, R. (1923) 'Coercion and distribution in a supposedly non-coercive state', *Political Science Quarterly*, 38: 470.

Hale, R. (1952) *Freedom Through Law: Public Control of Private Governing Power*. Oxford University Press.

Halpérin, J. L. (2011) 'French courts and public intervention in the economy during the nineteenth and the twentieth centuries', in *The Financial Crisis of 2008: French and American Responses*, Proceedings of the 2010 Franco-American Legal Seminar, University of Maine School of Law, pp. 130–50.

Hancher, L. and Moran, M. (1989) *Capitalism, Culture, and Economic Regulation*. Oxford University Press.

Hansard (1998) Parliamentary Under-Secretary of State, Foreign and Commonwealth Office (Baroness Symons of Vernham Dean), 28 April. Ref. 180-428-05, Column 160.

Harris, J. W. (1997) *Legal Philosophies*. Butterworths.

Harvey, D. (2005) *A Brief History of Neoliberalism*. Oxford University Press.

Hayek, F. (1944) *The Road to Serfdom*. G. Routledge & Sons.

Hayek, F. (1960) *The Constitution of Liberty*. Routledge & Kegan Paul.

Hellwig, M. (2009) 'Systemic risk in the financial sector: an analysis of the subprime-mortgage financial crisis', *The Economist*, 157 (2): 129–207.

Hill, J. (1982) 'The European Economic Community: the right of member state withdrawal', *Georgia Journal of International and Comparative Law*, 12: 335.

Hill, J. (2011) *Regulating Executive Remuneration after the Global Financial Crisis: Common Law Perspectives*, Sydney Law School Research Paper No. 11/91. Available on http://ssrn.com/abstract=1956294 (last accessed 17 March 2013).

Hofstadter, R. (1960) *The Age of Reform*. Vintage.

Hogarth, J. (2006) *Financial Education and Economic Development*, presented at the Improving Financial Literacy International Conference. Available at http://www.oecd.org/finance/financialeducation/37742200.pdf (last accessed 17 March 2013).

Hood, C., Rothstein, H. and Baldwin, R. (2001) *The Government of Risk: Understanding Risk Regulation Regimes*. Oxford University Press.

Hope, K. and Hadjipapas, A. (2013) 'ECB presses Cyprus to impose bank levy', FT.com, 17 March. Available on http://www.ft.com/cms/s/0/a2eac7d0-8f11-11e2-a39b-00144feabdc0.html#axzz2Nk1UfQ2q (last accessed 17 March 2013).

Hornbeck, J. (2010) *Argentina's Defaulted Sovereign Debt: Dealing with the 'Holdouts'*, CRS Report for Congress No. R41029. Congressional Research Service.

Horwitz, M. (1974) 'The historical foundations of modern contract law', *Harvard Law Review*, 87: 917.

Huntington, S. (2002) *The Clash of Civilizations and the Remaking of World Order*. Free Press.

Inman, P. (2010) 'FSA warns against heavy-handed EU regulation of hedge funds', *The Guardian*, 8 February. Available on http://www.guardian.co.uk/business/2010/feb/08/fsa-european-directive-hedge-funds (last accessed 18 March 2013).

Ireland, P. (2003) 'Property and contract in contemporary corporate theory', *Legal Studies*, 23: 453.

ISDA (2012) OTC Derivatives Market Analysis Year-end 2011, 6 June. Available on http://www2.isda.org/attachment/NDQzNQ==/Market%20Analysis%20060612.pdf (last accessed 17 March 2013).

Jackson, J. (2012) *Financing the US Trade Deficit*, Report RL33274, 16 November. Congressional Research Service. Available on http://www.fas.org/sgp/crs/misc/RL33274.pdf (last accessed 17.3.13)

Joyce, M., Tong, M. and Woods, R. (2011) 'The United Kingdom's quantitative easing policy: design, operation and impact', *Quarterly Bulletin*, Q3, Bank of England.

Kelsen, H. (1967) *Pure Theory of Law*. University of California Press.

Kelsey, J. (2011) 'The TPPA, financial instability and governments' regulatory space'. Available on http://aftinet.org.au/cms/sites/default/files/TPPA%20&%20FINANCIAL%20INSTABILITY.pdf (last accessed 18 March 2013).

Kerr LJ (1987) 'Arbitration v Litigation: the Macao sardine case', *International Business Law*, 15: 156.

Kessler, D. (2010) *Regulation vs Litigation: Perspectives from Economics and Law*. University of Chicago Press.

Keynes, J. (1926) *The End of Laissez-Faire*. Hogarth Press.

Keynes, J. (1981) *Collected Writings*, Vol. 20, *Activities 1929–31*. Macmillan.

King, M. (2005) 'Epistemic communities and the diffusion of ideas: central bank reform in the United Kingdom', *West European Politics*, 28 (1): 94–123.

Kolko, G. (1963) *The Triumph of Conservatism*. Free Press.

Krugman, P. (2008) *The Return of Depression Economics*. Penguin.

Krugman, P. (2012) 'Earth to Ben Bernanke', *New York Times*, 24 April. Available on http://www.nytimes.com/2012/04/29/magazine/chairman-bernanke-should-listen-to-professor-bernanke.html?pagewanted=all (last accessed 16 March 2013)

Lapavitsas, C. (2009) 'Financialised capitalism: crisis and financial expropriation', *Historical Materialism*, 17 (2): 114–48.

Law, J. (1750) *Money and Trade Consider'd with a Proposal for Supplying the Nation with Money*.

Lewis, M. (2011) *The Big Short*. Penguin.

Linzert, T., Nautz, D. and Bindseil, U. (2004) *The Longer Term Refinancing Operations of the ECB*, Working Paper Series, No. 359. European Central Bank.

Lipshaw, J. (2010) 'The epistemology of the financial crisis', *Southern California Interdisciplinary Law Journal*, 19: 299.

Locke, J. (1690) *Second Treatise on Civil Government*.

London G20 (2009) Summit, April. Available at http://www.londonsummit.gov.uk/en/summit-aims/timelineevents/summit-outcomes, http://www.londonsummit.gov.uk/en/summit-aims/summit-communique/ (last accessed 28 May 2009).

Lowi, T. (1979) *The End of Liberalism: The Second Republic of the United States*. W. W. Norton.

McBarnet, D., Voicelescu, A. and Campbell, T. (2007) *The New Corporate Accountability: Corporate Social Responsibility and the Law*. Cambridge University Press.

McCulley, P. (2008) 'The liquidity conundrum', *CFA Institute Conference Proceedings Quarterly*, March.

Mackintosh, J. (2012) 'Eurozone offers more Greek myths', FT.com, 27 November. Available on http://www.ft.com/cms/s/0/f98dc4fc-38b3-11e2-981c-00144feabdc0.html#axzz2Nk1UfQ2q (last accessed 17 March 2013).

McLean, B. and Nocera, J. (2010) *All the Devils Are Here: The Hidden History of the Financial Crisis*. Portfolio.

McNamara, K. (1998) *The Currency of Ideas – Monetary Politics in the European Union*. Cornell University Press.

Majone, G. (1989) *Evidence, Argument, and Persuasion in the Policy Process*. Yale University Press.

Manne, H. (1997–8) 'The judiciary and free markets (1997–1998)', *Harvard Journal of Law and Public Policy*, 21: 11.

Marciano, A. (2009) *Law and Economics: A Reader*. Routledge.

Marois, T. (2011) 'Emerging market bank rescues in an era of finance-led neoliberalism', *Review of International Political Economy*, 18 (2): 168–96.

Marrier, P. (2008) 'Empowering epistemic communities: specialised politicians, policy experts and policy reform', *West European Politics*, 31 (3): 513–33.

Mashaw, J. (1982–3) 'Rights in the federal administrative state', *Yale Law Journal*, 92: 1129.

Mason, P. (2012) 'Amid scars of past conflict Spanish far right grows', *BBC News*, 18 December. Available on http://www.bbc.co.uk/news/world-20773516 (last accessed 18 March 2013).

Mattei, U. and Nader, L. (2008) *Plunder: When the Rule of Law is Illegal*. Wiley-Blackwell.

Maxfield, S. (1997) *Gatekeepers of Growth: The International Political Economy of Central Banking in Developing Countries*, 3rd edn. Princeton University Press.

Mayer, C. (2011) 'Germany: grappling with the euro, and with its own complicated history', *Time Magazine*, 27 September. Available on http://www.time.com/time/world/article/0,8599,2095157,00.html (last accessed 17 March 2013).

Melody, W. (1997) *Telecom Reform: Principles, Policies and Regulatory Practice*. Technical University of Denmark.

Miller, D. (1976) *Social Justice*. Clarendon Press.

Miller, D. (2012) *Consumption and Its Consequences*. Polity.

Minsky, H. (2008) *Stabilizing an Unstable Economy*. McGraw-Hill.

Moloney, N. (2010) 'EU financial market regulation after the global financial crisis: more Europe or more risks?', *Common Market Law Review*, 47: 1317–83.

Morgan, B. and Yeung, K. (2007) *An Introduction to Law and Regulation: Text and Materials*. Cambridge University Press.

Muchlinski, P. (1999) *Multinational Enterprises and the Law*. Blackwell.

Munchau, W. (2009) *The Meltdown Years: The Unfolding of the Global Economic Crisis*. McGraw-Hill.

Nautz, D. and Schmidt, S. (2009) 'Monetary policy implementation and the federal funds rate', *Journal of Banking and Finance*, 33 (7): 1274–84.

Nesvetailova, A. (2010) *Financial Alchemy in Crisis: The Great Liquidity Illusio*. Pluto Press.

Newman, P. Eatwell, J. and Milgate, M. (2002) *New Palgrave Dictionary of Economics*. Palgrave Macmillan.

Nickerson, D. and Phillips, R. (2003) 'Regulating financial markets: assessing neoclassical and institutional approaches', *Journal of Economic Issues*, 37 (2): 443.

Nordvig, J. and St-Arnaud, C. (2011) *Currency Risk in a Eurozone Break Up – Legal Aspects*. Nomura, Fixed Income Research.

Novak, W. (1993) 'Public economy and the well-ordered market: law and economic regulation in 19th century America', *Law and Social Inquiry*, 18: 1.

Nozick, R. (1974) *Anarchy, State and Utopia*. Blackwell.

O'Keeffe, D. (2004) *Economy and Virtue: Essays on the Theme of Markets and Morality*. Institute of Economic Affairs.

OECD (2001) *Foreign Direct Investment and Sustainable Development*, No.79 Financial Market Trends. OECD.

Office of Fair Trading (2013) 'OFT acts against leading payday lenders and proposes to refer the sector to Competition Commission', Press release, 6 March. Available on http://www.oft.gov.uk/news-and-updates/press/2013/20-13#.UUcBWByeOSp (last accessed 18 March 2013).

Open University (2011) W822 Business and Human Rights Study Guide 2, Open University.

Panitch, L. and Leys, C. (2004) *The Socialist Register 2005: The Empire Reloaded*. Merlin Press.

Parkin, B. and Czuczka, T. (2011) 'Merkel's party votes to allow exits from euro', Bloomberg, 14 November. Available on http://www.bloomberg.com/news/2011-11-11/german-cdu-is-set-to-back-motion-allowing-euro-member-exit-1-.html (last accessed 17 March 2013).

Parsons, C. (2002) 'Showing ideas as causes: the origins of the European Union', *International Organization*, 56 (1): 47–84.

Pashukanis, E. (1987) *Law and Marxism: A General Theory*. Pluto Press.

Perry-Kessaris, A. (2011) 'Reading the story of law and embeddedness through a community lens: a Polanyi-meets-Cotterrell economic sociology of law?', *Northern Ireland Legal Quarterly*, 62 (3): 401–13.

Perry-Kessaris, A. (2012) *Socio-Legal Approaches to International Economic Law*. Routledge.

Pestritto, R. (2005) *Woodrow Wilson: The Essential Political Writings*. Lexington Books.

Peters, G. (1995) *The Politics of Bureaucracy*. Longman.

Pigou, A. (1952) *The Economics of Welfare*. Transaction.

Polanyi, K. (1957) *The Great Transformation*. Beacon Press.

Popkin, R. and Stroll, A. (1986) *Philosophy*, 2nd edn. Made Simple Books.

Porzecanski, A. (2005) 'From rogue creditors to rogue debtors: implications of Argentina's default', *Chicago Journal of International Law*, 6 (1): 333–43.

Posner, R. (1972) *Economic Analysis of Law*. Little, Brown.

Posner, R. (1974) 'Theories of economic regulation', *Bell Journal of Economics and Management Science*, 5 (2): 335–58.

Posner, R. (2009) *A Failure of Capitalism*. Harvard University Press.

Proctor, C. (2010) 'The euro-fragmentation and the financial markets', *Capital Markets Law Journal*, 6 (1): 5–28.

Prosser, T. (1986) *Nationalised Industries and Public Control: Legal, Constitutional and Political Issues*. Blackwell.

Putnam, R. (1977) 'Elite transformation in advanced industrial societies: an empirical assessment of the theory of technocracy', *Comparative Political Studies*, 10 (3): 383–412.

Quinn, J. and Hall, J. (2009) 'Goldman Sachs vice-chairman says: "Learn to tolerate inequality"', *The Telegraph*, 21 October. Available on http://www.telegraph.co.uk/finance/financetopics/recession/6392127/Goldman-Sachs-vice-chairman-says-Learn-to-tolerate-inequality.html (last accessed 14 March 2013).

Rand, A. (1957) *Atlas Shrugged*. Random House.

Rawls, J. (1971) *A Theory of Justice*. Oxford University Press.

Rehn, O. (2011) Speaking Points at the Press Conference on the Annual Growth Survey, 12 January. Available on http://europa.eu/rapid/press-release_SPEECH-11-11_en.htm (last accessed 13 March 2013).

Reich, R. (2009) *Supercapitalism: The Battle for Democracy in an Age of Big Business*. Icon Books.

Reinert, K., Rajan, R., Glass, A. and Davis, L. (2009) *The Princeton Encyclopedia of the World Economy: I–W*. Princeton University Press.

Renner, K. (1976) *The Institutions of Private Law and Their Social Functions*, rev. edn. Routledge.

Reuters (2010) 'Timeline: Greece's economic crisis', 3 March. Available on http://www.reuters.com/article/2010/03/03/us-eurozone-greece-economy-timeline-idUSTRE62230T20100303 (last accessed 17 March 2013).

Reuters (2012a) 'Factbox: terms of the Greek bond swap laid bare', 7 March. Available on http://www.reuters.com/article/2012/03/07/us-greece-swap-factbox-idUSTRE8260K620120307 (last accessed 17 March 2013).

Reuters (2012b) 'Euro zone cut fiscal deficit in 2011, debt up', 22 October. Available on http://www.reuters.com/article/2012/10/22/us-eurozone-debt-idUSBRE89L0B120121022 (last accessed 17 March 2013).

Reuters (2012c) 'Greece considers bond buyback from PSI holdouts', 12 December. Available on http://www.reuters.com/article/2012/12/12/greece-buyback-psi-idUSB4E7I600O20121212 (last accessed 17 March 2013).

Rittich, K. (2004) The future of law and development: second generation reforms and the incorporation of the social', *Michigan Journal of International Law*, 26: 199.

Röpke, W. (1960) *A Humane Economy*. Wolff.

Roubini, N. (2011) *Crisis Economics: A Crash Course in the Future of Finance*. Penguin.

Roubini, N. and Mihm, S. (2011) *Crisis Economics*. Penguin.

Ruggie, J. (1975) 'International responses to technology: concepts and trends', *International Organization*, 29 (3): 557–83.

Ruggie, J. (1982) 'International regimes, transactions, and change: embedded liberalism in the postwar economic order', *International Organisation*, 36 (2): 379–415.

Ruggie, J. (2008) *Protect, Respect and Remedy: A Framework for Business and Human Rights*, Report of the Special Representative of the Secretary-General on the Issue of Human Rights and Transnational Corporations and Other Business Enterprises. Available on http://www.reports-and-materials.org/Ruggie-report-7-Apr-2008.pdf (last accessed 18 March 2013).

Sandel, M. (2012) *What Money Can't Buy: The Moral Limits of Markets*. Allen Lane.

Schlichter, D. (2011) *Paper Money Collapse: The Folly of Elastic Money and the Coming Monetary Breakdown*. John Wiley & Sons.

Schumer, C. (2009) 'Cantwell announce "shareholder bill of rights" to impose greater accountability on corporate America', Press release. Available on http://www.schumer.senate.gov/new_website/record.cfm?id=313468 (last accessed 17 March 2013).

Schwarcz, S. (2011) *Ex Ante Versus Ex Post Approaches to Financial Regulation*, The Chapman Dialogue Series and Law Review Symposium Keynote Address. Available on http://scholarship.law.duke.edu/faculty_scholarship/2354/ (last accessed 17 March 2013).

Scott, H. (1998) 'When the euro falls apart', *International Finance*, 1 (2): 207.

Scott, H. (2010) 'Reducing systemic risk through the reform of capital regulation', *Journal of International Economic Law*, 13 (3): 763–78.

Securities and Exchange Commission (2010a) 'SEC charges Goldman Sachs with fraud in structuring and marketing of CDO tied to subprime mortgages', 16 April. SEC #2010-59, Washington, DC. Available on http://www.sec.gov/news/press/2010/2010-59.htm (last accessed 16 March 2013).

Securities and Exchange Commission (2010b) 'Goldman Sachs to pay record $550 million to settle SEC charges related to subprime mortgage CDO', 15 July. SEC #2010-123, Washington, DC. Available on http://www.sec.gov/news/press/2010/2010-123.htm (last accessed 16 March 2013).

Shavell, S. (1984) 'Liability for harm versus regulation of safety', *Journal of Legal Studies*, 13 (2): 357–74.

Shiller, R. (2008) *The Subprime Solution*. Princeton University Press.

Sindzingre, A. (2004) *Institutions and Economic Development: A Theoretical Critique*, mimeo, presented at the International Conference 'Economics for the Future', September 2003, pp. 17–19.

Singletary, M. (2012) 'Improving your financial literacy is a good investment', *Washington Post*, 27 March. Available on http://articles.washingtonpost.com/2012-03-27/business/35448184_1_financial-questions-national-financial-literacy-month-financial-crisis (last accessed 17.3.13).

Smith, A. (1776) *The Wealth of Nations*.

Sornarajah, M. (2010) *The International Law on Foreign Investment*. Cambridge University Press.

Soros, G. (2010) 'The euro will face bigger tests than Greece', FT.com, 21 February. Available on http://www.ft.com/cms/s/0/88790e8e-1f16-11df-9584-00144feab49a.html#axzz2Nk1UfQ2q (last accessed 17 March 2013).

Stigler, G. (1971) 'The theory of economic regulation', *Bell Journal of Economics and Management Science*, 2 (1): 3–12.

Stiglitz, J. (1989) 'Markets, market failures and development', *American Economic Review*, 79 (2): 197–203.

Stiglitz, J. (1998) 'Central banking in a democratic society', *The Economist*, 142 (2): 199–226.

Stiglitz, J. (2003) *The Roaring Nineties*. Penguin.

Stiglitz, J. (2010) *Freefall*. Penguin.

Stout, L. (2011) 'Derivatives and the legal origin of the 2008 credit crisis', *Harvard Business Law Review*, 1: 1

Strange, S. (1994) *States and Markets*, 2nd edn. Pinter.

Sullivan, R. (2009) *Insights into the Global Financial Crisis*, Vol. 2009(5). Research Foundation Publications, CFA Institute.

Sunstein, C. (1993) *After the Rights Revolution: Reconceiving the Regulatory State*. Harvard University Press.

Sunstein, C. (1999) *Free Markets and Social Justice*. Oxford University Press.

Teivanen, T. (2002) *Enter Economism – Exit Politics*. Zed Books.

Thompson, H. and Runciman, D. (2006) 'Sovereign debt and private creditors', *New Political Economy*, 11 (4): 541–55.

Tienabeso, S. (2012) 'Warren Buffett and his secretary talk taxes', *ABC News*, 25 January. Available on http://abcnews.go.com/blogs/business/2012/01/warren-buffett-and-his-secretary-talk-taxes/ (last accessed 14 March 2013).

Tomlins, C. and Grossberg, M. (2008) *The Cambridge History of Law in America*. Cambridge University Press.

Torcal, M. and Montero, J. (2006) *Political Disaffection in Contemporary Democracies: Social Capital, Institutions and Politics*. Routledge.

Treanor, J. (2010) 'Bankers' threat to quit City "blackmail", says Michel Barnier', *The Guardian*, 13 December. Available on http://www.guardian.co.uk/business/2010/dec/13/banking-bonuses-fsa-regulations (last accessed 13 March 2013).

Trebing, H. (1987) 'Regulation of industry: an institutionalist approach', *Journal of Economic Issues*, 21: 1707–35.

Tricker, B. (2012) *Corporate Governance: Principles, Policies and Practices*, 2nd edn. Oxford University Press.

Trubek, D. and Santos, A. (2006) *The New Law and Economic Development*. Cambridge University Press.

Voiculescu, A. and Yanacopulos, H. (2011) *The Business of Human Rights: An Evolving Agenda for Corporate Responsibility*. Zed Books.

Wade, R. (2008) 'The first-world debt crisis of 2007–2010 in global perspective', *Challenge*, 51 (4): 23.

Waelde, T. (1996) 'Investment arbitration under the Energy Charter Treaty', *Arbitration International*, 12 (4): 429.

Wagner, M. (1999) 'International investment, expropriation and environmental protection', *Golden Gate University Law Review*, 29: 466.

Waibel, M. (2011) *Sovereign Defaults before International Courts and Tribunals*. Cambridge University Press.

Wall Street Journal (2009) 'The new wage controls: one more sign that the levelers are now in charge', 15 June, p. A13. Available on http://online.wsj.com/article/SB124476565985708427.html (last accessed 17 March 2013).

Wapshott, N. (2011) *Keynes, Hayek: The Clash that Defined Modern Economics*. W. W. Norton.

Warburton, P. (2000) *Debt and Delusion*. Penguin Books.

Watson, M. (2002) The institutional paradoxes of monetary orthodoxy: reflections on the political economy of central bank independence', *Review of International Political Economy*, 9 (1): 183–96.

Wearden, G. and Fletcher, N. (2012) 'Eurozone crisis as it happened: Greek debt deal brings relief, and criticism', *The Guardian*, 27 November. Available on http://www.guardian.co.uk/business/2012/nov/27/eurozone-crisis-greece-debt-deal-agreed (last accessed 17 March 2013).

Webel, B. (2010) *The Dodd-Frank Wall Street Reform and Consumer Protection Act: Issues and Summary*, CRS Report for Congress No. R41350. Congressional Research Service.

White, W. (2008) 'Past financial crises, the current financial turmoil, and the need for a new macrofinancial stability framework', *Journal of Financial Stability*, 4 (4): 307–12.

Wintour, P. and Sayal, R. (2012) 'Andrew Mitchell resigns following allegations he called police "plebs"', *The Guardian*, 19 October. Available on http://www.guardian.co.uk/politics/2012/oct/19/andrew-mitchell-resigns-police-pleb (last accessed 14 March 2013).

Wolgast, E. (1987) *The Grammar of Justice*. Cornell University Press.

Wonga.com. Available on http://www.wonga.com/money/how-to-wonga/ (last accessed 21 February 2012).

Wood, S. and Clarkson, S. (2009) *NAFTA Chapter 11 as Supraconstitution*, CLPE Research Paper 43/2009.

Zito, A. (2001) 'Epistemic communities, collective entrepreneurship and European integration', *Journal of European Public Policy*, 8 (4): 585–603.

Žižek, S. (2008) '*Use Your Illusions*', *London Review of Books*, 14 November. Available on http://www.lrb.co.uk/2008/11/14/slavoj-zizek/use-your-illusions (last accessed 16 March 2013).

Index